WRITING AND AMERICA

Crosscurrents

General Editors:
Professor J.B. Bullen, University of Reading
Dr Neil Sammells, Bath College of Higher Education
Dr Paul Hyland, Bath College of Higher Education

Writing and America

Edited by
Gavin Cologne-Brookes,
Neil Sammells and David Timms

LONGMAN
London and New York

Addison Wesley Longman Limited,
Edinburgh Gate, Harlow,
Essex CM20 2JE, United Kingdom
and Associated Companies throughout the world.

Published in the United States of America
by Addison Wesley Longman Publishing Inc., New York

First published 1996

ISBN 0 582 214165 CSD
ISBN 0 582 214173 PPR

British Library Cataloguing-in-Publication Data

A catalogue record for this book is
available from the British Library

Library of Congress Cataloging-in-Publication Data

Writing and America / edited by Gavin Cologne-Brookes,
  Neil Sammells, David Timms
      p. cm. -- (Crosscurrents)
    Includes bibliographical references and index.
    ISBN 0-582-21416-5 (csd). -- ISBN 0-582-21417-3 (ppr)
    1. American literature--History and criticism. 2. National
characteristics, American, in literature. 3. Literature and
history--United States. 4. United States--Historiography.
5. United States--In literature. I. Cologne-Brookes, Gavin, 1961-
II. Sammells, Neil. III. Timms, David. IV. Series: Crosscurrents
(London, England)
PS169.N35W75   1996
810.9--dc20   95-49355
                                                            CIP

Set by 7 in 10/12 Sabon
Produced by Longman Singapore Publishers (Pte) Ltd
Printed in Singapore

Contents

General Editors' Preface

Crosscurrents is an interdisciplinary series which explores simultaneously the new terrain revealed by recently developed methodologies while offering fresh insights into more familiar and established subject areas. In order to foster the cross-fertilisation of ideas and methods the topic broached by each volume is rich and substantial and ranges from issues developed in culture and gender studies to the re-examination of aspects of English studies, history and politics. Within each of the volumes, however, the sharpness of focus is provided by a series of essays which is directed to examining that topic from a variety of perspectives. There is no intention that these essays, either individually or collectively, should offer the last word on the subject – on the contrary. They are intended to be stimulating rather than definitive, open-ended rather than conclusive, and it is hoped that each of them will be pithy, and thought-provoking.

Each volume has a general introduction setting out the scope of the topic, the various modes in which it has been developed and which places the volume as a whole in the context of other work in the field. Everywhere, from the introduction to the bibliographies, pointers will be given on how and where the ideas suggested in the volumes might be developed in different ways and different directions, and how the insights and methods of various disciplines might be brought to bear to yield new approaches to questions in hand. The stress throughout the books will be on crossing traditional boundaries, linking ideas and bringing together concepts in ways which offer a challenge to previously compartmentalised modes of thinking.

Some of the essays will deal with literary or visual texts which are well-known and in general circulation. Many touch on primary material which is not easily accessible outside major library collections, and where appropriate, that material has been placed in a portfolio of documents collected at the end of each volume. Here again, it is hoped that this will provide a stimulus to discussion; it will give readers who are curious to explore further the implications of the arguments an opportunity to develop their own initiatives and to broaden the spectrum of their reading.

The authors of these essays range from international writers who are established in their respective fields to younger scholars who are bringing fresh ideas to the subjects. This means that the styles of the chapters are as various as their approaches, but in each case the essays have been selected by the general editors for their high level of critical acumen.

Professor Barrie Bullen
Dr Paul Hyland
Dr Neil Sammells

Acknowledgements

We would like to thank the contributors to this book for their commitment and patience in responding to our requests and queries. Thanks are also due to colleagues at Bath College of Higher Education for their interest and support, especially to Tracy Brain and Richard Kerridge for valuable suggestions on reading parts of the manuscript.

GCB
NS
DT

We are grateful to Zomba Music Publishers Ltd for permission to reproduce an extract from 'Born in the USA' words and music Bruce Springsteen © 1984 Bruce Springsteen (ASCAP)/Zomba Music Publishers Ltd. for UK & Eire. Regina Barreca's essay makes use of some material previously published in her contribution on 'Social Comedy' in *The Oxford Companion to Women's Writing in the United States*, edited by Cathy N. Davidson and Linda Wagner-Martin, Oxford University Press, New York and Oxford, 1995.

We have unfortunately been unable to trace the copyright holder of 'Warehouseman Blues' by Jack Dupree and would appreciate any information which would enable us to do so.

In Memoriam
Les Arnold, 1943–1992

Writing and America: an introduction

Gavin Cologne-Brookes

'A nation is an act of the imagination', writes Terry Eagleton, ' "a country of the mind", rather than a tract of land or collection of individuals. It is in effect a myth – and it needs that myth making mechanism known as literature to sustain it'.[1] If Eagleton is right and countries are, to use Seamus Heaney's specific example, 'Englands of the mind',[2] such views are perhaps most applicable to the topic of Writing and America. Certainly, this vision is often evident in American writing. To use the example of Wallace Stevens, in 'The Idea of Order at Key West' the inhabiter or reader of a landscape 'is the maker of the song she sang', and humanity the 'artificer of the world'. Effectively, 'whatever self' a landscape or country has, it becomes 'the self' that is 'her song'.[3] As Stevens puts it in 'The Comedian as the Letter C', a poem at least tangentially about the reaching and reading of America, that is perhaps 'worth crossing seas to find'.[4]

On the other hand, in the same poem Stevens suggests an opposing way of viewing America. In the opening lines, mankind – as with Eagleton and Heaney – is 'the intelligence of his soil, / The sovereign ghost'. But later in the poem Stevens reverses this to assert that 'his soil is man's intelligence' (line 280). In varied ways, all the essays in Writing and America illustrate one or both observations. While America is written into being, American writing, which totals up into the idea of America, is itself shaped by the physical geography of the land.

Writing America

The idea of America – the 'New World' as described by and subsequently named after a Florentine merchant, and colonized by wave on wave of free emigrants from Europe and Asia and enslaved Africans – is synonymous with the writing that has formed America. Over the past five centuries, America has been literally written and rewritten into existence from within and beyond its boundaries. The writings of and about the country are a palimpsest in which texts do not so much erase their predecessors as (rewrite, distort, develop or annotate them) to create the multi-layered readings of the nation. *Writing and America*, a volume of essays by scholars on both sides of the Atlantic and from a variety of disciplines, charts a range of these responses from colonial times to the present, offering samplings of the multifarious sources and renewals evident in this writing and rewriting of a nation.

This volume's premise, moreover, is that what Eagleton calls the 'myth making mechanism' is not just literature. Rather, many forms of writing go into that 'act of the imagination' that we call a nation. For a start there are the documents that have created official America. The central legal and political concepts that define America as a nation dedicated (here and there and now and then) to 'life, liberty and the pursuit of happiness' are on paper in the form of the Constitution and the Bill of Rights. But just as the Constitution is itself organic, growing and moulded by the needs of new generations and new challenges, so too an enormous range of other texts – from Presidential addresses to advertisements for Pepsi; from Supreme Court judgements to the songs of Paul Simon – have contributed to what President Clinton, in his suitably abstract Inaugural Address, called 'the mystery of American renewal': (the ideological and rhetorical construction and reconstruction of America and Americanness.)

If the nation's sense of self owes much to its indigenous texts, and the perpetuation of certain key concepts dating back to the European colonists' rejection of British sovereignty, it also owes a good deal to European ideas of America. The British Romantics, for instance – notably Blake, Coleridge and Southey – revealed a view of America that influenced Americans in the attempts of the new Republic to differentiate itself from the Old World. In addition, on both sides of the Atlantic, constructions of America not only owe much to the visions and revisions evident in American texts, but also to a host of external viewpoints. These range from the actual travel writings or diaries of, say, Alexis de

Tocqueville, Dickens, Camus and Jonathan Raban, to the imagined or more symbolic American landscapes of Franz Kafka, Vladimir Nabokov and Michel Butor.

An equally large body of writing, including some of the above, has expressed clear dissent from the often-accepted understanding of American nationhood. While feminist writers and black writers ⬅ have objected to a traditionally 'white male' vision of the 'American', to dissent in one form or another has been a key role played by all kinds of American poets, novelists and playwrights from Emily Dickinson and Herman Melville, through Zora Neale Hurston and Richard Wright to Arthur Miller, Kathy Acker and E. L. Doctorow.

If subversion of the *status quo* is common to a great deal of writing and almost all humour, in America a perennial source of dissent has also been region. Much of the writing has a regional flavour: while Joan Didion's Californians and Bernard Malamud's Jewish Brooklyn shopkeepers have little in common, the upstate New York of Richard Russo's *Mohawk* (1986), Joyce Carol Oates's *Foxfire* (1993), or William Heyen's poetry, for all their distinct differences, share a recognizably common regional culture. But for historical reasons to do, respectively, with notions of the frontier and the 'peculiar institution' of slavery, the West and South have been the most vocal regions of dissent, and therefore those regions most examined from a regional perspective.[5] The very style and subject matter of Mark Twain's *Adventures of Huckleberry Finn* (1884) proclaims a desired freedom from what was then, and perhaps still is, the power-nexus of the north-eastern United States, in favour of the southwestern region of Twain's Missouri boyhood. Writing of the Deep South, too, has traditionally asserted – before and beyond the abolition of slavery – that, as W. J. Cash put it, 'the South is another land'.[6]

In some cases this is plainly so. Take, for example, the reactionary Agrarian poets of the 1920s and 1930s, centring at first around the Nashville Fugitives, including poets such as Donald Davidson, Allen Tate and John Crowe Ransom. Their position is overtly stated in the essay collection *I'll Take My Stand* (1930). The tenor of the movement was to uphold the 'agrarian tradition' of the South as a way of life markedly different from that of the supposedly urban North. But it is also true of such distinctly southern voices as Thomas Wolfe, Robert Penn Warren,

Flannery O'Connor, Eudora Welty and Peter Taylor. Moreover, the layering of textual 'voices' that make up the South's peculiar history is well illustrated in such William Faulkner novels as *Light in August* (1932) and *Absalom, Absalom!* (1936), which burrow down into a southern past very often too deep and dark to distinguish history from myth.

Indeed, much of this regional sense of identity has traditionally been couched in terms of regional myth. The western myth of the frontier, articulated by Frederick Jackson Turner in 'The Significance of the Frontier in American History' (1893), had its southern counterparts in the *ante bellum* myths of benign, patriarchal slavery and Walter-Scott style chivalry, as satirized by Twain. These myths in turn transformed into the *post bellum* southern myths of the Lost Cause and a way of life, as Margaret Mitchell would have it, Gone with the Wind. The title of Richard Gray's book on American southern writing, *Writing the South* (1986) – a book 'written in the belief that the South *is* primarily a concept' rather than being 'significantly different from the rest of the nation' – pinpoints this intimacy between writing and the mythology of region, and, by extension, between writing, myth and America's overall sense of nationhood.[7] Equally, the essays in this book are as often about Writing America as about Writing *and* America since, in its various parts and as a whole, America is written into being.

Certainly, then, there are 'official' texts that, like sacred script, seek to unify what might otherwise fly apart, and works that defy such unifying urges. The Pledge of Allegiance, Irving Berlin's 'God Bless America' or the nation's motto, *E Pluribus Unum*, can be set against more obviously centrifugal texts. These include not only regional writings that defy notions of national unity, but also forms of political dissent from Thoreau's *Walden* (1854) to Norman Mailer's *Why Are We in Vietnam?* (1967), as well as postmodern novels like Barry Hannah's *Ray* (1980), Ishmael Reed's *The Terrible Twos* (1982), or Kathy Acker's *Blood and Guts in High School* (1984). Yet so strong is the idea of America, and so powerful the will to achieve American identity in a country diverse in geography, climate, ethnic and cultural origin, and historical experience, that the urge is often simultaneously toward unity *and* diversity. 'Do I contradict myself?' asked Whitman. 'Very well then . . . I contradict myself.'[8] From Whitman on, American writers have often embraced the contradictions inherent in the American myths of freedom and equality, unity and diversity, patriotism and individualism.

Race, gender or background are no bar to this. F. Scott Fitzgerald, whose *The Great Gatsby* (1925) has been so central to the traditional twentieth-century American literary canon, defined 'a first-rate intelligence' (ironically in 'The Crack-Up' (1936)) as 'the ability to hold two opposed ideas in the mind at the same time, and still retain the ability to function'.[9] But perhaps the clearest examples of conscious struggle between the conflicting ideals of embracing a democratic vision yet asserting one's individual struggle occur in the writing of those who see themselves, or are seen as, racially, culturally, sexually or by gender outside the historically constructed American norm. For to rebel, in a country where the individual's search for freedom and success is the official ideal, is paradoxically to operate within a predominant national myth.

To take the examples of first women's writing and then black writing: it disturbs Marya, in Joyce Carol Oates's *Marya, A Life* (1987), 'that virtually nothing of what she read had been written by women', so she determines, with that typical American urge to remake, that '*she* would change all that'.[10] In doing so, however, Marya embarks on an intellectual as well as a social version of the quintessentially American, Horatio Alger story of rags-to-riches. Equally, in *The Souls of Black Folk* (1903), W. E. B. Du Bois describes the 'double-consciousness' of black Americans, whereby 'one ever feels his twoness – an American, a negro; two souls, two thoughts, two unreconciled strivings', a contradictory sense of identity which is echoed by many black American writers who preceded or followed Du Bois.[11]

The contradictory tensions of being an American are notably apparent in the polemical essays of James Baldwin. Again and again, in *Notes of a Native Son* (1955), *Nobody Knows My Name* (1961) and elsewhere, Baldwin affirms national ideologies even as he denies them, attacks them even as he celebrates them. 'In order to survive as a human, moving, moral weight in the world', he writes in his celebrated 1963 essay, *The Fire Next Time*,

America and all the Western nations will be forced to re-examine themselves and release themselves from many things that are now taken to be sacred, and to discard nearly all the assumptions that have been used to justify their lives and their anguish and their crimes so long.[12]

For all his anger, Baldwin's call for radical re-examination is also the perennial American call, exemplified in the writings of Emerson and Thoreau, to throw off the shackles of the past. His emphasis on renewal, on self-analysis, and indeed his ultimate optimism, are fundamental American traits. In the act of invoking the need to undo the work of the American past and the current *status quo*, he thus illustrates his very Americanness as a writer. Faced, moreover, with white Americans' assertion of hierarchical difference from blacks, his writing exemplifies Du Bois's sense of 'double-consciousness'. Mixed with his own call for black self-assertion, he sought that *other* quintessentially American ideal: unity and equality. 'The one thing that all Americans have in common', he writes in *Nobody Knows My Name*, 'is that they have no other identity apart from the identity which is being achieved on this continent'.[13]

In such ways, Baldwin encapsulates the contradictions of the American vision as eloquently as any American writer. His career was built on the anguish and indignation of being subject to the contradiction of loathing and loving America; of believing in the potential of its ideals, yet despairing at the chasm between the ideal and the real. American writers can only ever harness the ideals of the nation to their own ends. They can never depart from the national myth, since that myth is contradictory, asserting both a drive toward national unity, but also theoretically blessing the individual's struggle toward personal freedom. Therein lies the contradiction involved – in artistic terms anyway – in writing and rewriting America.

In the same essay, for instance, Baldwin writes of black American music, so influential on 'white' rock music, but this time to assert racial *difference*, at least of interpretation. 'In all jazz, and especially in the blues', he says, 'there is something tart and ironic, authoritative and double-edged'. However, he continues, 'white Americans seem to feel that happy songs are *happy* and sad songs *sad*, and that, God help us, is exactly the way most white Americans sing them'.[14] Too, in the very assertion of difference, Baldwin uses American, or white, or even

Christian language, though – as in his use of the phrase 'God help us' – we are in little doubt of his irony.

Of course, while differing racial experiences may exacerbate misunderstanding, all texts are open to conflicting interpretations depending on the reader's predisposition. Yet American voices in particular are often misread or 'rewritten' not just because of the differing experiences of writer and reader, singer and listener, but because, as with Baldwin, the contradictory pulls toward assent and dissent are inherent within the work. When, for example, American concert crowds in the 1980s waved American flags as Bruce Springsteen sang 'Born in the USA', a first response might be that they saw it as merely a new version of 'The Star Spangled Banner'. But were they necessarily asserting a raucous nationalism as simplemindedly, or singlemindedly, as in Britain Proms audiences and church congregations sing Blake's 'Jerusalem'? Is it conceivable that, knowing the lyrics, many of them were waving their Stars and Stripes ironically, on behalf of their young American predecessors sent to slaughter in Vietnam?

Quite possibly many were doing both. As with the similarly misreadable social call-to-arms of 'Jerusalem', and its attack on industrialization, 'Born in the USA' ostensibly sends out a message of national pride, yet is unquestionably about the hard facts of being a working class American. Such lyrics as 'Got in a little hometown jam so they put a rifle in my hand / Sent me off to a foreign land to go and kill the yellow man', clearly attack American foreign policy in the late 1960s for its use and abuse of so many of Springsteen's generation, American and Vietnamese. Similarly, subsequent lyrics describe the veteran returning to find no work available at the refinery and, aside from the penitentiary, 'nowhere to go'.[15]

This kind of incorporation of national myths within a text that undercuts those myths is a common occurrence in American writing. In poetry, for instance, Robert Frost's much-anthologized 'The Road Not Taken' would seem to owe its popularity to its ostensible celebration of the American individualist ideal. Echoing Thoreau, the speaker asserts that, of two paths, he 'took the one less traveled by, / And that has made all the difference'. It is only, perhaps, on reflection that the reader notices that the speaker is looking back with a 'sigh' and that the title points to the road *not* taken.[16] Frost, in other words, is writing about the dangers and difficulties that complicate an individual's choice as to whether to follow social expectations or defy them. In all kinds of American writing, is irony indeed defined, in the words of a Julian Barnes character, 'as what people miss'?[17]

As in Baldwin, Springsteen and Frost, pinpointing irony in American writing is an elusive enterprise because various contradictory sentiments are at war within the author, the work, and the audience. In Springsteen's song, for instance, the reference to 'the yellow man' is potentially readable as racist. Seen in the context of his songs as a whole, such a view would be perverse, and the line becomes an ironic allusion to the racism that helps explain the absurdity of the Vietnam War. On the other hand, this album brought Springsteen's music to a new, younger generation, with less interest in Springsteen as a spokesman for a generation of working class Americans sent to Saigon in the 1960s and early 1970s and, if alive, often out of work in 1980s America. His popular success, moreover, was not just due to the more obviously 'pop' singles from the album – notably 'Dancing in the Dark' – which markedly contrasted with album tracks like 'Working on the Highway' and 'Darlington County', let alone such songs as 'Factory' and 'Atlantic City' from earlier albums.[18] It was also due to a pervasive mood in America of renewed, belligerent nationalism. Tired of their country's perceived weakness in the face of the Iranian hostage crisis under Carter's administration, many Americans fell in behind Reagan's reaffirmation of national self-belief. This included a return to strong denunciations of Soviet Communism as what Reagan called 'the Evil Empire', and thereby a reassertion of America as leader of the 'free world'. It also led to a rewriting of the Vietnam War in popular mythology as something that, in the hands of Sylvester Stallone, sometimes looked absurdly like victory.

Indeed, is the question of how to hear 'Born in the USA' any easier to answer when we consider that this album appeared in 1984, and the 1980s was also Stallone's big decade, with *First Blood* released in 1982 and *Rambo: First Blood, Part II* in 1985? Gung-ho nationalism, pumping iron, and Reaganite America's renewed sense of strength were synonymous, so that even Springsteen, whose 1960s physique apparently led to a failed physical that kept him out of Vietnam, now worked out and wore a Ramboesque bandanna.[19] The problem with 'Born in the

USA' – and, for that matter, 'Jerusalem' – is that it is all too easy to grasp the less subtle of two contradictory possible meanings.

The point, in any case, is that writing in and of America has not only always been open to definitions as diverse as those attributed to the gold doubloon Ahab nails to the mast in *Moby-Dick* (1851), or indeed to the whale himself, but often explicitly holds 'two opposed ideas', or contradictory readings, within it. In the nineteenth century, what Christine Bolt calls the 'popular catch-phrase' of the nation's 'manifest destiny', to advance across to the Pacific and populate the entire continent from the Forty-Ninth Parallel down to the Gulf of Mexico and the Mexican border, depended for its popularity on the given points of view of the continent's inhabitants.[20] Indeed, in the light of the environmental crisis, the word 'destiny' has proved to be ever more clearly double-edged. Jonathan Weiner, for example, in *The Next One Hundred Years* (1990), writes of the greenhouse effect caused by the mass deforestation of the United States in the latter half of the nineteenth century, in which woodsmen, pioneers and settlers converted forests with scattered meadows 'into an essentially continuous grassland with scattered trees'. As part of a pioneer explosion that included not only the 33 million emigrants to the United States between 1821 and 1924 but also 'South America . . . Australia, New Zealand, the Indus Valley, Siberia, Inner Mongolia, and Manchukuo', 'manifest destiny' helped change the biosphere.[21] Such phrases, including key euphemisms like 'equality', 'liberty' and 'happiness', are endless battlegrounds of meaning because of the contradictions they seek to subsume.

Quite aside from popular catch-phrases, in a written America, as in the writing of or between any nations, no major river or byway of any political relevance is uncontestable as to its symbolic meaning. The Mississippi, as Neil Schmitz says of *Huckleberry Finn*, 'is for Huck the end of his journey', but for Jim 'the means of his deliverance elsewhere', just as, variously for others, it is the East–West divide or a trade route.[22] The symbolism of the Rio Grande at El Paso is different for the American border guard or the Mexican wetback. Similarly, while the Atlantic passage may, indeed, as Jonathan Raban puts it in *Hunting Mister Heartbreak* (1991), have seemed '*the* great European adventure' if you were an emigrant, it must have seemed rather different for those in transport to slavery.[23]

America has traditionally been defined – in the manner of all definitions – through opposition; as another great outsider, Emily Dickinson, noted, 'internal difference' is 'where the Meanings, are –'.[24] It is not, therefore, coincidental that Baldwin and Springsteen were writing of events at either end of the 1960s. For during this period the arguments over this sense of writing, rewriting, and therefore defining, America renewed in vigour. Arguably, the fact that the relationship between writing and nationhood nowadays seems such an issue owes much to events of that decade.

With America's outward identity, and so its foreign policy, defined by the supposed Communist menace, the 1960s became a decade of increasing domestic turbulence. In particular, black Americans, along with many white Americans, were hacking away at the racist structures and attitudes that had helped define America's social identity structure for centuries. In political terms, key events around the time included the Supreme Court's 1954 ruling of the doctrine of 'separate but equal' as unconstitutional, a move that eventually led to the end of racial segregation in schools. As well as this there was the increasing visibility of the Civil Rights Movement – aided by public events like the 1963 equal rights march on Washington – the escalation of the Vietnam War, and the assassinations of President Kennedy, Martin Luther King, Jr. and Robert Kennedy. But in literary and cultural terms – in terms of Writing and America – the pivotal point was perhaps the 1967 publication of William Styron's *The Confessions of Nat Turner*, a white southern novelist's depiction of a black slave's insurrection from the protagonist's viewpoint.

Styron partly based his version of Nat Turner on his talks with Baldwin, who had drafted parts of *The Fire Next Time* and *Another Country* (1962) while a guest of Styron's. Baldwin, after all, as we have seen, called for a national merging of identity, so, in one sense, Styron appeared to echo this by merging his white sensibility with a supposed black sensibility to form an interracial American mind. At first, the novel won positive reviews, mostly from white critics, but also from blacks such as Baldwin and John Hope Franklin. Moreover, having made the cover of *Newsweek* and been praised by Baldwin for having 'begun the common history – ours', Styron's novel won the Pulitzer Prize for 1968.[25]

Within the year, however, a black backlash occurred. Most notably, a book of essays by black intellectuals appeared, edited by John Henrik Clarke. Entitled *William Styron's 'Nat Turner': Ten Black Writers Respond*, the essays challenged, and in some cases attacked and sought to discredit, Styron's novel. Many of the arguments had to do with the novel's perceived historical inaccuracy. The charges included the claim that Styron had moulded his figure to suit his own white, 'racist' purposes and ignored evidence from the original record of the confessions, written by Turner's white lawyer, Thomas Gray, and Herbert Aptheker's historical account in *American Negro Slave Revolts* (1939), that suggested a quite different – more heroic – picture of the insurrectionist.

While that controversy was in many ways rooted in the climate of the 1960s, in another sense the arguments it engendered, not least the far broader question of who writes history, have never really gone away. In 1992, Albert Stone published *The Return of Nat Turner: History, Literature and Cultural Politics in Sixties America*, specifically devoted to the role of the Turner controversy in that decade, and Stone elsewhere goes so far as to suggest that the novel had an 'initiating role in redirecting attention to the actual and symbolic function of history within our multicultured culture'.[26]

Certainly it has had wider repercussions as a cultural watershed since it hit on an issue that has proved fertile soil for argument in subsequent years: the fact that history does not exist per se, but is *made*, and had been made, with particular relevance for America as a multi-ethnic democracy, largely by white males of which Styron was palpably yet another. Many of the contributors, who included not only literary critics, but novelists, teachers, a political scientist, a historian, a librarian and a psychiatrist, argued not merely that Styron wrote the wrong book, the wrong version, but that he had no *right* to embark on the project in the first place, and so continue the long line of white definitions of black history.

The volume's significance lay in the fact that white Americans could no longer expect the unchallenged right to shape history to (arguably) suit their own ends. Ironically, the contradictions involved in what Styron was trying to do are the same contradictions evident in his model, Baldwin, and the contradictions involved in any national attempt to weld one social voice with another. At what point does the joining of voices become the usurpation of one voice by the other? 'The American Negro can no longer, nor will he ever again, be controlled by white America's image of him' is a bold statement, made in 1961 and ushering in what has become a dramatic opening up of the literary canon across American and European campuses, yet it was made by the very person – Baldwin – whose call, elsewhere, for 'reconciliation' and 'fusion' helped instigate Styron's controversial leap of the imagination.[27]

Within a couple of years Hayden White published his pioneering exploration of the narratives of history, *Metahistory* (1973), and history never seemed quite the same again. Nor, indeed, did the American past. It came to be acknowledged openly that, to use the words of the American physicist John A. Wheeler, 'the past is theory. It has no existence except in the records of the present. We are participators, at the *microscopic* level, in making that past as well as the present and the future'.[28] Perhaps Wheeler overstates the case. Wheeler himself, after all, helped to invent nuclear fission and to design the atomic and hydrogen bombs. Not only, therefore, may he have made rather more than a '*microscopic*' contribution to the future, but the existence of such devices proves the past to be more than 'theory'. Nevertheless, it remains true that, from the 1960s onward, writers of all kinds have increasingly acknowledged what modernists like William Faulkner had implicitly shown decades earlier: that our *access* to what we can know of (as) 'history' is first and foremost *textual*. It came to be seen, not as the linear progression of a national destiny, but as an amalgam of assertions – including not only writing but voices, film, painting, photography, or any 'signifying' media – expressing varied versions of past events.

Writing and America has consequently become a vexed issue as to the possibility of describing a uniform American identity at all. How far, the question became, can one American culture understand or know another? To what extent is the nation brought into being and developed through writing, and who has the right – the power – of the pen and computer? Paralleling this there has been a shift away from a white male dominated version of America to a rewriting of the nation, and certainly of its history, in terms of greater pluralism. Such traditional histories of the nation as Allan Nevins and Henry Commager's *America: The Story of a Free People* (1942) were once considered earnest endeavours of historical scholarship. Yet they present selected facts of American history as a narrative recording the triumph of white settlers over 'savages' who were 'too few and too backward to be a grave impediment to colonization'.[29] To use the titles of Westerns from either end of the 1960s, 'Once Upon a Time in the West' American history, fuelled by Hollywood and often directed by John Ford, explained 'How the West Was Won'. But, as the title of a 1993 television documentary exemplifies, in more recent years attention to ancient cultures across the continent has revealed 'How the West Was Lost'.[30]

Ford, as director and sheriff, with Wayne as his star, dominated the Western myth in the 1940s and 1950s. They were backed up by a posse of classic Westerns, such as Fred Zinneman's *High Noon* (1952) and George Stevens's *Shane* (1953), both about how a good white man defeats bad white men. In neither film do Native American Indians assume enough relevance to even gather, as happened in so many other Westerns, from nowhere on the horizon. But as the 1960s progressed, revisionist Westerns began to appear. As well as Sergio Leone's *Once Upon a Time in the West* (1968), such films would notably include Arthur Penn's 1970 version of Thomas Berger's novel, *Little Big Man* (1964). Abounding with Vietnam parallels and traversing cultures, it stars Dustin Hoffman as a supposedly 121-year-old man whose claims include having been adopted and brought up by Indians before returning to white society, eventually to become the sole survivor of Custer's catastrophe at the Little Big Horn.

Where once, too, literary scholars saw Melville, Hawthorne, Twain, Whitman and Dickinson as the key figures, the field has since diversified to include hitherto marginalized or forgotten voices of the American past, and new, multicultural voices of the present. Consequently, students are as likely now to read the work of Frederick Douglass, Louise Erdrich's Native American Indian novels about the Chippewas of North Dakota, or the Chinese-American writing of Maxine Hong Kingston, as the 'dead, white, male' canon of tradition.

It remains true that the supposed hegemony of white males

(with Dickinson as the 'token' female) was not all it seemed, and revisionists have themselves sometimes merely produced hierarchies of their own. Many of the traditional canon of nineteenth-century American writing – Whitman, Melville, Hawthorne, Thoreau, Twain, Poe – can be viewed as outsiders or dissenters in one way or another, while Dickinson, of course, speaks for herself; a counter tradition of subversion is therefore evident long before the opening up of the canon.

In broader cultural terms, one example of this revising of the polemical revisionists is Christina Sommers's claims of intellectual dishonesty on the part of high-profile American feminists. In *Who Stole Feminism?* (1994), Sommers critically examines the arguments and evidence presented by commentators including Naomi Wolf, Catharine MacKinnon, Susan Faludi and Gloria Steinem. The results of Sommers's research are sometimes startling; she whittles down the impression Wolf gives, in *The Beauty Myth* (1991), that each year '150,000 American women die of anorexia'[31] to a figure of less than 100.[32] But they further remind us of how text-bound such arguments become, and how easily readers are manipulated by historical and social statistics presented as fact.

Indeed, Sommers's own revisionism lumps together figures of diverse approach and persuasion, so she herself perpetuates this centripetal categorizing that so easily shapes American writing. There is a vast difference in ideas and tone between Catharine MacKinnon's *Toward a Feminist Theory of the State* (1989), informed as it is by legal theory and practice, and more journalistic 'bestsellers' like *The Beauty Myth* or Faludi's *Backlash* (1991). In MacKinnon's words, the problem with a 'generalized, universal' discourse is that it fails to 'solve the disagreements, resolve the differences, cohere the specifics, and generalize the particularities'. Instead, it submerges specificity, and silences particularity.[33]

For the purposes of this volume, though, the point is less the critical, cultural or historical arguments and counter-arguments themselves, than how texts of all kinds are always constructed by critics and commentators to suit contemporary ideologies. This is something that, among others, Paul Lauter writes about with regard to Herman Melville as a writer who, despite revisionists and hostile students, 'has remained atop the academic canon'. In a 1994 essay in *American Literature*, Lauter explores Melville's rise in critical estimation in the 1920s as representing 'the ascent of the ideology we call "modernism" and of the academy and its adjuncts in the hierarchy of cultural authority'.[34]

A result, however, of such challenges to the canon, the law, 'official' history and the *status quo*, has been that the multicultural nature of the American past and American writing is being honoured as never before. America is not – any more than any other country – a democracy of political or social equality, as the riots in Watts in the early 1990s attest, and the establishment remains predominantly white and male. But a large grouping of influential black literary, academic and political figures does now exist. One obvious literary leader is the 1992 Nobel Prize-winner, Toni Morrison, who writes in *Playing in the Dark* (1990) of how her study of canonical American writing revealed the various 'self-evident ways that Americans chose to talk about themselves through and within a sometimes allegorical, sometimes metaphorical, but always choked representation of an Africanist presence'.[35] American writing, it is now commonly acknowledged, has always been fundamentally shaped by the relationship in a society of different ethnic groups, primarily but not exclusively African and Caucasian.

The nation, then, is indeed 'an act of the imagination'. Vast and diverse as it is in its people and its geography, it is unified by an idea shaped and reinforced by writing. The emphasis of this volume, and a major intellectual focus in the past two decades, is precisely therefore that, to quote Woody Guthrie, 'this land is made' and remade, not natural. Constantly evolving, the idea of America nevertheless contains key factors in its continuation that, like human evolution, allow it to reproduce and evolve while still retaining the recognizable concept that we know as America. The writing of America, in whatever form, is also, then, the making of the American mind.

American writing

That said, Eagleton's assertion that a nation is 'an act of the imagination' is only a partial truth. Stevens, who is less certain, is more accurate. A nation is more than a notion. Eagleton's point may be precisely that of the opening line of 'The Comedian as the Letter C': 'Nota: man is the intelligence of his soil'. But Stevens's revision of this, at the start of Section Four of the poem – 'his soil is man's intelligence' – acknowledges that, in fact, the land shapes the mind, and not just the mind the land. For neither writing about America, nor writing about its writing, can long ignore the country's geography. In a very real sense, America *is* 'a tract of land', and the physical facts shape the idea.

This is especially well illustrated in America's rich tradition of travel writing. This includes, among the innumerable indigenous works, such 'road' books as Nathan Asch's *The Road* (1937), John Steinbeck's *The Wayward Bus* (1947), Jack Kerouac's *On the Road* (1957), and William Least Heat-Moon's *Blue Highways* (1983). As well as these, one must include well-known accounts by outsiders such as those mentioned earlier, from de Tocqueville to Raban, and a host of uncelebrated, largely forgotten journeys, like Ernest Young's *North American Excursion* (1947), describing a meandering ride from the St Lawrence to San Diego just before America entered the Second World War.

Also there are the myriad road movies, pioneered by Frank Capra's classic, *It Happened One Night* (1934), where Claudette Colbert's encounter with Clark Gable unravels by way of a very different experience of Greyhound Bus travel from, say, the marginalized bus journey Julia Roberts's character, Laura, takes in Joseph Ruben's *Sleeping with the Enemy* (1990). Such films would include, among many others, Dennis Hopper's *Easy Rider* (1969) and Ridley Scott's feminist revision of the typical buddy system, *Thelma and Louise* (1991). But American travel writing also includes 'river' writing, from Huck and Jim's escape down the Mississippi to Raban's journey the length of it from Minnesota to Louisiana, as described in *Old Glory* (1981), to John Hildebrand's *Reading the River* (1988), an American's canoe voyage down Canada's Yukon. It includes, too, 'train' writing, from the Buster Keaton film *The General* (1926) to Paul Theroux's *The Old Patagonian Express* (1979).

Indeed, the closer you look the more the travel motif crosses all sorts of boundaries in American writing, from canonical novels like *Moby-Dick* and *Huckleberry Finn* through Westerns like Ford's *The Searchers* (1956) and George Roy Hill's *Butch Cassidy and the Sundance Kid* (1969) to historical accounts of

Atlantic and Westward migration. Even such films as Chaplin's *The Gold Rush* (1925), or Michael Cimino's *Heaven's Gate* (1980), are, on one level, part of the travel genre. So too, in a very different sense, are the narratives of escaped slaves like Frederick Douglass, or Dee Brown's account of 'the long walk of the Navahos' in *Bury My Heart at Wounded Knee* (1970).[36] American history and writing has always been, in practical terms and in perception, about being on the move to somewhere else, whether a new land – enforced or chosen – a greater or lesser future, freedom from shackles, increasing enclosure, or outer space.

One might, in all these cases, have chosen quite different examples – Zora Neale Hurston, Ralph Ellison, Saul Bellow – of American writing specifically or tangentially merging geographic travel with what Bellow's Henderson, in the mythical Africa of *Henderson the Rain King* (1959), calls 'mental travel'.[37] The very multiplicity of possibilities testifies that the landscape has shaped the idea as much as the idea has given meaning to the landscape. While travel writing is a universal genre, geographic circumstances inevitably shape traditions. It seems no coincidence that one could take Paul Theroux's ill-advised attempt to journey by train around the British coast, described in *Kingdom by the Sea* (1983), and profitably compare it with Tobias Smollett's travel novel, *The Life and Adventures of Sir Launcelot Greaves* (1762). Theroux's book, a bad-tempered tract mainly about frustrated connections, and Smollett's novel about a Quixotic knight who travels in full armour down the Great North Road, known nowadays as the A1, share a sense of getting nowhere slowly.

In America, on the other hand, the relationship between writing and landscape has developed quite differently. The relative vastness and diversity of the land, and the near-endless lengths of its major roads and rivers, incorporate a culture that changes only as slowly as a raft can drift. In other words, one key to the links between the writing, the culture and the geographic land mass is the unity amid the diversity. Certainly nowadays, to enter a shopping mall in San Diego or Omaha, Cincinnati or Tampa, is likely to be an almost identical experience. This sense of America as an extraordinarily homogeneous culture appears in some recent travel writing. In *American Heartbeat* (1993), for instance, the British journalist

Mick Brown laments that all American shopping malls are 'pretty much the same; all with a Gap, a Florsheim's Shoe Shop, a Radio Shack' and 'a boutique filled with expensive and useless gifts'.[38]

As an Iowan decamped to Britain, Bill Bryson offers an expatriate view that is nevertheless often similar to Brown's. In *The Lost Continent* (1989), he writes about the uniformity of 'small town America', especially, in this case, in the Midwest. 'About all that separates them', he notes, 'are their names'.

> Every fourth or fifth community will be a county town, built around a square. A handsome brick courthouse with a Civil War cannon and a monument to the dead of at least two wars will stand on one side of the square and on the other side will be businesses: a five and dime, a luncheonette, two banks, a hardware store, a Christian bookstore, a barber's, a couple of hairdressers, a place selling the sort of mens' clothing that only someone from a very small town would wear. At least two of the businesses will be called Vern's. The central area of the square will be a park, with fat trees and a bandstand and a pole with an American flag and scattered benches full of old men in John Deere caps sitting around talking about the days when they had something else to do other than sit around and talk about the days when they had something else to do.[39]

One might, indeed, as easily be reading here about Garrison Keiller's Wisconsin in *Lake Wobegon Days* (1985) as Bryson's Iowa, or, indeed, call to mind the town square in Robert Zemeckis's *Back to the Future* (1985).

A reaction to this could be that it illustrates how a nation *is* 'an act of the imagination' that has nothing to do with geography. In the 1930s, Antonio Gramsci responded to Luigi Pirandello's 1929 declaration that 'Americanism is swamping us' by pinning the question down to how the weight of America's 'economic production' might compel Europe to overturn its own 'economic and social basis'. For Gramsci 'the elements of a "new culture" and "new way of life" ' that were 'being spread around under the American label' were 'just tentative feelers'.[40] But we have reached the stage where American signs and logos, to a living generation from Paris to Moscow to Hong Kong, will seem merely global: Macdonald's and Burger King; Budweiser and Michelob. Many dividing lines are so blurred – multinational companies, the Rolling Stones, Baskin Robbins Ice Cream – that, conversely, some things seen as American are in fact not. Even Budweiser, apparently the world's 'largest selling beer', and seen by Americans like Will Anderson in *Beer, USA* (1986) as integral to national identity, is for many Europeans a Czechoslovakian brew.[41] So many distinctions have collapsed that E. M. Forster's nightmare vision of a world where few travel because 'thanks to the advance of science, the earth was exactly alike all over' and Peking 'just like Shrewsbury' can seem all too real.[42]

Maybe the 'act of the imagination' known as America really is fulfilling its 'manifest destiny' and spilling way beyond its defined 'tract of land'; maybe uniformity – for good and bad – is what lies ahead. If so, perhaps Kevin Costner's oscillating accent in *Robin Hood: Prince of Thieves* (1991), which veers between a West Coast vernacular and an 'English' accent reminiscent of the 'Mind the Gap' voice on the London Underground to come out as disc-jockey midatlanticism, is not bad cinema but the way future generations will speak, and write. Such a concern is certainly evident with Mick Brown, who in *American Heartbeat* views America as already written for his generation by popular music. His subsequent switching between fascination and hostility during his travels – a common European attitude to America – results partly from the expectations engendered by such music.

But an American paradox has always been the country's extraordinary uniformity *and* endless variety. Another explanation for Costner's confused accent in *Robin Hood* is evident on hearing him read the diary of Lieutenant John Dunbar in *Dances with Wolves* (1990). Flat as the prairies he rides across, his actual accent is not just irretrievably American, but specifically (and problematically, given Dunbar's intrepid journey to the then-frontier) a West Coast accent, originating from somewhere around the Los Angeles suburb of Compton. This also reminds us that American *writing* retains a wide range of regional and ethnic dialects, from what Anthony Burgess once called the magnolia blossoms of William Styron's southern prose to the Jewish inflections of Isaac Bashevis Singer or Philip Roth, or black dialects used by Toni Morrison or Maya Angelou.[43]

Different texts can suggest different Americas entirely – uniform or diverse. While the likes of Bryson and Brown lament uniformity, this is also a country that *is* as diverse in outlook as geography. It is, after all, a land of which writers from Whitman to Nik Cohn can write about the endless variety of travelling up or down a single, famous avenue: Manhattan's Broadway. Robert M. Greenberg in *Splintered Worlds* (1993) emphasizes the effect on Whitman of his trips on omnibuses 'the whole length of Broadway', quoting Whitman's claims of 'the influence of those Broadway omnibus jaunts and drivers' on 'the gestation of "Leaves of Grass" '.[44] That such infinite variety remains the case is evident from Cohn's *Heart of the World* (1992), an account of a Broadway walking odyssey from the Battery, aiming for the Bronx.

So perhaps America, and American writing, is best discussed in terms of these various forms of moral, cultural and physical paradox. This is not least the case because the writings that launched the idea of America are deeply entrenched in part-Christian, part-Lockean Enlightenment ideals. These serve (at least rhetorically) to temper, even as they give credence to, the nation's capitalist drive. As such, Michel de Montaigne's vision of the self, coinciding with the early morning of colonization, seems to encapsulate America's subsequent development. We are, he says in his *Essays* (1581), 'double in ourselves' so that 'what we believe we do not believe, and cannot disengage ourselves from what we condemn'.[45] Not only is the country driven by high, abstract ideals and therefore troubling dilemmas, but it also exudes this sense of being double or multiple in itself: a place of many in one, one in many. The land, the writing and the culture contain a simultaneous pull towards unity and diversity, built as the latter two are on the contradictory ideals of individual freedom and social equality.

Ultimately then, what holds America together as a nation are the two things, writing and land mass; the idea and the geography both go into the shaping of the idea of America in mind and experience. Therefore, this volume deals with not just Writing America, nor just American Writing, but Writing and America. It is true that America is made out of its writing, out of the *idea* of America – a nation *is* an 'act of the imagination'. As Lincoln put it in the Gettysburg Address, America, in particular, is a nation dedicated to a 'proposition'. It is also true that without writing, and the traditions and history it captures, inhabitants of South Dakota, Nevada, Delaware or Arkansas might appear to have nothing but language in common, and those of Alaska and southern Florida not always that. But in the end a country, especially one which, as America does, so celebrates its land- and cityscapes, is a marriage between idea and fact, between its myths and history, and its defined boundaries and physical actualities. To return to Stevens, in the end, the truth of a country lies in the contradictory pull between his first assertion, which is also Eagleton's, and his revision of that later in the poem. A nation's identity is constructed from its texts and countertexts, but also its contexts. 'Man is the intelligence of his soil' – or 'when she sang, the sea, / Whatever self it had, became the self / That was her song' – *and* 'his soil is man's intelligence'.

Writing and America

Such, then, is the background to *Writing and America,* a volume which seeks to reflect many of the facts and tensions suggested here, and in doing so to address the issue of language – of writing – as the problematic, imperfect, yet fundamental tool for understanding America as a geographic and psychological entity.

The contributions to the volume are a blend of specific case-studies of writers such as James Fenimore Cooper and William Carlos Williams, who form a focus for discussions of American nationhood, with essays on more general topics including colonial notions of America as the Promised Land, the discourses of nationhood in the new Republic, and the sense of nationhood in American historiography and in the formation of the American literary canon. The collection also investigates the notion of stable nationhood, focusing on writers until recently beyond the canon.

It seeks as well to integrate the various component disciplines that make up American Studies, deliberately setting out to overcome conventional boundaries; historians write about literary texts, literary critics examine the construction of history. It aims, among other things, to give a sense of variety; to explore in-depth as well as broadly; to touch on, in one way or another, most kinds of writing, ranging from fiction to film, philosophy to politics, law to literary criticism, to create, in effect, a Bakhtinian heteroglossia of merging and clashing opinions like the country itself.

Christopher Mulvey's 'American constitutions and literary traditions', describes the ideological and rhetorical role of the Constitution in America's definition of itself, and discusses the significance of the fact that a central expression of American identity is *written*. Offering a broad sweep through history, Mulvey explores the Constitution and literary tradition, examining the historical contexts that link the formation of the Constitution to More's *Utopia* (1516). He shows how the Utopian ideal gained a new lease of life with the discovery of America. He also discusses the ongoing rewriting of constitutions and the fact that laws came to be seen to be made not natural, like America itself.

A companion essay, in that it too deals with what might loosely be termed Writing and Politics, is David Seed's 'Writing out of Communism: recantation memoirs of the Cold War'. Taking Whittaker Chambers's *Witness* (1952) as a focal point, he explores the links between the varied discourses of the 1950s that take Communism as their theme, and in particular examines the way fictional tropes shape the descriptions of historical and political 'fact' in the period.

Similarly, two essays look at issues concerning Writing and Gender. In 'A sense of the ludicrous: women and humour in American literature', Regina Barreca explores the contrasting roles of women as objects and as creators of humour in American writing and culture generally through the nineteenth and twentieth centuries. In doing so she examines the way women's humour interrogates and subverts the contradictory ideology of American masculinity, and explores the strategy she sees as evident in women's writing for concealing the humour in their texts.

In 'The two narratives of the Western', Antony Easthope takes an opposing tack to the extent that he rebukes a feminist reading of the Western, pointing out the positive aspects of the Western myth. The essay focuses on the West as a fictional locus of the ideal of American masculinity, and examines a variety of texts, historical and literary, writing and film, from the late nineteenth century through to *Dances with Wolves* of 1990, to expose the way they construct the notion of the American man.

This is followed by two essays devoted to issues of Writing and Race. In 'Narratives of the Native American', Robert Burchell examines the changing perception of the American Indian in historical and fictional writings from the earliest settlement of America through to the twentieth century. Burchell seeks to illustrate the way various forms of American writing have ideologically constructed the Native American to serve political ends, and as a point of definition for the American self.

Mary Ellison's 'African American song in New Orleans: the voice of the people' journeys through slave songs to black freedom songs, an evolution from necessary double-speak of the kind Baldwin describes, to a joyous celebration where, in Ellison's view, 'now the lyrics could be unambivalent'. Again in line with Baldwin's point, she explores black assertion and white mimicry as having to do, not just with words on a page, but with intonation. She also examines the blues from such figures as Lonnie Johnson, Fats Domino and Professor Longhair to the likes of Snooks Eaglin and Earl King, and looks at black and Native American traditions and the Mardi Gras, seeing in the various songs and lyrics 'the diversity and common cultural core that united America as a whole'.

Alan Munslow, in 'Writing history: Frederick Jackson Turner and the deconstruction of American history', then looks at the issue of writing and history. In doing so, he discusses the work of Frederick Jackson Turner on the significance of the frontier, and directly addresses the question of history as a literary artifact with reference to the work of Michel Foucault, Hayden White and Louis Althusser.

In '*Hawthorne*, James and History', David Timms explores the confusions and contradictions evident in Henry James's *Hawthorne* (1879). He argues that James's assertion of the importance of a realist approach to writing is belied by James's own predilection, in that study and in his novels of the time, for metaphoric language and deep scepticism of 'the visible world of things'. For Timms, James not only 'subverts his own realist principles by his very techniques in the book', but his fiction is always at odds with his theory. For all James's admiration of Emile Zola and Honoré de Balzac and the well-charted changes in his fictional practice, he remains heir to the same intellectual influences as Hawthorne.

The final two essays broadly focus on the issue of writing and place. In 'Revisioning the American landscape: from Utopia to eco-critique', Kate Fulbrook and Renee Slater begin by surveying ways of imagining America in the European consciousness from before the discovery of the continent through the Romantic movement to the more recent European views of Sartre and Baudrillard. They then focus on new and dissident views of reading the American landscape, in particular those of Scott Momaday and Barry Lopez. They also discuss the Puritan view of the American wilderness, and the influence on visions of the American landscape of the writings of Vespucci, Bacon, Locke, Washington Irving, Hawthorne, Cooper and James. Finally, they look at the contemporary situation through such writers as Wendell Berry, Peter Matthiessen, Annie Dillard and Gary Snyder.

In 'William Carlos Williams and the reconstruction of America', Les Arnold examines Williams's attempts to reconstruct America, rescuing it from authorized histories and rebuilding it upon previously ignored sources. Arnold explores *In the American Grain* (1925) as a starting point for Williams's ambitious proposal, moving through his examination of various literary models in the 1930s, before focusing on the construction of the American city in *Paterson* (1946).

Echoing several of the other contributors, Arnold makes the point that Williams seeks 'to represent the American writer's task as initially one of destruction' that should 'seek always to disturb, disrupt and finally subvert'. This dismantling, and subsequently reconstructing, process does indeed seem to be at the heart of much of *Writing and America*, and of American writing, whether that be through ethnic or gender-orientated rewriting, or the kind of rewriting of culture and history that, say, the poet William Heyen engages in, in collections devoted to disturbing and disrupting official versions of such issues as the Holocaust, the environment, the destruction of the buffalo, and the Gulf War. Such writers – numerous as they are – continue the (counter) tradition of re-imagining, rewriting and reassessing documents and data. Several contributors, indeed, point to the fact that *re*writing America is a constant need, illustrating that ever-rewritable palimpsest of the American past in the very process of being written.

Finally, one of the strengths of this collection is that, while the plethora of issues that can arise from a topic like Writing and America is infinite, the variety of contributions distil issues in broad areas. The aim is thus to offer argument, evidence and examples for further discussion. Among the issues only touched on here or in essays, are, for instance, American drama from Howells through to O'Neill and Miller, and on into the present with the likes of Naomi Wallace and her Gulf War play, *In the Heart of America* (1994); writing in such areas as, say, sociology, psychology or science; small journals; postmodernism; religions and cultures aside from Amerindians or the Amish – such as Jewish or Mormon communities, or the Melungeons in the Clinch Mountains of the Appalachians in Tennessee – not subsumed by American culture or the American self as constructed in mainstream writing and culture; and sports writing, not least the mythologies surrounding baseball and basketball, a genre which is another area of identity for the American self and, judging by the O. J. Simpson trial, has a major impact on American culture and America's writing of itself. One could go on, since that is the nature of the subject. Beginning as an apparently definable area of exploration, like the land itself, once past the port of entry it expands ever wider. But *Writing and America* seeks, among other things, to offer a guide, a map of possible routes, and some insights along the way.

Notes

1. Eagleton T A 1993 Merrie state of mind. *Guardian* 2 (14 December): 8.
2. Englands of the mind. In Heaney S 1984 *Preoccupations: selected prose 1968–1978*. Faber, London, p 150.
3. The idea of order at Key West. Stevens W 1955 *The collected poems of Wallace Stevens*. Faber, New York, p 129.
4. The comedian as the letter C. Stevens 1955 pp 27–35.
5. Stampp K 1956 *The peculiar institution*. Random House, New York.
6. Cash W J (1941) 1960 *The mind of the South*. Random House, New York, p vii.
7. Gray R 1986 *Writing the South: ideas of an American region*. Cambridge University Press, Cambridge, pp xii, xi.

8. Whitman W (1855) 1986 *Leaves of grass*. Penguin, Harmonds-worth, p 85.
9. Scott Fitzgerald F (1945) 1965 *The crack-up, with other pieces and stories*. Penguin, Harmondsworth, p 39.
10. Oates J C 1987 *Marya, a life*. Cape, London, p 152.
11. Du Bois W E B (1903) 1963 *The souls of black folk: essays and sketches by WE Burghardt Du Bois*. Dodd, Mead & Co, New York, p 3.
12. Baldwin J (1963) 1964 *The fire next time*. Penguin, Harmonds-worth, p 44.
13. Baldwin J (1961) 1967 *Nobody knows my name: more notes of a native son*. Dell, New York, p 42.
14. Baldwin 1964 p 42.
15. Bruce Springsteen Born in the USA. *Born in the USA*, CBS 1984.
16. The road not taken. In Frost F 1963 *Selected poems of Robert Frost*. Rinehart, New York, pp 71–2.
17. Barnes J 1989 *A history of the world in 10½ chapters*. Cape, London, p 54.
18. Bruce Springsteen Factory. *Darkness on the edge of town*, CBS 1978; Nebraska. *Nebraska*, CBS 1982.
19. Springsteen tells this story about being drafted in 1968 for Vietnam before the song War (*Bruce Springsteen and the E Street band live 1975–85*, CBS 1985).
20. Bolt C 1974 *A history of the USA*. Macmillan, London, p 525.
21. Weiner J 1990 *The next one hundred years: shaping the fate of our living earth*. Rider Books, London, pp 52–4.
22. Schmitz N 1983 *Of Huck and Alice: humorous writing in American literature*. Minnesota University Press, Minneapolis, p 103.
23. Raban J 1991 *Hunting Mister Heartbreak: a discovery of America*. HarperCollins, New York, p 2.
24. Dickinson E There's a certain slant of light. In Johnson T H (ed) 1970 *The complete poems of Emily Dickinson*. Faber, London, p 118.
25. Sokolov R A 1967 Into the mind of Nat Turner. *Newsweek* (16 October): 69.
26. Stone A E 1987 The return of Nat Turner: history, literature and cultural politics in sixties America. *Prospects* **12**: 252.
27. Baldwin 1967 p 72.
28. Wheeler J A 1984 This participatory universe. In Allen L Hammond (ed) 1984 *A passion to know: twenty profiles in science*. Scribners, New York, p 185.
29. Nevins A and Commager H S 1942 *America: the story of a free people*. Oxford University Press, Oxford, pp 7, 4.

30. Sergio Leone (dir) 1968 *Once upon a time in the West* (*C'era una volta il West*) and Henry Hathaway, John Ford, George Marshall (dir) 1962 *How the West was won.* The 1962 classic Western starred John Wayne, James Stewart, Richard Widmark, Henry Fonda and that all-American girl-next-door, Debbie Reynolds. Leone's 1968 film in contrast is a revisionist Western. It too starred Fonda, as well as Charles Bronson, but countercasts Fonda as a sadist.

31. Wolf N 1992 *The beauty myth: how images of beauty are used against women.* Anchor Doubleday, New York, p 182.

32. Sommers C 1994 *Who stole feminism? How women have betrayed women.* Simon & Schuster, New York. See also Greig G 1994 Get your facts straight sisters. *Sunday Times* (Style and travel section, 14 August): 4–5.

33. MacKinnon C A 1991 *Toward a feminist theory of the state.* Harvard University Press, Cambridge, Mass, p xv.

34. Lauter P 1994 Melville climbs the canon. *American Literature* **66** (1): 20, 3.

35. Morrison T 1990 *Playing in the dark: whiteness and the literary imagination.* Harvard University Press, Cambridge, Mass, p 17.

36. Brown D (1970) 1990 *Bury my heart at Wounded Knee: an Indian history of the American West.* Vintage, London, pp 13–36.

37. Bellow B (1959) 1981 *Henderson the rain king.* Penguin, Harmondsworth, p 157.

38. Brown M 1993 *American heartbeat: travels from Woodstock to San José by song title.* Penguin, Harmondsworth, p 84.

39. Bryson B 1993 *The lost continent: travels in small town America.* Abacus, London, p 16.

40. Hoare Q, Nowell Smith G 1972 *The prison notebooks* by Antonio Gramsci. Lawrence and Wishart, London, p 317.

41. Anderson W 1986 *Beer, USA.* Morgan and Morgan, New York, p 166.

42. Forster E M 1980 The machine stops. In *Collected short stories.* Penguin, Harmondsworth, p 117.

43. Burgess A 1979 Brooklyn Liebestod. *Observer* (9 September): 15.

44. Greenberg R M 1993 *Splintered worlds: fragmentation and the ideal of diversity in the work of Emerson, Melville, Whitman and Dickinson.* Northeastern University Press, Boston, Mass, pp 124–5.

45. Of glory. In Montaine M 1913 *The Essays of Michel de Montaigne* trans Charles Cotton (1685–86) rev W C Hazlitt (3 vols). G Bell & Sons, London, vol 2 p 337.

PART I

1 *American constitutions and literary traditions*

Christopher Mulvey

Socrates: 'Come then, let us invent a state.'

Plato, *The Republic*

Eighteenth-century American claims to have written a new constitution have a parallel in seventeenth-century British claims to have inherited an 'Ancient Constitution', the origins of which were said to be 'time out of mind'. The strength of such a claim was considerable whether or not the British claimants meant what they said. They probably did, but that is immaterial. The effect of the claim was to make the British Constitution immemorial and therefore unquestionable. This was a powerful argument of legitimation even if it could be used as much by those who wished to overthrow a present constitution as by those who wished to defend one. By contrast the Constitution of 1789 was presented as something new and in that process the historical roots of the American Constitution were denied just as the historical roots of the British Constitution were denied. Both strategies were effective in solving problems of sovereignty, commitment, and continuity: issues which face shapers of nations. A denial of historical origins and a claim for the universal validity of the selected model of constitution induced the trope of timelessness. With a document so presented, men and women could govern their lives, and for a document so presented they could, if necessary, be asked to die. This last condition is the difficult one to effect but it is one which the United States Constitution in due course achieved.

Socrates' challenge to Adeimantus in Book I of Plato's *Republic* to 'invent a state'[1] is a good invitation to a debate about the matter, but a dangerous start to the real thing. What can be made can be unmade, especially if it is seen to be the work of ordinary people. It is best for constitutions to be author-less. And it is very good for them to seem to be changeless since citizens and subjects alike will then be the more ready to accept and to obey them. The drafters of the Constitution of the United States overcame the problem of authorship by diffusing authority as widely as possible. The drafters when they had written it moved not to publish it but to adopt it. Its authority came by a process of ratification and the final authors were the People of the United States; the 'Supreme Fiction' works as long as people believe it works.

In the late-twentieth century and after 200 years of operation, the United States Constitution can claim something of the timelessness of the British Ancient Constitution. For the majority of people the late-eighteenth century is 'time out of mind'. The British dismiss Chinese pity for the novelty of a people who trace their origins to the fifth century AD and for everyday history 1789 is old enough, but in 1789 some other claim had to be made to authenticate a constitution.

In a manoeuvre matching the disappearance of its author, the Constitution forgot its origins. Any constitution that operates without direct show of force may be presumed to have some call upon a people's loyalty. What constitutions need to do initially is to provide sufficiently good government long enough for the necessary myths to take root. The historical origins of a con-stitution need not then become a weak point in its call for co-operation; in due course co-operation should mature into loyalty. The origins of the American Constitution nonetheless lay in a historical process. From the late-medieval through the early-modern period, Western states ruled by law were evolving towards the condition of liberal, property-based democracies. This was a process which developed most rapidly in environ-ments that enabled political treatise and political experiment to influence each other. It was not by chance that British North America produced what is called the world's oldest written constitution for there a culture of constitutional treatise writing and constitutional experimentation had offered an exchange of what might work with what had worked over a period of almost 200 years before a final form was found. This was a cultural evolution which was accelerated by deliberate, intelligent search for the best models. But the planning did not have to be towards anything for it to be successful; over time observers would only be looking at those constitutions which further the process. Ontology is more important than teleology.

The US Constitution's origins in treatise and contract

In particular, two kinds of texts shaping the Constitution of the United States can demonstrate this process, though a full discussion of either would take more space than is available here; even a partial discussion of one of them will have to be more assertion than demonstration. Nonetheless Sir Thomas More's *Utopia* (1516) permits a starting point for an investigation backwards to Plato's *Republic* (c.375 BC) and forwards to the Constitution of the United States of America to demonstrate the Utopian nature of that document. This is one of the generic lines on which the Constitution can be placed. Another line runs backwards from *Magna Carta* (1215) to Aristotle's *Constitution of the Athenians* (c.335 BC) and forwards from *Magna Carta* by way of the company charters to the Constitution of the United States.

The two lines might be thought of as the sacred and the profane origins of the Constitution because the writing of a political treatise has traditionally been valued above the drafting of a charter. However, it is arguable that no more actual intelligence has gone into the first than has gone eventually into the second. It is fair to say 'eventually' because the charter, like other legal instruments, has an incremental, evolutionary nature. It is able under the right circumstances to shed those elements in its composition that inhibit its operation, to adopt those elements that re-drafters recognize as beneficial, to adapt to a variety of economic and political niches, and to accumulate its wisdom. The right circumstances are circumstances which once they have emerged are likely to be maintained by the operation of the institutions which they have brought into being. The subsequent evolution of the documents becomes self-reinforcing in powerful and unpredictable ways as the documents multiply their variety of forms of operation and consequently increase the varieties of conditions of experiment.

The development of the legal instrument, either charter or constitution, creates a subtext, controlling the supertext which is the charter or constitution held in the hand and immediately read. This kind of literary tradition is not the traditional literary tradition. There are no great names in a subterranean tradition. It is adaptive and evolving. It works inexorably, incrementally, insistently; it cannot forget its way because it is making the way as it goes forward. It is not deterministic either. It is influenced by external conditions and events and as these change so it changes. Legal instruments, business letters, trade journals have literary formulations in common and they share something with the folk story; in particular they bury authors, conceal origins, internalize influences and offer themselves as common currencies.

In none of these forms is originality much valued. Invention will be concealed, or, failing that, passed off as discovery. The internalizing of influences creates an implicit tradition like that in music before the invention of the record-player. Hans Heinrich Eggerbrecht calls this 'the spontaneous tradition, whereby the past was still contained within the new and one merged into the other'.[2] It is difficult to realize that state now, but Monteverdi heard only his immediate predecessors and Bach heard no Monteverdi. Mozart heard only those works of Bach that he dug out and played to himself in the Master's old chapel. Beethoven heard little Mozart. But the influence of one musician upon another was nonetheless real and strong; it was carried by intermediaries. The twentieth-century musician works in a simultaneous rather than an internalized tradition – this must influence composition substantially. Writing has provided the opportunity for the composers of written pieces to work in either tradition, and this is especially true since the invention of printing. However, contract lawyers could not expect to gain much advantage from having before them the whole tradition of contracts, and they have not attempted it. It is quite sufficient to have the latest version before them; they may presume that for most instances it contains its accumulated advantages.

For this reason, starting from scratch with the writing of contracts is more likely to produce unwanted economic and/or political results than modifying existing documents or formulae, but it is also for this reason that original thinkers want to start again. And it is also, in cultures which admire originality, creativity, and imagination, the inventive political thinker who is admired above the document drafter. There is less testing in practice of philosophers' constitutions than of lawyers' contracts, though there has been some testing, and in the Americas especially. However, even though there have been tests of the invented constitutions of philosophers, the impulse to originality has made philosophers dislike trial and error, condemn tinkering and fixing, and made them ready to go back to first principles, to start again. First principles themselves evolve, so philosophers do in practice respond to some accumulations of what – for want of a better word – I will call *wisdom*; even so, the generic line through political theory is always more discontinuous than that through legal practice. The philosopher having read widely in the canon of best instances will commonly proceed to write as fresh a statement as can be made; the lawyer having read deeply in the precedents will commonly draft as close a restatement as can be made. The lawyer who does otherwise runs the danger of being called a philosopher.

An English philosophical tradition and the American Constitution

Because they want to be original, philosophers read the work of their predecessors, more so than poets who, up to the seventeenth century in England certainly, were working more within an implicit than an explicit tradition. Emrys Jones's *New Oxford Book of Sixteenth Century Verse* shows how frequently poems written in that century were not first published until the nineteenth or even the twentieth century.[3] But More read Plato before writing *Utopia*, and Bacon read Plato and More before writing *The New Atlantis*. J. C. Davis's *Utopia and the Ideal Society: A Study of English Utopian Writing 1516–1700* makes clear just how explicit was this tradition of Utopian writing as one author followed on another developing plans for ideal societies.[4] He identifies a chain of five major seventeenth-century English Utopian texts: Robert Burton's *Anatomy of Melancholy* (1621), Francis Bacon's *New Atlantis* (1627), Samuel Gott's *Nova Solyma* (1650), Gerard Winstanley's *The Law of Freedom* (1652), and James Harrington's *The Commonwealth of Oceana* (1656).

But the distinction between an explicit or declared tradition and an implicit or internalized tradition is not absolute and one can overlap the other. Davis lists close to 150 items (some are versions and variations of the same title) in his bibliography of Utopian writings from 1516 to 1700. Not all of these were as widely read as others. No doubt Davis is the only person to have read all the titles in his list, and his list is not a complete one. What this means is that by the seventeenth century, the Socratic invitation to invent a state had been taken up by well over a hundred writers in the English-speaking world. The practice of state-inventing was just as widespread in the Latin-writing world, though by the 1630s writers were increasingly turning to vernaculars.

The genre took on its own momentum and not everyone needed to have read all examples for all examples to have had some modifying influence upon the form. At the very least every new venture made speculation about the ideal state more commonplace and implementation more thinkable. At the same time there is evidence that even the explicit tradition could become effectively implicit and begin to operate in a sub-terranean, subtextual way. This particular tradition starts with Plato and there is no doubt that the philosophers, from Sir Thomas More through to John Locke and beyond, had read and thought about *The Republic*. But there is considerable doubt as to whether or not the writers of the US Constitution were familiar with Plato. Gore Vidal for one disputes the idea that the framers of the Constitution were influenced by great intellectual forces. In an essay called 'The Second American Revolution', he notes how few are the references in the writings of these men to intellectual masters. He has made a count of namings in *The Federalist Papers* (1788) and notes that Locke is not mentioned once, and Plato is mentioned only once.[5]

Bernard Bailyn has an interesting supplement to this observation. In *The Ideological Origins of the American Revolution* he writes 'John Adams, who in 1774 had cited Plato as an advocate of equality and self-government . . . was so shocked when he finally studied the philosopher that he concluded that *The Republic* must have been meant as a satire.'[6] This certainly was not the first nor the last time that an idealist finally turned to Plato to have a rude awakening. Bailyn's story about Adams is significant of the way in which the active intellectual who is also a lawyer operates. Plato had been a touchstone because he was known to have written the original statement of the ideal *polis*. But without having read Plato, Adams was happy to quote him. Plato was operating through a tradition that was only implicit, but was having a radical effect on the idea of the ideal state in North America. When Adams actually read Plato, he found that the Plato of tradition was contradicted by the Plato of the text. Adams reconciled the contradiction by calling Plato's work a satire and so negated the negation.

Certain ideas had been central to a tradition of the Utopian state as this had been modified by More out of Plato. These ideas had included a belief in centralized decision making and a belief in the common ownership of property. By the middle of the seventeenth century the first of these had become generally modified, so that a concept of the tripartite operation of the state's powers was becoming more and more generally accepted. With this acceptance came a recognition that unless those powers were divided among different centres in the state then Plato's worst scenario, tyranny and domination by the tyrant, would result. Precisely because in early republican thinking Plato's prescriptions appeared to lead directly to a tyranny based in caste, they were repulsive to John Adams.

But if Plato's thinking was caste-bound, he also offered the powerfully attractive idea of the common ownership of property. This was to dominate nineteenth- and twentieth-century socialism, and 'Communism' was the name to be given to the twentieth century's most virulent form of Utopianism. It was not an idea popular with the property owners who framed the American Constitution, but as Jack Pole has pointed out, it was not popular with any of those taking part in the constitutional debates of the 1770s and 1780s. In his essay 'The Ancient World in the New Republic: the Founder's Use of History', Pole suggests that the absence of a debate about property ownership in 1787 should provoke surprise in the twentieth-century historian. This is particularly the case since, as he argues, the British North Americans were inheriting a tradition in a literature of ideal commonwealths which said that land tenure should be governed by regulation to control purchase and inheritance, so that inequalities would not develop. But even this relatively moderate restriction on property ownership met with no sympathy from those engaged in the American constitutional debate. 'The silence of the Anti-Federalists on this theme is all the more remarkable when one considers', says Pole, 'that James Harrington had incorporated an agrarian law, so fundamental that he turned an adjective into a noun and called it "the Agrarian", into the stabilising structure of his *Oceana* (1656)'. Pole is as emphatic about the influence of Harrington on these debates as he is about the ineffectiveness of Harrington's advice on property control. 'Harrington stood at the source', says Pole, 'of the Anglo-American Commonwealth tradition, and one member of the Massachusetts's constitutional convention of 1779–80 had gone so far as to suggest that the name of the Commonwealth should be changed from Massachusetts-Bay to Oceana'.[7]

This to-ing and fro-ing of influences will need to be examined further since it is clear that 'the Anglo-American Commonwealth tradition', as Pole calls it, was achieving a consensus somewhat different from those of Europe, including the English or British. The role of John Locke in helping to shape the American consensus on the matter of property and land inheritance can be shown to be strong, and not only as the philosopher of the rights of private property. Locke's influence can also be seen in the pragmatic tradition of contract evolution. He was a philosopher given a chance to write a working constitution. John Locke's 'First Set of the Fundamental Constitutions of South Carolina' of 1669 united the theoretical-philosophical with the empirical-statutory tradition. But it comes at a midway point in the development of the one and the evolution of the other. The starting point for the Anglo-American commonwealth tradition was 150 years old by then and in order to put Locke in his place, it would be best to start at the beginning made by Sir Thomas More.

Ancient, medieval and Renaissance Utopias

Sir Thomas More was both a philosopher and a lawyer, but he wrote as a philosopher when he composed *Utopia*, published first in Latin in 1516. *Utopia* did not present itself as an outline for a new society and government, but rather as a satire on the society and government that More knew. He satirized actual government and society by describing a land, Utopia, where things were ordered very differently from England. Utopia was a land of freemen and slaves, where goods were held in common, where there was a national system of education for men and women alike, where everyone had to work, where religious toleration was practised, and where the good of the individual was sacrificed to the common good.

More's philosophical model for *Utopia* was Plato's *Republic*. The form of that book was the dialogue. But the teller of the story, a navigator, provided another more immediate model: that of the Renaissance navigator's narrative. The narrative of Amerigo Vespucci had been published in 1507 and Sir Thomas More's narrator Raphael Hythlodaye (or 'Nonsenso') claimed to have sailed with Vespucci himself.[8] Amerigo Vespucci was not only unknowingly to provide the everyday name for the regions discovered to European knowing by Columbus, Cabot, and da Gama; he also provided the philosopher's name for these regions. In the letter on his third voyage to Lorenzo Pietro Francesco di Medici of March or April 1503, he said:

> In past days I wrote very fully to you of my return from new countries, which have been found and explored with ships, at the cost and by command, of this Most Serene King of Portugal; and it is lawful to call it a new world, because none of these countries were known to our ancestors, and to all who hear about them they will be entirely new.[9]

America, *Mundus Novus*, the New World, was More's Nowhereland. His Utopia is an island off the coast of the Americas and the text *Utopia* is one of the first texts in Anglo-American literature, albeit in Latin. Although it was 'about' England, it was no less 'about' America, a land, or a space, or a place that was not just a 'U-topia' or 'no-where' but was also a 'eu-topia' or 'sweet place' about which philosophers might dream, speculate and scheme. As such it was very much a 'some-where', very much a place sailed to, and looked at, and entered upon. The book *Utopia* derived from Plato, and not only from *The Republic* but also from the *Timaeus* and the *Critias*. And in the later dialogues, Plato developed his myth of the island of Atlantis and its conflict with the ideal commonwealth of ancient Athens where the principles of government expounded in theory in *The Republic* were put into practice in a lost world of authoritarian dreaming. This ancient Athens, like Atlantis itself, was a land which could not exist, and was indeed nowhere. But in bringing together the dialogue of Plato and the narrative of Vespucci, More was making one of those alterations in first principles which philosophers periodically achieve. For Atlantis had really not existed for Plato but Utopia really did exist for More and, more particularly, for his readers. They would have to associate it with the lands being all the time more discovered, uncovered, recovered during the sixteenth century. Within 100 years of the publication of *Utopia*, men and women from England had begun to live in the Americas in a continuous, social way, making 'nowhere' their homes and having to rethink the meaning of 'the land to the West' from starting points which were Atlantic landfalls rather than European landends.

The speculations of these English men and women would need to be very different from the speculations of medieval writers about the Land of Avalon or the Land of Cockaigne. Geoffrey of Monmouth had described in the *Vita Merlini* (c.1159) an '"island of fruits" . . . where the soil [yielded] harvests without sowing and where the inhabitants [were] noted for their longevity. Morgan [ruled] the island, assisted by her eight sisters; all skilled in leechcraft and other learned arts'. Avalon was also called the 'Insula Pomorum' – 'the Island of Apples' – and this has been linked with Celtic myth and the Celtic words for that fruit. Avalon was still further linked with Glastonbury in Somerset and with Celtic myths of 'Summerland', and with the whole magical-mystery tour of Arthurian legend.[10]

The Land of Cockaigne was a medieval Utopia of a more robust kind, not so much a dream of the courtier as a dream of the peasant 'where life was a round of luxurious idleness. . . . In Cockaigne, the rivers were of wine, the houses were built of cake and barley sugar, the streets were paved with pastry and the shops supplied goods for nothing . . . roast geese and fowls wandered about inviting folks to eat them, and buttered larks fell from the skies like manna'.[11] The Land of Cockaigne has been associated with the Land of the Cockney but it appears that it was first discovered in the stories of medieval Germany. It is a myth which retains its energy and zest. The name plays wonderfully with the land of modern drug-induced euphoria and it had as little to do with rational planning for a better world as do the dreams of the twentieth-century cocaine user.

More's Utopia was a very real place by comparison. There was nothing magical about it and nothing particularly self-indulgent. Few courtiers and no peasants must have dreamt of going there. It was the beginning of a new dream of reason. Further, the effect of the discovery of a whole continent and many, many lands in the West was to dissolve the mists of myths. Discovery discredited the undiscovered and very largely replaced it. Both Atlantis and Avalon became America.

Utopian places and New World spaces

Sir Thomas More was a religious as well as a philosophical man and his *Utopia* was a didactic document. More's satire was generalized to address England as a typically Christian and European state which was failing to meet the ideals that its Christian, European status required of it. The critique was as Christocentric as it was Eurocentric and More's title said precisely that things were done better nowhere. But from More's text there developed a line of politico-philosophical writing which, if we look back through More to Plato, increasingly offered descriptions of new lands, new worlds, and new states which were more and more real. They were states that did not exist but they might now be thought of as states which could exist. *The Republic* and *Utopia* increasingly become starting points for descriptions of forms of government which their writers hoped to see implemented as new orders. Men began to draft constitutions for new states somewhere not nowhere.

By the seventeenth century, the speculative construction of commonwealths became a regular project among thinkers. Tammaso Campanella's *City of the Sun* (1623) was followed by Francis Bacon's *New Atlantis* (1627). Joabin, the good Jew of the city of Bensalem in the land of Bacon's New Atlantis, makes direct reference to More's *Utopia*, saying: 'I have read in a book of one of your men, of a Feigned Commonwealth', and Bacon had it as his original plan 'to have composed a frame of Laws, or of the best state or mould of a commonwealth'.[12] James

Harrington's *The Commonwealth of Oceana* (1656) moved speculative thinking about the ideal commonwealth towards practical application. Harrington was writing in the period of the English Commonwealth and he dedicated his work to the Great Protector, Oliver Cromwell. The English had been brought to the point of recognizing that their political system was not given but made and they were in the process of making it again.

The line through More to Harrington by way of Bacon and Campanella is strong and the fact that the first three texts in this great tradition were all written in Latin emphasizes the fact that this was a European, not merely an English, tradition. A common feature of these fictional commonwealths is that they are placed on islands, Utopia and Oceana in the Atlantic, the City of the Sun and New Atlantis in the Indian and Pacific Oceans. All of them are made isolated so that they develop in a vacuum of political force. They are all little Americas, or new worlds isolated from the old. By contrast, while the commonwealths developed in the English new world were sufficiently far from Europe to permit the growth of new forms, they were sufficiently in touch with each other to allow a limited evolutionary struggle to take place so that newly emerging forms got some real testing in an America which was not a nowhereland.

All four writers in this Utopian tradition were imprisoned. More was imprisoned and executed many years after he had published *Utopia*; Bacon was imprisoned and disgraced just before he wrote *The New Atlantis*; Campanella was imprisoned and tortured and wrote *The City of the Sun* in jail; Harrington was first questioned by Cromwell about *Oceana*, then imprisoned by Charles II. In prison, Harrington became insane.[13] This is a genre with a special history, one engaged in by men who excited the anger of princes. The Englishman no more than the Italian could experiment with constitution framing and state making; such schemes needed to be disguised as satires, fantasies, and dreams. Nonetheless the danger remained that the writer so dreaming could be perceived as subverting the state. Cromwell liked that no better than Charles I or Charles II.

But in the space of the New World, Utopian thinking could sometimes lead to Utopian experiment without challenging the authority of the monarchs of the Old World, and the English began in the seventeenth century to catch up with the Spanish in the epic arts of city founding, state shaping and eventually nation making. When Europeans looked at the Americas they called them empty despite their extant cultures, civilizations and polities. But those cultures, civilizations, and polities were not recognizable by people trained to think that only that which derived its origins from Europe was a political reality. Lands were full to the European state and constitution makers, even of a Utopian order, only when they had populations with European densities and weaponry of European strength. These were principles, or practices at least, which obtained for all continents, not just the Americas. They obtained particularly in Europe itself where any state which weakened in numbers or arms was immediately subjected to invasion by its neighbours. The fact that all European-American state-making experiments started with violations of those human rights that the best of the experiments was eventually to 'declare' meant that all the experiments, Utopian and pragmatic alike, were trapped in an original sin for which neither suffering nor passion has so far made atonement.

Utopian experiments in British North America

Utopian experiment in the British North American colonies can be divided into three phases: the Puritan experiments from the 1620s onward in the founding of a religious commonwealth in the Massachusetts Bay area; the American rationalist Utopias which began with the establishing of South Carolina in 1669; and the federal experiment which began with the Declaration of Independence and the drafting of state constitutions in 1776 and ended with the ratification of the Constitution of the United States in 1789. The second phase, from the restoration of Charles II to the reign of George II, is the recognized Utopian phase of colonial foundations, and it is significant that the Massachusetts or New England foundations are not traditionally called 'Utopian'. There may also be good reason to deny the term *Utopian* to the venture which resulted in the ratified Constitution of the United States in 1789. But these colonial and federal foundations were deliberate attempts to establish societies which were an improvement on known, actual societies and all of them intended to put into reality ideals of humanity and government and the good life.

AMERICAN UTOPIAN EXPERIMENTS: PHASE 1

The Puritan ventures of the 1620s were similar in many respects to those experiments regularly called 'Utopian' which led to the foundation of so many communities in the Early American Republic. The doctrine of St Paul that Christian communities were 'bound together for the common good' was an important justification for many of these groups and a starting point for idealism. Among the pre-twentieth-century sects that have survived to the present is the Church of Jesus Christ of Latter Day Saints, and the Mormons offer some useful points of comparison with the earliest religious communities of Massachusetts. Of all the several hundred American Utopian groups of the nineteenth century, the Mormons alone attempted to leave the United States polity and to set up an idealized, independent state as much beyond the jurisdiction of Washington as the Massachusetts Bay Colony was beyond the jurisdiction of London. The members of the Bay Colony had to acknowledge theoretical control but in effect they were moving to a state of self-rule similar to that of the Mormons on the Great Salt Lake in 1848. When Washington began to reclaim rule over the territory which it called Utah but which the Latter Day Saints called Deseret, it did so with much less effort and with more complete success than London had achieved in Massachusetts, but the Puritans' movement to the wilderness had much in common with the Saints' movement to Deseret.

When the English Puritans had obtained their charter from Charles I in 1629, their crossing of the Atlantic in a fleet of seventeen ships with close to 1,000 men, women and children constituted one of the largest organized crossings of its kind and it established a model for successful settler-colonial ventures. It was the same model in terms of large, mixed numbers under firm control and central organization that the British Government was to adopt in the next century when it set up the penal colony of Botany Bay.[14] The effects of large numbers, of mixed genders, of mixed ages, of forward planning, of agreed purpose, and of subordination of individual to community interest had as good results in both cases. Utopian or not, the Commonwealth of Massachusetts and the parallel commonwealths of New England established a strong pattern of interaction between theoretical proposition and practical experiment in state shaping. In the next phase, this interaction was to operate with an explicitly Utopian self-awareness.

AMERICAN UTOPIAN EXPERIMENTS: PHASE 2

In 1665 Charles II gave to Sir George Carter and seven other distinguished men of the Kingdom

> all that Province, Territory, or Tract of Ground, called *Carolina*, scituate, lying and being within our dominions of America, extending from the *north* end of the Island, called Luke Island, which lyeth in the *Southern Virginia* seas, and within six and thirty degrees of the *northern* latitude; and the *west*, as far as the *south seas*; and so respectively as far as the river of *Mathias*, which bordereth upon the coast of *Florida*, and within one and thirty degrees of the *northern* latitude, and so *west* in a direct line, as far as the *south* seas aforesaid.[15]

So the king that day gave away 900,000 square miles of land that was not his. Among the beneficiaries of this charter was Sir Anthony Ashley Cooper, later to become the Earl of Shaftesbury, and he directed John Locke to draw up a document which came to be called the 'Fundamental Constitutions of Carolina'. This scheme represented a consciously planned attempt to devise a constitution for good government. Sir Arthur Ashley Cooper could call on John Locke to write the constitution because Locke was physician to the great man's household. Although constitution writing must have come as an unusual job, American business was to become a central preoccupation for Locke and his master through to 1672 (in which year Shaftesbury was made president of the Council of Trade) and beyond. Locke's 'duties in regard to all manner of colonial questions occupied him for the next two years. He seems to have had some thoughts of visiting America, and he was a shareholder for some time in a company formed to settle the Bahamas'.[16] It has been counted remarkable that one of the prominent features of this constitution was the creation of an hereditary nobility with the titles of landgraves, caciques, lords of the manor and below them freeholders, serfs, and slaves. The eight grantees, the Lords Proprietors, were to constitute a Palatine Court. Titles were to go with property alongside strict laws regulating land inheritance.[17]

Locke's constitution was not a success and has been mocked for its aristocratic bias. But it is not surprising that a gentleman-servant in an aristocratic household introduced an aristocratic element in his ideal commonwealth and it was not obvious in 1669, as it would become after 1776, that aristocracy was antithetical to the North American zone. Locke's commonwealth, like More's, included slaves and slaves might well have been thought to be as much complementary to a scheme that included aristocrats as one that included freemen. John Locke learned something from this venture in state making and his *Treatises of Government* (1690) show how much. Those texts contained many of the presumptions about government held by constitution writers in the next century.

Seventeenth-century British North America saw one more proprietorial experiment in idealized government, the foundation of Pennsylvania. The Lord Proprietor, William Penn, received a charter from Charles II on 14 March 1681 which made Penn 'absolute proprietor' of a large tract of land and imposed certain restrictions on the Proprietor in terms of requiring a legislative assembly in the colony, obeying certain acts of the English Parliament, submitting to certain vetoes of the Royal Privy Council, and abiding by legal appeals to the Crown. Within these restrictions William Penn had a free hand and he used it to describe and establish a new kind of state. To the extent that Penn was a Quaker and to the extent that his Quakerism shaped his model state, Penn's was a religio-Utopian venture. In 1682 he constructed a Frame of Government that guaranteed religious freedom, and he went on to lay out a Utopian city named for Brotherly Love and conclude a treaty of friendship with the peoples in possession, the Native Americans. He did not presume the Lockean *tabula rasa* of Carolina. In the long run, it made little enough difference to the American Indians, but it was a better start. Penn's Frame of Government was more effective altogether than the Carolinian Fundamental Constitutions and remained in operation in modified form until 1776.[18]

The final colonial Utopian experiment took place in land reabsorbed by the Crown when the Carolinas, by then plural, were surrendered by the proprietors in 1729. A member of the English Parliament named James Edward Oglethorpe had become in that year chairman of the parliamentary committee on debtors' prisons. His brief involved him with the problems of pauperism and the relief of those imprisoned for debt. His parliamentary interests further involved him with matters of trade and British naval supremacy. This combination of concerns led him to look with interest at land newly available for appropriation. Heading a consortium of 20 associates he sought in 1732 a charter from George II for a new independent colony to be called Georgia.[19]

Oglethorpe had a religious purpose, like William Penn, but he wished to protect persecuted Protestant sects and so his declaration of religious toleration extended only to those of the Protestant faiths and explicitly excluded Catholics. At the same time, he was more liberal than South Carolina on the issue of freedom: the importation of slaves into the new colony was forbidden. Oglethorpe also introduced legislation on the use of alcohol in the colony. Distilled liquors were seen as an evil and the importation of rum and brandy were banned from the beginning. In addition to banning slaves, rum and brandy, Oglethorpe's constitution also set special limitations on land tenure. The original grant to the Georgian Trustees was to run to 1752 and on 4 July of that year the Trustees surrendered control of the colony to the Crown. Oglethorpe's special provisions concerning labour, liquor, and land had all proved unworkable. With the collapse of each one the colony's prosperity had been boosted.[20]

The relationship between Utopian experiment and state prosperity is a crucial and not a straightforward one; in particular, it would be wrong to argue that the Georgian experiment demonstrated the pointlessness of a Utopian constitution. The drafting and redrafting of Georgia's colonial charter and the reshaping of its constitution were major lessons for constitution makers before the round of drafting and redrafting of constitutions which took place following the Declaration of Independence.

AMERICAN UTOPIAN EXPERIMENTS: PHASE 3

The British in North America or, as we can call them in 1787, the Americans had become very practised performers in the constitutional genre by the time Madison and his friends put pens to paper. By that date, James Bryce said, the Americans had already produced 117 constitutions.[21] The framers of the Constitution had the advantage of publications (appearing in Philadelphia particularly) which were called 'Constitution Collections'. These would present the colonial and state constitutions adopted to date. Like Elizabethan sonnet collections, they showed the aspiring writer what to do, what was expected, and what won praise. We know that the Constitution drafted in 1787 and ratified in 1789 is a good example of the genre because constitutions have an advantage which sonnets do not have and that is that there are legal procedures to judge whether or not constitutions are believed to be well written.

Practical planners and theoretical schemers alike may have exploded the term *Utopia* but there still remain senses which retain more of the ideal than of the ridiculous and so it is fair to explore the ways in which the Utopianism set in motion by Sir Thomas More in 1516 might be seen to shape the political experiments which led to the founding of the United States of America and which make it a serious question to ask to what extent the Constitution framed in 1787 was a Utopian statement.

The Constitution is not Utopian, if Utopian means impractical, impossible, or mythical. The Constitution has lasted too well; it has outlived four French constitutions and one Soviet one, at least. It is true that there are many reports of its imminent collapse; but like Mark Twain's death these may be exaggerated. And even were it to collapse tomorrow, it would have proved itself workable for two centuries. It is not Utopian, if Utopian cannot involve a conservative vision of the human animal as a flawed political being. It is not Utopian, if Utopian means perfectionist. Its authors, especially its principal author, James Madison, were conservative men, and, even if they were not religious men, they agreed with St Paul that man was prone to evil. But if Utopian can mean a statement in a tradition which goes back through various experimental English-language constitutions of the eighteenth and seventeenth centuries and then back through Sir Thomas More to Plato about how the state might best be organized, then there may be a case for calling the Constitution Utopian.

The third phase of Utopian state making in the British North Americas was also to be the final stage because with the adoption of the Constitution of the United States in 1789, the space in which constitution making was possible without insurrection became as limited as that in Europe. The window of experiment closed and the new document had to take on the majestic proportions of a nation's charter. It needed the aura of an Ancient Constitution, wrapped in mystery and magic. It could not be seen to be a changeable, working or experimental document. It veiled its origins and its authoring in myths of universality and timeless- ness. The law-smiths and contract-wrights who had become so accomplished in colonial practice were set aside as the servants of the People until new generations arrived who would elevate those authors to the status of culture heroes and national icons.

The constitutional genre beyond 1789

It is true that in the new territories of the United States the old space for constitution writing remained open, in a limited sense. Through the nineteenth century and into the twentieth there succeeded new ventures in the genre of constitution writing. But only the examples of the First Texan and the Confederate constitutions could match that of 1789 in attempting nation making. Neither the Texan nor the Confederate constitution was successful, but notably these are the two American nineteenth-century constitutions about which some mystery and magic still hover. In the twentieth century only the drafting of the post-1945 Japanese Constitution exercised the epic version of the genre, which involves the act of nation making. That drafting was done in a space made by atomic explosion. That it was an exercise in the British North American tradition is made clear in its opening clause where the phrase 'We, the Japanese People' rings strangely. As Kyoko Inoue points out in *MacArthur's Japanese Constitution: A Linguistic and Cultural Study*, this phrase caused alarm to the Japanese team but it was insisted upon by the American team.[22] The Japanese saw it, correctly, as a threat to the sovereignty of the Emperor. The nature of the American people's original claim to the great authorizing formula is made clear by the Japanese reshaping of 'WE the PEOPLE of the United States'.

Notes

1. Richards I A 1966 *Plato, Republic.* Cambridge University Press, Cambridge, p 42.
2. Eggerbrecht H H 1980 Historiography. In *The new Grove dictionary of music and musicians* (20 vols). Macmillan, London, vol 8 p 596.
3. Jones E (ed) 1991 *New Oxford book of sixteenth-century verse.* Oxford University Press, Oxford.
4. Davis J C 1981 *Utopia and the ideal society: a study of English utopian writing 1516–1700.* Cambridge University Press, Cambridge.
5. Vidal G 1990 The second American revolution. In Ollman B, Birnbaum J (eds) 1990 *The US constitution.* New York University Press, New York, pp 169–70.
6. Bernard B 1967 *The ideological origins of the American revolution.* Harvard University Press, Cambridge, Mass, pp 24–5.
7. Pole J The ancient world in the new republic: the founders' use of history. In Kroes R, Van de Bilt E (eds) 1988 *The US constitution after 200 years.* Free University Press, Amsterdam, p 6.
8. More T 1988 *Utopia* trans P Turner. Penguin, Harmondsworth.
9. Vespucci A 1894 *The letters of Amerigo Vespucci and other documents illustrative of his career* ed C R Markham. Hakluyt Society, London, p 42.
10. *Encyclopaedia Britannica* 1964 edn 2: 886.
11. *Encyclopaedia Britannica* 1964 edn 5: 997.
12. Bacon F 1974 *The advancement of learning and the New Atlantis* ed A Johnson. Clarendon Press, Oxford, p 237.
13. Morley H (ed) 1988 *Ideal commonwealths.* Daedalus/Hippocrene Press, Santry, Cambs, pp xi–xiii.
14. Johnson P 1991 *The birth of the modern: world society 1815–1830.* Weidenfeld and Nicolson, London, p 249.
15. The second charter guaranteed by King Charles II to the proprietors of Carolina. In Carroll B R (ed) 1836 *Historical collections of South Carolina* (2 vols). Harper, New York, vol 2 p 38.
16. *Dictionary of National Biography.* 34: 29.
17. The first set of the fundamental constitutions of South Carolina: as compiled by Mr John Locke. In Carroll 1836 vol 2 pp 361–90.
18. Morris R B 1970 *Encyclopedia of American history.* Harper and Row, New York, p 48.
19. *Dictionary of National Biography.* 42: 43.
20. Morris 1970 p 64.

21. Bryce J 1914 *The American commonwealth* (2 vols). Macmillan, New York, vol 1 p 30.
22. Inoue K 1991 *MacArthur's Japanese constitution: a linguistic and cultural study of its making.* University of Chicago Press, Chicago, p 184.

2 Writing out of Communism: recantation memoirs of the Cold War

David Seed

As early as 1938 a new kind of autobiographical memoir began appearing in the United States.[1] These volumes described how their authors had ceased to believe in Communism and were produced partly in response to such historical events as the Franco-Soviet Pact (1934), the Moscow trials (1936–38), and the Nazi-Soviet Pact of 1939. These memoirs reversed the paradigm of 'how I became a Socialist' narratives from the turn of the century where the pattern of religious conversion (a perception of social or individual faults leading to a pivotal experience of rebirth and a subsequent reforming zeal) was transposed on political ideology.[2] These new works, however, were inverted conversion narratives, which reflected a general movement towards the Right in postwar America. Instead of describing how their authors found the true faith they recount the loss of the false one. As Hannah Arendt put it, they work 'to make a confession, own up to a conversion, and form a solid political group'.[3] Collectively they express a disillusionment with the ideals of the socialist movement and with Stalinism in particular. As the investigative agencies of the USA increased their efforts at tracking down any signs of Communist subversion, these memoirs began to function as public testimonies delivered as extensions of the official proceedings of, for instance, the House Un-American Activities Committee (HUAC).

The most famous of these memoirs was Whittaker Chambers's *Witness* (1952), which focused on one of the most notorious cases of the period – that of Alger Hiss. Chambers had joined the

Communist Party in 1925 and then gone underground from 1932 to 1938 when he served in several Russian-sponsored circles of espionage. Most notably he acted in a Washington-based group which by his testimony included a young State Department lawyer named Alger Hiss. Although Chambers gave information on these spy rings to the FBI in 1939 no action was taken and it was not until 1948 when Chambers was summoned before HUAC that the Hiss case began. Later that year Hiss was indicted for perjury but his first trial in 1948 resulted in a deadlocked jury. The second trial ran from November 1949 to January 1950 and led to a conviction followed by a prison term starting in 1951. The case attracted so much attention, in the process casting retrospective fame over Lionel Trilling's fictionalization of Chambers in his novel *The Middle of the Journey* (1947), that when *Witness* was published the *Saturday Review* brought out a special issue because the book was felt to lie 'at the core center of one of the most important public debates in American history'.[4] In what follows, the emphasis will be placed not on the factual evidence of the case but on the rhetorical strategies used by Chambers in *Witness*, Hiss in his rejoinders, and their contemporaries in their writings to engage in public witness during an era of mounting fear before what was referred to as the 'Communist conspiracy'.

Cold War rhetoric

The foreword to *Witness* expands the significance of the confrontation between Hiss and Chambers into a clash between the two main faiths of the twentieth century. Thus a particular legal case becomes the capitalized 'Great Case' of the age, a stylistic emphasis which Hiss was later to note with annoyance. Not only does Chambers build up the drama of the particular legal proceedings; he also tilts a Marxist conviction of historical change towards a melodramatic confrontation of titanic political forces: East and West, Communism and Capitalism. The imminence of change gives the present its dimension of crisis: 'It is our fate', Chambers warns, 'to live upon that turning point in history' which will decide whether the world will become free or Communist; and in 1953 he defined a Communist starkly as the 'soldier, in uniform or business suit, whom you or your children have faced, or will face . . . in military or civil combat'. Chambers's historical claim for the Hiss case was completely endorsed by Bennett Cerf who assessed *Witness* for Random House. His report declares that like Rousseau's *Confessions* 'it reflects the entire political thinking of a generation at one of the big turning-points in the world's history'.[5]

Since Chambers's foreword offers an expository prelude to his narrative it is crucial to note the style he deploys to express political possibilities. Again and again, the latter are reduced to stark, mutually exclusive alternatives: 'God or man', Freedom or Communism, and so on. The following lines are characteristic:

> Communists are that part of mankind which has recovered the power to live or die – to bear witness – for its faith. And it is a simple, rational faith that inspires men to live or die for it . . . It is not new, it is, in fact, man's second oldest faith. Its promise was whispered in the first days of the Creation under the Tree of Knowledge of Good and Evil: 'Ye shall be as gods' (p. 9).

Such passages build themselves around contrasts, opposing notions or qualities which are so antithetical that by implication no compromise between them seems possible. Communists, liberals and fellow travellers alike are lumped together as the force of darkness. Rhetorically, Chambers is exploiting what Philip Wander has called 'prophetic dualism', a set of values which, he argues, informed US foreign policy in the 1950s: 'In its perfected form prophetic dualism divides the world into two camps. Between them there is conflict. One side acts in accord with all that is good, decent, and at one with God's will. The other acts in direct opposition. Conflict between them is resolved only through the total victory of one side over the other.'[6] This division, he continues, results in a whole series of political consequences such as an identification between compromise and appeasement, and Wander derives the Manichaean world view from American fundamentalism. Chambers's rhetoric links him ideologically not only with the public pronouncements of Eisenhower but also with the more florid outbursts of McCarthy, to whom setbacks in foreign policy were 'defeats'. And because such events could not be viewed as morally neutral within a cosmic engagement between Good and Evil, they had perforce to become evidence of a malevolent force at work: the present situation 'must be the product of a great conspiracy, a conspiracy on a scale so immense as to dwarf any previous such venture in the history of man. A conspiracy of infamy so black that, when it is finally exposed, its principals shall be forever deserving of the maledictions of all honest men.'[7] McCarthy's 1951 attack on General George C. Marshall exploits a rhetoric of size which recurs in *Witness* and which in effect situates the experiences of its author at the centre of twentieth-century politics.

Chambers deploys a battery of intensifiers to strengthen his ideological message. He casts himself first of all as a respondent to enquiries: formulations recur on the pattern of 'you will ask . . . '. His answers take shape dialogically, refuting the cruder presumptions of what constitutes Communism, and then proceed to reinforce themselves by repetition, short assertive phrases, and rhetorical triplets. Chambers essentially fills out the broad parameters he introduces in his opening pages, and insists on the force and appeal of Communism as a 'vision'. It emerges as a quasi-religion except that, as we can see from the passage quoted in the preceding paragraph, Chambers locates it metaphorically within Christian mythology as the voice of the serpent. By so doing he cues the reader into a response to Communism as evil and sets up the main motif of his narrative, which is to distinguish between true and false witness. He also in the process raises a major contradiction which his book never really resolves, namely how the Cold War rhetoric of militant combat can coexist with the Quaker quietism Chambers later adopted.

The early collapse of Chambers's family life deprived him by his own account of a buttress between himself and an alien world. His father's withdrawal into fantasy (his room housed five editions of the *Arabian Nights*) creates a void in the young Chambers's life which he implicitly filled for his own children. More importantly, though, the resultant dissatisfaction forced Chambers to leave home and find work as a labourer in Baltimore. That experience gave him his first contact with the poor and accelerated his drift towards socialism. When *Witness* was first published, Irving Howe praised it as a confession but remarked that 'as autobiography, the book is embarrassing; Chambers's memoir of his family seems a needless act of

masochism'.[8] On the contrary, the accounts of his brother's
suicide and his father's death help to conflate Chambers's
personal destiny with his perception of cultural collapse following
the First World War. Recoiling from a 'dying world', he turns to
a faith which promises life and a community of believers. The
memoir in Section 5 of his experiences within the Communist
Party infuriated the reviewer for *Masses and Mainstream* so much
that he placed *Witness* within a tradition of 'Big lie' literature
which included the propaganda of the Nazis. Specifically,
Chambers was taken to task for trying to 'separate Marxian
Socialism from its historic-social basis' and thus for missing the
point that any conspiracy lay in the social system itself.[9] There is
some truth in the charge in so far as Chambers explicitly
proposes faith to be an issue prior to economics rather than vice
versa; but Milton Howard makes out a case that Chambers is in
effect attacking a native populist tradition including figures like
Tom Paine and Whitman. By so doing he sidesteps the main issue
within Chambers's depiction of the American Communist Party,
namely that its programme was subject to the vagaries of Stalin's
consolidation of power.

Chambers's dissatisfaction with party organization ironically
coincided with his being appointed editor of the journal *New
Masses*, which itself more or less coincided with his invitation to
go underground. That narrative becomes complicated at this
point by a new series of contrasts forced on Chambers. Of
necessity he had to resign from the party and take up the
ostensible life of a bourgeois while continuing to serve in the
party's clandestine apparatus. A gap opened up here between
surface and depth, appearances and what they conceal. This
opposition is expressed spatially when Chambers descends into
the New York subway (a 'catacomb' of tunnels) to make his first
contact. As his disenchantment with the underground grows it is
referred to variously as a 'pit' or 'Hades' and these spatial
metaphors result in a new awareness on Chambers's part of
historical processes being hidden. The fact that he received his
order to go underground anonymously fills him with melodramatic 'implications of undefined power' and gradually he
learns the existence of a party-within-the-party, with its own
jargon, code names for members, and set of signals for
communication. Just as Section 4 outlines the moves and

organization of the Communist Party to an unfamiliar reader, so the next sections take us into a secret area, thereby performing an exposé similar to the FBI dramatized movie-documentary on Russian espionage, *Walk East on Beacon* (1952). More importantly, the text itself performs an act of disobedience, since Chambers tells us: 'I was never to write anything about my work'. At one and the same time then his narrative captures the retrospective immediacy of his secret operations and by its very existence reminds the reader of his later defection.

The second half of *Witness* deals primarily with Chambers's part in the Hiss case and for many pages autobiography and the public record coincide as he simply quotes from the proceedings before HUAC and a New York grand jury. His period with *Time* is depicted partly as a quiet interlude ('The Tranquil Years') and partly as a largely unsuccessful attempt to sharpen that journal's hostility towards the Soviet Union. The psychological pressure of dealing with the investigative agencies, once the process had begun, was so severe that retrospectively Chambers became alien to himself: 'I see not myself, but someone who is not I' (p. 532). This is not an expression of the gap between early and late selves which occurs frequently in autobiographies, but rather an elaboration of the term 'informer' which Chambers carefully pushes towards passivity by describing himself as a slave to the police, motivated only by the public good. The initial contact having been made, Chambers even dehumanizes himself into an animal being led to the slaughter. Such figures conveniently minimize his own initiative and usher in a line of references to fate and doom. Now he becomes isolated ('I seemed absolutely alone') as the bemused spectator to a power clash between the Justice Department and HUAC; and in terms ironically anticipating Hiss's own, Chambers finds himself recast as the 'defendant in a great public trial'. Just as Hiss was later to exaggerate his isolation before forces working through Chambers, so Chambers found in Hiss the representative of a concealed enemy.

Situating the self

Chambers's political account concludes with Hiss being charged and ultimately convicted of perjury. If that was all *Witness* attempted, then the book would be not much more than a historical document, but Chambers also narrates his attempts to locate himself within his national culture and his search for a 'community of worship'. Here we could draw a contrast with the autobiography of one of Chambers's contemporaries – one he actually knew – Joseph Freeman. Freeman was born a Ukrainian Jew in Czarist Russia and in *An American Testament* (1938) he describes his progress from a medieval culture to a modern pluralistic one. Freeman is bewildered by the number of potential selves he could adopt and he expresses this mixture of desire and frustration in spatial terms: thus after the First World War 'we wanted to feel at home everywhere, and felt at home nowhere'.[10] Travel takes on a heightened symbolic importance for its educative value and relevance to Freeman's attempts to situate himself. Each place simultaneously offers new values and new dissatisfactions. So Greenwich Village temporarily liberates him from middle class values but at the same time reminds him that it is the enclave of a Bohemian caste. He finally manages a reconciliation between poetry and politics which neither Chambers nor Richard Wright could manage by making a decision of selflessness: 'Subordinate everything personal and trivial and important, to transcend yourself in a great goal.'[11] Wright never achieved such a reconciliation and his autobiography *American Hunger* (written in the 1940s, published 1977) ends with a confrontation between party discipline and writerly ambitions which forced Wright to leave the Communist Party. In the event Freeman's commitment too was short-lived. He left the socialist movement and took up a job on *Time* for which he had to be screened by none other than Chambers.

For Chambers too, belonging was a major issue but his autobiography addresses the problem in a more literal way than Freeman's. The 'Foreword' to *Witness*, a letter to Chambers's children, concludes by describing scenes from their home life in the late 1940s and it is symbolically crucial for him that this home was a farm. Early in the narrative proper Chambers indicates this significance as follows: 'The men and women Communists and fellow travellers who staffed this Fifth Column were dedicated revolutionists whose primary allegiance was no longer to any country – nor to those factors which give a country its binding force: tradition, family, community, soil, religious faith' (p. 33). For Chambers an individual's adoption of the cause of international Communism was a corruption or deviation from a norm summed up by the key words in his list. All these values are exemplified in the descriptions of Chambers's own farm life, but it is an idyll shot through with pathos because these 'golden days' are lost in the irrecoverable past. (For that reason Chambers refers to himself and his wife through the role-names 'Papa' and 'Mama'.) These images of domesticity echo throughout *Witness* and carry their own internal drama. Again and again the warmth and light of the domestic interiors are posed against a threatening outside darkness, a place of solitude, fear and above all danger, all the more potent because not specified.

The farm, then, becomes a means of articulating Chambers's desired location within American culture. One of his earliest literary undertakings was to compose a series of poems about his past: 'I wished to preserve through the medium of poetry the beautiful Long Island of my boyhood before it was destroyed forever by the advancing City' (p. 165). Writing attracted Chambers by its capacity to arrest time, but in practice he can never manage this. Instead a rhythm establishes itself throughout *Witness* of Chambers gaining and then losing a particular location. Chambers's loss of the Long Island countryside carries mythic undertones of expulsion from a primal paradise and he casts urbanization as an antagonistic force which displaces him not only from the land but from his very country: 'It cut my roots and left me more than an alien, a man without soil, and, therefore, without nation' (p. 165). By identifying his personal fate with that of a region, Chambers implicitly diagnoses a conflict within his own culture, and establishing a life for himself as a farmer symbolically enacts his sporadic attempts to regain access to a lost centrality within American life.

The special authenticity which Chambers attributes to farming life aligns with a tradition of national self-images stretching back to Crèvecoeur, who rhapsodized over the fact that America was a nation of independent smallholders. A work which helpfully clarifies the implications of Chambers's *Witness* is the collection *I'll Take My Stand* published by the Southern Agrarians in 1930. This document takes a defensive stance against the 'Communist menace' which, while recognized, is pushed into second place by the forces of industrialization. Andrew Lytle's sketch 'The Hind

Tit' describes a day in the life of a farming family, stressing its piety, bonding and sensitivity to natural signs that would be lost on a city-dweller. The introduction to the volume spells out one of the issues at stake: 'The theory of agrarianism is that the culture of the soil is the best and most sensitive of vocations.'[12] Chambers too places himself within a national tradition of working the land and like the Agrarians attempts to create an enclave of pious industry against the encroachments of modern mechanization: 'The farm is our witness, it is a witness against the world. By deliberately choosing this life of hardship and immense satisfaction, we say in effect: The modern world has nothing better than this to give us' (p. 517). Chambers does not seek a complete withdrawal. How could he when he was dependent for subsistence on his salary from *Time* magazine? Later he was to write that 'a conservatism that cannot face the facts of the machine and mass production, and its consequences in government and politics, is foredoomed to futility and petulance'.[13] Rather, he designates the farm a 'sanctuary' or 'haven', a place to which he can retreat from the publicity of the Hiss case and a place of spiritual renewal.

Spiritual autobiography

Chambers's descriptions of his farms render them as places of laral piety and help to indicate that the true genre of *Witness* is prophetic autobiography. G. Thomas Couser has argued that this is a mode characteristic of the USA and outlines its general features as follows. The individual conflates personal and communal experience, consciously creating exemplary patterns of behaviour. History is seen as God's will in action and the author identifies his/her period as one particularly requiring exhortation. A role is thus opened up for the autobiographer to speak for God to the community and communal achievements are frequently measured against individual standards. Couser stresses the historical moments of such works: 'Prophetic autobiography flourishes in times of crisis – when change threatens communal values or when historical developments demand new modes of interpretation.'[14]

Point for point these general features are realized in *Witness*.

Chambers with supreme arrogance identifies himself with his age: 'I committed the characteristic crimes of my century.' He identifies his period as one of unique change, repeatedly refers his experiences to the larger currents of modern history, and ultimately attributes contemporary crisis to twentieth-century secularism. In an article on the theologian Reinhold Niebuhr, Chambers sought to define a position where the contradictions of capitalism can only be resolved on an extra-economic level through faith.

Witness possesses a strong teleological emphasis throughout. In Section 9, a brief bridging passage between his period as a Communist and his subsequent life, Chambers makes this narrative issue explicit:

> In the end, the only memorable stories, like the only memorable experiences, are religious and moral. They give men the heart to suffer the ordeal of a life that perpetually rends them between its beauty and its terror. If my story is worth telling, it is because I rejected in turn each of the characteristic endings of life in our time – the revolutionary ending and the success ending. I chose a third ending. (p. 450)

Chambers evokes this third ending through predictions ('later I was to meet . . .', etc.) which shift priority off present instances onto a future event of paramount importance. In this context the future event is of course the Hiss case and its deferral informs the perspective from which Chambers describes – by no means unsympathetically – his years within the Communist Party. Thus what was probably unacceptable to the *Masses and Mainstream* reviewer was a description which places the party as a phase *within* a sequence, not its culmination as ultimate goal.

Among the writers whom Chambers admits as an influence here figures Dostoevsky – the Chambers family library included *The House of the Dead*, *The Idiot*, and *Crime and Punishment* – and a number of reviewers noted this debt. The case was put with the greatest hostility by Philip Rahv who complained that 'Chambers seems to have appropriated lock, stock, and barrel, the entire Dostoevskyan polemic against socialism as the culminating movement of Western rationalism and secularism, leading through the rejection of God to the deification of man'. He notes important elements of the novelist's thought which

Chambers ignores, and concludes: 'to Chambers the idea is everything; men nothing'.[15] Rahv has pinpointed an issue that caused considerable disagreement among the reviewers of *Witness*: how to cope with its frequently inflated style. The responses varied from acceptance (Marcus Duffield saw the book as the 'apologia of a soul that has struggled for serenity') to modification (Arthur M. Schlesinger accepted the general discussion of faith but found the real issue to be in the 'sense of human limitation, of human fallibility') and downright rejection.[16] In the latter camp Mary McCarthy objected to the 'studio atmosphere of sublimity and purpose' and Brendan Gill, for the *New Yorker*, objected that the book's tone failed because it revealed a 'piety as rigid and obtuse as the godless Communist piety he has abjured'.[17]

The general problem which all these comments address can be explained (though not entirely answered) by reminding ourselves of Chambers's ultimate spiritual purposes. When he glosses his experiences as a labourer in Washington with the words 'the wretched of the earth had stretched out their hands and claimed me for their own' (p. 151), the statement not only seems to be offensively self-aggrandizing (are they looking for a messiah in Chambers?) and a reference to Victor Hugo's *Les Misérables*, but also shifts the rhetorical register from circumstantial realism on to a more symbolic plane. So what Rahv calls Chambers's 'lust for the Absolute' leads him to shift the level of *Witness* to and fro between the secular and the spiritual. Often he can manage this movement by keeping the two dimensions in separate sections of his text. At other times he rings the changes on the different meanings of his title. Roughly speaking, the first half of the book plays on secular significances of evidence, vouching for information, and authenticity of report. Then in Section 12 (appropriately entitled 'The Bridge') a crucial shift of meaning occurs: 'I began to grasp the degree to which I was not merely a man testifying against something. I was first of all a witness for something' (p. 699). From this point on Chambers's narrative picks up and strengthens earlier hints that he has been chosen to testify for his faith, if necessary by martyrdom. A strong suggestion of this role is given as early as Section 1 where Chambers's loss of faith in Communism is described as an entirely positive process of virtual transfiguration repeating the biblical stories of Lazarus and Jonah. This figure, of descent followed by ascent, structures first, his period within the Communist Party and, later, his experiences during the Hiss case. After a dark night of the soul Chambers plumbs the depths of despair, attempts suicide, and then rises to new heights of spiritual confidence.

A key progression throughout *Witness* is Chambers's growing capacity to distinguish an authentic faith from a spurious one (Communism). We have already seen how he phrases his commitment to the Communist Party as the adoption of a set of ideals but Chambers must distinguish his own work from that of socialist autobiographies like Joseph Freeman's by depicting Communism as an obstacle to self-fulfilment, not its culmination. Chambers's references to Communism as if it were a religion should not be read as a contradiction within his narrative so much as the expression of a trope which became commonplace in the 1950s. Richard Crossman's 1949 volume of autobiographies by six former Communists, *The God that Failed*, saw a specific analogy between Stalinism and the Catholic Church: 'The Communist novice, subjecting his soul to the canon law of the Kremlin, felt something of the release which Catholicism also brings to the intellectual wearied and worried by the privilege of freedom.'[18] A related analogy was pursued at ironic length by Howard Fast in his memoir *The Naked God* (1958), which rationalizes his recent departure from the party by defining its true essence. He does this in a mock-anthropological analysis of the 'magical practice' informing the Communist Party, which emerges as absurdly tribal and irrational. Fast turns party rhetoric on its head and insists that magic is not a metaphor but an actuality, achieving a caricature of 'magic formulas and power words'.[19] Chambers sadly did not possess the sense of irony necessary for such effects, one reason being that faith was too pressing an issue for him. He could not stand back like Crossman or Fast and apply a religious or magical analogy from an essentially secular viewpoint: *Witness* shows that his spiritual commitment is immanent from the very beginning.

Chambers's interest in literature has been noted here, and the pages of *Witness* are peppered with references to Whitman, Rilke and other figures. Within the general context three specific writers stand out as influences on his life: Dostoevsky as already noted, Victor Hugo, and George Fox. Pride of place in Chambers's childhood reading was reserved for *Les Misérables* which he describes as a '*Summa* of the revolt of the mind and soul of modern man against the materialism that was closing over them' (p. 134). While Hugo's impact on Chambers should be noted, the influence of George Fox and Quaker autobiography is more important since it clearly affected the organization of *Witness*. Fox's *Journal* accelerated Chambers's move towards the Quakers in recoil from the Communist Party by giving him a speaking text, 'less a book than a voice'. When Chambers starts attending Quaker meetings the meeting house symbolically has both doors open, thereby granting him access to the 'community of worship' he had been seeking. The writings of such seventeenth-century Quakers as Fox and Francis Howgill renewed Chambers's faith in the inner self and helped shape his sense of his life as witness. The true believer, he writes, 'should make his own person a living testimony against the world, should thereby protest mutely' (p. 489). The Quaker meeting house became a special place of silent peace for Chambers, and his new-found faith enabled him to conflate spiritual and secular notions of witness in giving legal testimony at the Hiss hearings and also in adopting a symbolically plain demeanour. His own narrative at this point takes on a special significance. Like Fox's *Journal*, which defines its purpose in its opening lines as being 'that all may know the dealings of the lord with me', *Witness* follows an implicit analogy with the persecuted few who were seeking the truth and introduces pivotal moments within a spiritual sequence which culminates in a visionary experience Chambers has on an explanation of his farm. The whole book delays till that moment the significance of the image of a Russian revolutionary burning himself to death as a gesture of protest against imprisonment. As he wanders in the woods on his farm, this image recurs to Chambers's consciousness: 'That was the precipitating image. It linked the purposes of my past and present and made one meaning of my life' (p. 747). The experience is cast within a Quaker context of silent passivity and Chambers carefully stresses that he can only approximate significance which seemed pre-verbal. At any rate its experiential value links it with culminating moments of conviction within socialist autobiographies, where life takes on a newly meaningful shape and continuity.

Another ex-Communist who described his flight from the party as regaining a religious faith was Louis Budenz. Budenz grew up in a Catholic household, but lapsed at least from 1935 to 1944, when he rejoined the Church. Throughout his memoir *This is My Story* (1947) he describes his attempts to reconcile Catholicism and Communism, although he admits time and time again that he could only come near to achieving this aim by blinding himself to what was going on in Russia during the 1930s. A union activist and later editor of the *Daily Worker*, Budenz never penetrated the Communist underground to the depths of Chambers, but he saw enough to realize eventually that 'the Communist movement in this country, the agent of a foreign power, is committed to the maiming of the American nation and the atomization of the American people'. This conviction, expressed in the preface, is reinforced by Budenz's bald conclusion that 'Communism and Catholicism are irreconcilable'.[20] He presents the party as the enemy of reconciliation in labour disputes, indeed as the enemy of the body politic itself. Budenz figures it as a prison and a divisive force, an 'alien world' within America. Leaving the party, then, simultaneously liberates him and bonds him to groups of ascending size: to his family, the Church and the nation. His memoir, like Chambers's, therefore functions as a warning to the country at large.

The response to Hiss

Three years after his release from prison in 1954 Alger Hiss published his own account of his trials, *In the Court of Public Opinion*. It is difficult to imagine a work farther removed from Chambers's *Witness* in both subject and method. Hiss ironically took his title from a HUAC report that identified the Committee's purpose as an enabling one: to allow the American public to pass open judgement on those charged with Communist activities. Hiss, however, casts himself as the victim of a prevailing mood which had reversed presumptions about guilt and innocence: 'The fear of Communism had become so great, so unreasoning, that charges made before the Committee, when once spread across the newspapers of the nation, were widely accepted until completely discredited.'[21] Hiss's perception of a public prejudice, which was to increase in 1950 with the outbreak of the

Korean War, leads him into a contradictory stance in his book. On the one hand the title might make us expect Hiss to address an imaginary jury as Humbert does in *Lolita* (published two years earlier), to use his book as a forum for public testimony. The actual volume, however, pursues a rather different, more specialized tack.

In the Court of Public Opinion takes as its premise a principle of law that 'testimony, unlike ordinary conversation, is given in response to specific questions'.[22] Although Hiss states disingenuously in his conclusion that he had tried to 'let the record speak' (the 'record' by the time of his petition for appeal had grown to some 4,000 pages), he offers rather a running commentary on that record which highlights omissions (e.g. of FBI evidence), arbitrary inferences, and the stage-managed proceedings of HUAC. Professional lawyer as he was, Hiss depicts the ideal courtroom as a unique place of rational investigation and tries to articulate in his book a corresponding quiet reasonableness. For Herbert L. Packer this gave the book its main virtue but also its central weakness: 'Its lack of drama and color causes the reader's attention to flag, and this can be fatal to a book whose impact must depend on making the reader pay close and continuous attention to a very complicated narrative.'[23] Packer continues that Hiss does not address the real issue of his trials which was that of alleged Communist activity and Hiss refused to do so because he was writing on the presumption that his testimony should be responsive not volunteered, that is, given in answer to a series of questions or charges. His account thus concentrates overwhelmingly on the detail of the HUAC hearings and of his trials. Hiss simultaneously appeals to the 'real Court of Public Opinion' of the future and writes an account which demands of the reader a capacity to assess evidence and marshal testimony only available to a trained lawyer.[24]

Undoubtedly Hiss recoiled from the hysteria creeping into the contemporary press accounts which he quotes and the self-dramatizing tendency which he identified in *Witness* (he drily notes, for instance, Chambers's tendency to capitalize the term 'Case'), turning instead to a quieter, even understated style for his own purposes. But while he avoids Chambers's melodramatic rhetoric of 'forces' working through Hiss, Hiss himself reverses the allegation by stressing the inequality of the HUAC hearings

('they were many against one') and by throwing out dark hints
that 'others' were manipulating the gullible Chambers – the
'perfect pawn', as he was to call him – to their own ends.[25]
Towards the end of his narrative Hiss points out the constraints
of such hearings: 'We search for records – the FBI has them. We
ask questions – the FBI will not let people talk to us . . . We ask
people to certify information in files they have shown us – they
must consult counsel, and we hear no more from them.'[26] The
plural 'we' draws the reader into a common predicament of
searching in vain for information. Correspondingly the FBI
expands into all the forces attempting to block this search. The
sentences quoted exploit a starkly impressive contrast between
'we' and 'they', citizens and officialdom, but this is a local effect
which the book as a whole does not sustain. Indeed, Hiss could
have made a major issue out of the unavailability of information.
This had to wait until 1975 when the National Emergency Civil
Liberties Foundation began collecting documents on Hiss's behalf
as a preliminary step towards a writ alleging violation of his
constitutional rights, which was issued in 1978. The Foundation
then took a further step which testified at once to its conviction
that Hiss's case was historically crucial and to its faith in the
power of the printed word, by publishing the writ, memorandum
and supporting documents.[27] These volumes only repeated in
exacerbated form the problems confronting the reader of *In the
Court of Public Opinion*, for now s/he is expected to be adept
not only at weighing up the legal face of the writ but also at
assessing the bewildering array of reports and testimonials that
accompanied it.

Witness as theatre

Whittaker Chambers's narrative of his heroic attempts at bearing
witness supplied a kind of precedent for one of the most amazing
cases of the Cold War. In October 1954 negotiations began
between Harvey Matusow and the journalist Albert E. Kahn to
publish Matusow's account of his career as a professional
informant. The resulting volume, *False Witness* (1955), recounts
a depressing story of how Matusow gave evidence before HUAC
and other committees, and testified in the cases of the sinologist

Owen Lattimore and the labour leader Clinton E. Jencks, supplying a tissue of half-truths, innuendoes and downright lies. Matusow was warned when planning his book: 'It's not enough for you to reveal what you've done – you have to reveal yourself.'[28] Accordingly Matusow gives a brief autobiographical introduction which diagnoses his desires as springing from an inferiority complex. Beset by a conviction that he could never match up to his brother, Matusow turns to a series of organizations – Boy Scouts, army, American Youth for Democracy, and finally Communist Party – because they all offer him the possibility of being 'part of something'. Here the first major difference from Chambers emerges. Matusow stayed in the Communist Party only briefly, from 1947 to 1951 (when ironically he was expelled for being an FBI informer), not from any ideological commitment, but because it temporarily satisfied his desire to belong and to secure approval. His membership also supplied him with a tenuous justification for claiming to be an 'expert' on the party.

Matusow's career as informer began in 1951. Having re-enlisted in the army in an attempt to see active service in Korea, he found this desire blocked by official anxieties over his Communist past, and so Matusow manoeuvred his way into testifying before HUAC on American youth organizations. His experience as an informer for the FBI eased him effortlessly into his new role as witness and Matusow described his first appearance before HUAC as his 'opening night'. This was no passing phrase but one of the first signals in the text that Matusow regarded his testimony as a kind of theatre. Once again the description of his book's composition strengthens this point. Matusow insisted on dictating it because he needed the sharper sense of audience. 'Almost everything is a performance', he admitted to his publisher. 'But the lines were important, and the improvising.'[29] Matusow glosses his career throughout *False Witness* as if he were climbing the 'witness ladder' towards stardom. Newspaper reports of his performances function as reviews. He gets a 'break' in being allowed to testify on youth organizations; he invents a 'gimmick' (a combination of trickery and salesmanship) by improvising politicized nursery rhymes; and he is groomed repeatedly by other informers on how to behave in the courtroom. The trajectory of Matusow's career rises from

HUAC through local triumphs in Ohio to the ultimate peak when he joins McCarthy's inner circle of aides. So while he admits that 'being a witness before the Grand Jury was the highest honor in witnessdom', it was when serving on the McCarthy staff during the 1952 elections that Matusow had his real experience of political stardom.[30] Appropriately enough, once he had abandoned his career as a witness Matusow found employment as an actor for TV and radio.

Matusow's theatrical vocabulary deflects the reader's attention from the issue of truth onto tactics, and by so doing suspends the moral implications of the story until its conclusion, when he experiences a change of heart. Matusow had already followed this strategy when describing his activities as an informer by depersonalizing his friends into mere figures in his activities. In a similar spirit he compares legal proceedings now to a chess game, now to a drama where subtext and dress become as eloquent as his actual words. Specifically, Matusow writes that when addressing the women on a jury: 'I watched their faces as I told them I was a veteran of World War II and the Korean War. The undertone to all I had to say was: listen, listen hard, I could be your son. "Put these people away where they belong" were the words between the lines.'[31] This passage suggests that Matusow took a Nabokovian stance, being at once participant and observer. Thus the distinction in Matusow's book between the time of events and the time of narration chronologically restates a double role, where he is both leading actor and his own best audience. Louis A. Renza has identified a 'unique pronominal crux' which arises for the writer of an autobiography: 'how can he keep using the first-person pronoun, his sense of self-reference, without its becoming – since it becomes, in the course of writing, something other than strictly his own self-referential sign – a de facto third-person pronoun?'[32] Matusow's sense of theatricality easily copes with this problem by oscillating between the viewpoint of a protagonist and that of an observer. Accordingly, when he first goes to meet an FBI agent he shifts to the third person ('a very frightened me arrived at the Federal Court House'). And his repeated references to timing, delivery, appearance and tone all help to maintain a constant self-reflexivity in his narrative.

Matusow's regard for the official record is ironic in the

extreme. The first passage quoted in the preceding paragraph suggests that there is a whole dimension of significance which is immediately excluded once words are filtered out of their context. The relation of Matusow's glosses to passages from the official record in that respect resembles diegetic shift within a novel. Instead of quoting a factual statement and then adding more data – which Matusow rarely does, for the very good reason that much of his testimony was invented! – he draws the reader on to a rhetorical level of scrutiny where style becomes all. Paradoxically he insists on the truth of his own account while at the same time demonstrating the vulnerability of all written accounts to political distortion. Documents become 'documents', within scare quotes. One of the most important episodes in *False Witness* revolves around a prosecution of Communist leaders which necessitated assembling documentary evidence culled from a Marxist bookshop. Roy Cohn and Matusow select passages 'around the "theory" that the Communists used "Aesopian language" – or double-talk – in which they said the opposite of what they really meant', namely that if they state that they do not advocate the violent overthrow of the US government, this fact becomes evidence that they do.[33] The overriding expediency of proving that they are liable to prosecution under the Smith Act traps the Communist defendants in a Catch-22 where it has become impossible to prove innocence. Similarly, Matusow describes how he mastered the art of selecting and angling a radio programme towards desired ends, and records McCarthy's plan to script a TV 'soap opera' (McCarthy's own words) about Communist bookshops. As the distinction between judicial procedure and entertainment media blurs, the former emerges as a media circus where proceedings are determined by their publicity value for the press.

In his analysis of the phenomenon of stardom, Alexander Walker declares that 'a star seeks or accepts screen roles which seem to reflect the image he has of himself and which he knows his public have come to share'.[34] Where Chambers took pride in the solitude and suffering of his political life, Matusow dramatizes himself as a performer in a collective enterprise which carries barbed ironies for American society and even for the reader. Like Matthew Cvetic's *The Big Decision* (1959) and Elizabeth Bentley's *Out of Bondage* (1951), *False Witness* was written of course as an exposé and it was therefore understandable that the FBI and Justice Department should use every means in their power to try to suppress publication on the ostensible grounds that his book was a 'collective product of the Communist conspiracy'.[35] But the ironies of Matusow's narrative direct themselves against such a broad range of institutions and figures that his guilt slides onto a public so gullible or so paranoid about the Communist threat that they will believe even the most outrageous overstatements. Towards the end of his account Matusow recoils with revulsion from his self-image in a mirror. He then sets out to drive at suicidal speed across the Nevada desert, and as he races along kills a rabbit. This episode has a two-fold symbolism, summing up the damage done by his evidence and also signalling the death of Matusow's old self. As the latter vanishes he withdraws into his own text and challenges the reader: 'I am the mirror, you are the viewer, and this story is your reflection.'[36] Matusow overtly implicates the reader in his narrative. The very title *False Witness* – far more effective than his original *Blacklisting Was My Business* – draws the addressee, the recipient of testimony, into a position of complicity. As Steinbeck sadly reflected in his review of Matusow's book, 'such were the winds of the times that certain basic nonsense was allowed to pass unnoticed. . . . Well, Matusow has ruined the racket'.[37]

The McCarthy era was a period of cases – of trials, hearings and investigations. As David Aaron has demonstrated in *Writers on the Left*, pre-war political commitments became an embarrassment. Now writers, particularly former members of the Communist Party, were responding to a felt need to state their credentials in public as if writing against an implicit accusation of guilt. For that reason they were confronted with an issue of choice: did their main commitments lie with their country or with an international movement which, under the impact of domestic revelations and the Korean War, was emerging as antithetical to the national interest? A figure like the novelist Meridel Le Sueur, who doggedly argued that there was a native tradition of socialism, was rare indeed. Much more common was the strategy pursued by Chambers, Budenz and others whereby they retrospectively erased any intellectual appeal from Communism, presenting it instead as an alien and authoritarian movement.

Their period in the party is described as a time of self-delusion or intellectual slavery followed by liberating recantation. Whatever the writers' specific beliefs, religion emerges as the ultimate antithesis to Communism although questions of religion repeatedly blur into questions of nationality. The cultural location of the self is a central problem in these narratives because the writers' choice of place reflects their choice of society or nationality. Arthur Koestler shrewdly noted this issue during the Hiss trial and attributed the public anger towards Chambers as that of a tribe towards a renegade member which had betrayed it.[38] However, many variations were woven on the Manichaean discourse of the Cold War that discourse still remained intact as a series of oppositions between bondage and freedom, or the alien and the domestic. Such polarized antitheses carried with them a constant risk of intellectual rigidity or worse. Sidney Hook for one pointed out the irony that, although Chambers wrote *Witness* to attack the totalitarian claims of Stalinism, he was nevertheless opening the door to an equally sinister form of absolutism by consigning political opposition to the realms of evil.[39] The very extremity of this position grew out of a collective sense of insecurity paradoxical in a period of unparalleled economic and military growth, a sense of being under threat. 'Communists are not American', insisted J. Edgar Hoover categorically. There is a fundamental and irreconcilable opposition between the two: 'Communism stands for everything America abhors: slave camps, rigged elections, purges, dictatorship.'[40] The memoirs of former party members reinforced such polarities by narrating the reunion of the errant member with the dominant group, thereby facilitating prescriptions of so-called 'normalcy'. Such a consensus was, however, to come under severe strain with the social and cultural upheavals of the sixties.

Notes

1. Belfrage C 1989 *The American inquisition 1945–1960: a profile of the 'McCarthy era'* 2nd edn. Thunder's Mouth Press, New York, p 40.
2. Relevant comment on the connections between religion and politics in this context can be found in Hopkins C H 1967 *The rise of the social gospel in American protestantism 1865–1915* 2nd edn. Yale

University Press, New Haven, Conn.; Aaron D 1977 *Writers on the left* 2nd edn. Oxford University Press, New York; Homburger E 1986 *American writers and radical politics 1900–1939: equivocal commitments.* Macmillan, Basingstoke, pp 36–8, 43–4, 59, 125.

3. Arendt H 1953 The ex-communists. *Commonweal* (20 March): 595.
4. Editor's Note 1952. *Saturday Review* 35 (24 May): 8. Cf Trilling L 1975 Whittaker Chambers and *The middle of the journey. New York Review of Books* (17 April): 18–24.
5. Chambers W 1979 *Witness: the story of a middle class family* 2nd edn. Regnery, South Bend, Indiana, p 7; subsequent page references in text. Chambers W 1953 What is a Communist? *Look* 17(15): 28; Cerf B 1951 Report on Whittaker Chambers's *Witness.* MS Columbia University.
6. Medhurst M J et al 1990 *Cold War rhetoric: strategy, metaphor and ideology.* Greenwood Press, Westport, Conn, p 157.
7. Matusow A J (ed) 1970 *Joseph R McCarthy.* Prentice-Hall, Englewood Cliffs, NJ, p 59.
8. Howe I 1979 *Celebrations and attacks.* Deutsch, London, p 81.
9. Howard M 1952 The holy war on reason: what Whittaker Chambers means to America. *Masses and Mainstream* 5(7): 5.
10. Freeman J 1938 *An American Testament.* Left Book Club, London, p 134.
11. Ibid p 565.
12. 'Twelve Southerners' 1962 *I'll take my stand: the south and the agrarian tradition* 3rd edn. Harper & Row, New York, p xxix.
13. Buckley W F Jr (ed) 1969 *Odyssey of a friend: Whittaker Chambers's letters to William F Buckley Jr 1954–1961.* Putnam, New York, p 79.
14. Couser G T 1979 *American autobiography: the prophetic mode.* University of Massachusetts Press, Amherst, Mass, p 3.
15. Rahv P 1952 The sense and nonsense of Whittaker Chambers. *Partisan Review* 19(4): 472–3, 475.
16. Duffield M 1952 Review of *Witness. New York Herald Tribune Book Review* 25 May: 1; Schlesinger Jr A M 1952 Whittaker Chambers and His *Witness. Saturday Review* 24 May 35: 40.
17. McCarthy M February 1954 My confession. *Encounter* 2(2): 43; Gill B 24 May 1952 Review of *Witness. New Yorker* 28: 133.
18. Crossman R H S 1950 *The god that failed: six studies in communism.* Hamish Hamilton, London, p 12.
19. Fast H 1958 *The naked god: the writer and the communist party.* Bodley Head, London, pp 80–5.
20. Budenz L 1947 *This is my story.* Browne & Nolan, Dublin, pp 10, 359.

21. Hiss A 1957 *In the court of public opinion*. Knopf, New York, p 76. In his more recent memoir Hiss charges Nixon with tampering with the public: Hiss A 1988 *Recollections of a life*. Unwin Hyman, London, p 153.
22. Hiss 1957 p 133.
23. Packer H L 1962 *Ex-communist witnesses: four studies in fact finding*. Stanford University Press, Stanford, Ca, p 24.
24. Hiss 1957 p 150.
25. Hiss 1988 p 202.
26. Hiss 1957 p 384.
27. Tiger E 1979–80 *In re Alger Hiss* 2 vols. National Emergency Civil Liberties Foundation, New York.
28. Kahn A E 1987 *Matusow affair*. Moyer Bell, Mt Kisco, p 35.
29. Ibid pp 56, 57.
30. Matusow H 1955 *False witness*. Cameron & Kahn, New York, p 191.
31. Ibid p 129.
32. Renza L A 1977 The veto of the imagination: a theory of autobiography. *ELH* **9**: 9.
33. Matusow 1955 p 127. The phrase 'Aesopian language' comes from Lenin's preface to *Imperialism* where he explains that he had to express his political views obliquely so as to get round the Czarist censorship.
34. Walker A 1974 *Stardom: the Hollywood phenomenon*. Penguin, Harmondsworth, p 302.
35. Cvetic worked as an informer for the FBI; Bentley appeared before a federal grand jury in 1947 and then served as a government witness from 1948 until 1953. The very high proportion of dialogue in her memoir provoked ironic comments on her memory from reviewers.
36. Matusow 1955 p 235.
37. Kahn 1987 p 286.
38. 'This horror probably has its roots in the collective unconscious in past loyalties to church clan or tribe which even if apparently buried remain potent emotional forces': Koestler A 1955 *The trail of the dinosaur and other essays*. Collins, London, p 56.
39. Hook S 1952 The faiths of Whittaker Chambers. *New York Times Book Review* 25 May: 35.
40. Hoover J E 1958 *Masters of deceit: the story of communism in America*. Dent, London, pp 102, 103.

3 'A sense of the ludicrous': women and humour in American literature

Regina Barreca

Without being defined as such, the study of comedy in American writing has been the study of masculine comedy. Even a relatively new collection such as *The Big Book of American Humour* claims to deal with comedy 'from Woody Allen to Philip Roth' – not an astonishingly diverse crowd, apparently, if these two represent the poles of experience. Oxford's volume of American humour has as its cover a picture of the map of the US with a cigar protruding from a mouth drawn across the country. These collections contain one or two selections by women, and, unnervingly, often offer the same selection by women, as if only Dorothy Parker ever told a funny story, and as if she could only tell the same funny story over and over again.

What accounts for the absence of female figures in the discussion of American humour and comedy in literature? In her landmark work, *A Very Serious Thing: Women's Humour and American Culture*, Nancy A. Walker discusses some of the reasons why women have been excluded from the study of comic literature. Walker explains that while both male and female writers of humour are seen as 'outsider' figures, usually observing the dominant system only to point out its flaws, the 'outsider' role is especially important for the woman writer. 'The humorist is at odds with the publicly espoused values of the culture, overturning its sacred cows, pointing out the nakedness of not only the Emperor, but also the politician, the pious, and the pompous', declares Walker. She goes on to assert that

For women to adopt this role means that they must break out of the passive, subordinate position mandated for them by centuries of patriarchal tradition and take on the power accruing to those who reveal the shams, hypocrisies, and incongruities of the dominant culture. To be a woman and a humorist is to confront and subvert the very power that keeps women powerless, and at the same time to risk alienating those upon whom women are dependent for economic survival.[1]

It is difficult to laugh openly at the boss, the father, the teacher – any figure who holds power directly over you. And yet these figures of authority are the inevitable targets of women's humour, which laughs 'upward' in the hierarchy. Women laugh at the systematic appropriation and misuse of power by those who have no right to rule; they do not laugh at a victim, a scapegoat, or someone burdened by a trait they cannot help. For example, women's humour will laugh at the arrogance of the mayor rather than at the incompetence of the clerk; it will laugh at the pretensions of the professor rather than at the shy student who drops all his or her books; it will laugh at the competitiveness of the business tycoon rather than at the fears of the underling. Emily Toth sums this up when she writes that: 'Women writers rarely violate what I call the Humane Humour Rule . . . that is, "Thou shalt not make fun of something that a person cannot change".'[2] Women are, therefore, often in the position of satirizing traditionally masculine roles and behaviour.

Joanna Russ, author of *How To Suppress Women's Writing*, underscores these points by explaining why and how 'culture' is perceived as 'male':

Culture is male. This does not mean that every man in Western (or Eastern) society can do exactly as he pleases, or that every man creates the culture solus, or that every man is luckier or more privileged than every other woman. What it does mean (among other things) is that the society we live in, like all other historical societies, is a patriarchy. And patriarchies imagine or picture themselves from the male point of view. There is a female culture, but it is an underground, unofficial, minor culture, occupying a small corner of what we think of officially as possible human experience. Both men and women in our culture conceive the culture from a single point of view – the male.[3]

It is also true that the single point of view is not only male; the single point of view is that of the white, educated male. Some of the most powerful and provocative women writers of American literature are women of colour, and their writing shows the strain, tensions, and range of writing as outsiders who are even further away from the centre.

And yet – or should we say 'in response' – women writers of colour have produced some of the wittiest satires on American life we can read. Alice Childress, a twentieth-century playwright and author, continually draws her audience's attention to the ironies of a life that says black women aren't fully human. As Mary Helen Washington tells us, the usual plot for the woman in fiction does not allow the heroine to triumph because to triumph is to undercut her supposedly frail femininity; in such a case the female protagonist 'cannot savor the satisfaction of her actions because the very act of taking control of her life is also, for a woman, a fall from grace'.[4] And humour is the art of triumph, the art of power, and the art of control. These are not usually regarded as 'feminine' arts by a world which would condemn women to the needle and thread instead of the needle and threat. But women of all colours in America have a tradition of using humour to survive what is often a hostile environment.

We should add to these remarks those of prominent Americanist Nina Baym, who alerts us to the way women have been systematically driven out of the canon of American literature:

> Yet I cannot avoid the belief that 'purely' literary criteria, as they have been employed to identify the best American works, have inevitably had a bias in favour of things male – in favour, say, of whaling ships rather than the sewing circle as a symbol of the human community; in favour of satires on domineering mothers, shrewish wives, or betraying mistresses rather than tyrannical fathers, abusive husbands, or philandering suitors; displaying an exquisite compassion for the crisis of the adolescent male, but altogether impatient with the parallel crisis of the female.[5]

In other words, to be a woman is to be a marginalized member of our culture; women's humour is seen as the trivial being discussed by the unimportant in a frivolous manner.

Coupled with a dismissal of female humour, however, is a wariness about its possible dangers. To be a woman writer of comedy is to be doubly marginalized. A woman who uses humour to get her point across is seen as a troublemaker, an outsider who wants to disrupt the system because she can't belong to it, or even as a 'wisecrack' (a term employed by a recent film on female stand-up comics). Dorothy Parker, who actually wrote *hundreds* of stories, poems and essays, and who is one of the most important writers of comic fiction and essays from the 1920s to the 1950s, argues that irreverence is essential for the creation of humorous prose. 'There must be courage; there must be no awe. There must be criticism, for humor, to my mind, is encapsulated in criticism', writes Parker about comedy. 'There must be a disciplined eye and a wild mind. There must be a magnificent disregard of your reader, for if he cannot follow you, there is nothing you can do about it.'[6] Perhaps, one could argue, male readers simply found it too difficult to 'follow' female writers of comedy, and so declared them unfit practitioners of honour. It would be easier to say someone wasn't funny than to admit that you simply couldn't 'get' the joke.

It is a fact of American life that women have been often regarded as humourless creatures. Women are notorious – among men – for having no sense of humour. Books have been written (by men) on the subject and studies have been done (by men) to prove in absolute terms that women are deficient in this area. (One critic put it this way: 'Women are the unlaughing at which men laugh.'[7]) How can a whole sex be missing this important faculty? What do women readers do with the accusation that women have no sense of humour when we've grown up listening to the laughter coming from our mothers and aunts in the kitchen, our friends and colleagues in the classroom and the office? What do we do with the accusation when we've grown up reading books – from Louisa May Alcott's short stories, to Zora Neale Hurston's *I Love Myself When I Am Laughing*, to Anita Loos's *Gentlemen Prefer Blondes*, to Erma Bombeck's *Family – The Ties that Bind . . . And GAG*, to Cynthia Heimel's *If You Can't Live Without Me, Why Aren't You Dead Yet?* – that made us laugh out loud? What do we do with the accusation that women have no sense of humour? We have to dispel this concept, the very inaccuracy of which should make us laugh.

Obviously women do indeed have a sense of humour. Obviously, too, it's gone unnoticed because it differs from what has been for many years considered 'true' comedy, 'true' humour. Contrary to the popular cliché, a joke is not, in fact, always a joke. You remember 'true' comedy, don't you? Mother-in-law jokes. Breast jokes. Bum jokes. You know, true humour. When women didn't laugh at the jokes that offended them they were accused of being humourless, despite the fact that they obviously found *other* things very funny indeed. Mostly what they found funny were those issues highly prized by conventional culture: the cult of masculinity, the laws and rules of a patriarchal society, and the ritualized debasement of women. Those were the ideals and ideas worth a comic attack. One noted comedian said that men were afraid of women's laughter because they fear that women are making fun of their sexual equipment. 'What we're laughing at is always much funnier than that and far more absurd – we're laughing at the way men run the government, and the way that they act when they're sick.'[8]

It can be argued that women form a particular kind of alternative culture, with its own knowledge, folklore, traditions and assumptions, that differs from the dominant patriarchal culture. As Emily Toth has wryly noted, men and women have different approaches to what is of value in a culture. 'No woman would go off to sea and chase a white whale that had already chewed up other women and part of herself', Toth points out. 'Nor do women respond to adversity the way Mark Twain's heroes do, by running away from home. . . . Much of what seems heroic from one point of view seems silly from another.'[9] This would, of course, affect both the creation of and response to humour. Anthropologist Mahadev L. Apte proposes that 'humour is culture based in the sense that individual cultural systems significantly influence the mechanism that triggers the humour experience. Familiarity with a cultural code is a prerequisite for the spontaneous mental restructuring of elements that results in amusement and laughter.'[10] An argument can be made, therefore, that women have a tradition of humour that is grounded and defined, in significant ways, by the manner in which it differs from the masculine tradition. Freud has argued in *Jokes and the Unconscious* that jokes represent 'a rebellion against that authority, a liberation from its pressure. The charm of caricatures lies in this same factor: we laugh at them even if they are unsuccessful simply because we count rebellion against authority as a merit.'[11] Rebellion against the authority that men have historically possessed over women has always been a staple of women's humour. As Louisa May Alcott wrote of a harried female character in 1872, her 'sense of the ludicrous supported her through many trying scenes'.[12]

As Walker suggests: 'The writer assumes the reader's familiarity with her topics and themes, and assumes further a shared discomfort or anger at the oppression they mutually endure.'[13] Often, this submerged anger is covered or screened by humour, even though humour does not purge the writer's sense of distress. Flannery O'Connor wrote, in a 1955 letter to a friend, that 'I am interested in making up a good case for distortion, as I am coming to believe it is the only way to make people see'.[14] O'Connor is, in this sentiment, echoing a history of women writers who felt a need to 'distort' their truths in order to reach their audience. As Emily Dickinson writes: 'The Truth I do not dare to know I muffle with a jest.'[15] Dickinson also counselled her readers to 'Tell the Truth, But Tell it Slant' since 'Success in Circuit Lies'.[16] Often the most profound forces of rage, recognition, and power were carefully concealed by women writers in order that their words were not suppressed completely.

In part because they told the truth 'slanted' through humour, there is a great tradition of women's writing in America, going back to the colonial days of the mid-seventeenth century. At that time, for example, Anne Bradstreet's poetry was published as the first collection of original poems produced in America. But Bradstreet, despite this honour, was wary of the way she would be read – 'as only a woman'. In her 'Prologue', she confronts a fact that would remain shadowy but nevertheless persistent until illuminated by feminist critics more than 300 years later: that the processes of reading and writing are deeply and irrefutably informed by gender. Bradstreet is using the sort of sly subversiveness that becomes a characteristic of women's humour in America when she writes:

> I am obnoxious to each carping tongue
> Who says my hand a needle better fits,
> A poet's pen, all scorn I should thus wrong,
> For such despite they cast on female wits:
> If what I do prove well, it won't advance,
> They'll say it's stolen, or else it was by chance.[17]

That the success of her work will be written off as imitative or merely lucky is something of which Bradstreet is only too aware; her witty uncovering of the mechanism that will damn her as second-rate, however, proves again how first-rate she really is. Bradstreet's refusal to be treated as less able than her male contemporaries is another hallmark of American women's humour: wit is both evidence of – and born out of – a sense of defiance, and humour as a way to defend against the overbearing, overriding patriarchal culture.

Because of the ways in which women's humour differs from conventional masculine humour, it has often gone unrecognized or underestimated. Masculine comedy and humour in the American tradition often relies on particular methods or tropes, such as the 'tall tale' of exaggerated prowess in the Paul Bunyan tradition ('Why, you should've seen him, Ma. He done rounded up forty-thousand head of cattle and chopped down sixty forests all before lunchtime'), the philosophical/mysterious method of comic story-telling à la Mark Twain's 'The Mysterious Stranger', or the overtly political satire of Will Rogers ('Politics has got so expensive that it takes lots of money to even get beat with'). These three categories of humour are rarely explored by women writers, and can therefore be classified as 'masculine' forms of humorous writing.

But, you might ask, why regard it as 'masculine' comedy? Why make it gender-specific? Why not see comedy as the last frontier of the universal, humour as that glorious patch of hallowed ground where we all meet and laugh with equal joy? A charming thought, but dangerous in its attempt to seduce the reader into a belief that we all laugh at the same things, even when we happen to laugh at the same time, that we all see the same thing when we stand next to each other. The finite, tightly closed-off limits of traditional comedy are erased by the decentring, dislocating aspects of women's writing. Women's writing defies the usual categories, and is therefore often unseen – or when seen, ignored. American women's humour has an underground tradition of making trouble, even for those critics who would seek to classify it under broader headings.

While assuming ostensible conventionality, women's comedy subtly undercuts the defining features of the genre it seems to embody in order to repudiate the patriarchal, repressive nature of those limitations. In other words, women's humour is often elusive, evasive, and subversive. Judy Little calls such humour 'liminal', meaning that it is on the outskirts of acceptability, or that it exists on a boundary. Little argues in her 1983 book *Comedy and the Woman Writer* that women writers make use of liminal imagery when writing comic prose, since what they are saying is dangerous to the *status quo* but must still be understood and accepted to the extent that it must be heard. 'At its best, feminist comedy deals with absolutes, but not absolutely', claims Little, who goes on to say that women writers 'use liminal imagery to mock long-standing social and psychological institutions'.[18]

We know that a piece of writing by southern author Flannery O'Connor is humorous, for example, but her work is not easy to fit into the pre-existing categories or definitions, since it deals – perhaps – with death by drowning or with the theft of a false limb by a travelling salesman. Can you call a short story that deals with these issues ('The River' and 'Good Country People' respectively, in O'Connor's case) humorous? By calling the definitions into question, the compass of the question itself alters, depicting, finally, the ideological foundations embodied by and perpetuated by conventional comedy which often disregards or debases women's experience.

Traditionally, American humour written by men treats women one of two ways: it treats her like a goddess, or it assumes she is a whore. It should come as no surprise that humour written by women does not limit or reduce female existence to these clichés, but instead considers a woman's life to be as fully interesting, as fully multi-faceted, and as fully important as a man's. One way in which the woman writer can undercut the traditional stereotypes that reduce women to clichés is to make use of these stereotypes herself in order to undermine them. Walker argues that:

> What female humorists have done with these stereotypes, however, is to subvert them. The housewives who cannot reach perfection, such as those of Jean Kerr and Erma Bombeck, are in this situation because the standards for their performance are impossibly high; the lovelorn women of Dorothy Parker, Margaret Fishback, and others are victims of male indifference and the double standard; the dumb blonde, such as Lorlei Lee in Anita Loos's *Gentlemen*

Prefer Blondes (1925), is not so dumb after all, but uses the assets she has to turn matters to her own advantage, all the while laughing at the men who perceive her as stupid.[19]

In a book published over 100 years ago, *The Woman's Story As Told by Twenty American Women*, editor Laura Holloway declared in her introduction that 'the differences in population; the varieties of classes, and the broad distinctions in local colouring are vividly exhibited in the annals of American fiction, the largest contributors to which are women'.[20] Apparently as far back as 1889, when Holloway's book first appeared, women realized that there was a need to present women's stories separately, as well as a need to highlight the way in which women writers bring their differences to bear as gifts rather than threats to the larger community. Contemporary poet Adrienne Rich declares: 'Today women are talking to each other ... reading aloud to one another the books that have moved and healed us, analysing the language that has lied about us, reading our own words aloud to each other.'[21] But we can see that women have always had a story – and a joke – of their own.

Women's comic stories subvert the condition traditionally regarded as a prerequisite for humorous narrative: the assumption of a consensus opinion or shared values. It is standard practice for the author and reader to share a system of values into which a main character must be initiated. The traditional humorous story often begins when the main characters uninitiated behaviour sets him apart from his peers. But something else is at work in stories by women. Often the character learns to distrust and refuse to participate in the system of dominant values. In other words, the triumphant values are the ones espoused by the uninitiated female protagonists. Refusals are at the heart of such works as the filmscripts of Anita Loos. For the humour to work, there has to be a shared basis of particular experience – one of the reasons comedy doesn't seem as 'eternal' as tragedy is because comedy often relies on getting a particular play with words or the overturning of a particular rule. It also depends on gauging your audience accurately.

The shared experience of humour relies on the creation of the right sort of context. In her memoirs, *Kiss Hollywood Goodbye*, Anita Loos discusses the film *Red Headed Woman*, which she scripted for MGM. Loos describes the movie as having outraged 'ladies' clubs throughout the land' because 'our heroine, the bad girl of whom all good husbands dream, ended her career as many such scalawags do, rich, happy, and respected, without ever having paid for her sins'. But, most importantly, the film became a major hit only after Loos included a prologue 'to tip the audience off that the movie's a comedy'.[22] Since the plot centred on the break-up of a marriage, the preview audiences were not sure how to respond. Isn't such a topic tragic? One of the directors argued: 'You can't make jokes about a girl who deliberately sets out to break up a family,' to which Loos replied: 'Look at the family! It deserves to be broken up!'[23] Loos included a brief opening scene where the heroine, played by Jean Harlow, tries on a dress in a shop. She asks the saleswoman: 'Is this dress too tight?' The clerk says that indeed it is, and Harlow replies 'Good!' as she buys the garment. The audiences obviously felt better knowing it was okay to laugh. They had the film's permission to find laughable something usually considered an unfit topic for laughter. The story works not against the renegade woman-reader-heroine, but against those who would confine her in the attic of 'acceptable' behaviour, who would write her out of her own text. Behind the humble curtsey to the ruling culture, the writer also presents a wink to readers, an encoded signal to those who understand that the heroine's apparent submission does not negate her instinctive rebellion. The values shared by reader and heroine remain in ascendancy; the values of those in control are swept away.

These writers use their stories not to justify the ways of God to man, or to justify the ways of men to women, but rather to expose the problems inherent in such ways. Through intricate weavings of politics, aphoristic commentary, romance, and narrative, these short stories gain their profound power from small and large transgressions. These writers delightedly and unrelentingly expose the myths that have helped keep women 'in their place'; by understanding the social and economic basis for women's exclusion from the power structure, women can begin to undo the system by refusing to participate within their assigned roles.

'Women use comedy', argues contemporary Pulitzer Prize-winning playwright Wendy Waserstein. 'You use it to get a laugh but you use it deliberately, too.'[24] Humour is too potent a force to be used solely to make jokes about impotence; women's humour is often very political, but the political and the personal are inextricably entwined. When Charlotte Perkins Gilman wrote her 1913 classic, *The Yellow Wallpaper*, she used a chilling form of humour to get her point across. A young woman, locked in an attic by her physician husband until she can 'get well' and behave herself properly (by being a more traditional mother and by no longer wanting to write), tells her own tale of confinement and release. We are drawn to the heroine because she is clearly trying desperately to understand the rules she must obey, even as she grows to understand that the system – not she – is mad. We laugh not at the powerless victim but at a society that wants to grind her personality to dust. The victim is no longer a source of amusement, no longer a sort of comic scapegoat; instead, the world of physicians, domineering husbands, and barred windows is slyly attacked by the heroine's merely repeating the 'rules' under which she must live. Her husband is 'very careful and loving', she tells us, but that translates into the fact that he controls her every action and would like to control her every thought. He medicates her with a 'schedule prescription for each hour of the day' so that 'I take phosphate or phosphite – whichever it is, and tonics, and journeys, and air, and exercise, and am absolutely forbidden to "work" until I am well again'.

Early on in the tale, the narrator wonders: 'If a physician of high standing, and one's own husband, assures friends and relatives that there is nothing really the matter with one but temporary nervous depression – a slight hysterical tendency – then what is one to do?' She is trapped within a system that cannot accommodate her, and which ridicules her questioning of this effectiveness: 'John laughs at me, of course, but one expects that in marriage.' She wonders, almost faint with the thought of such an unfeminine idea, whether the fact that her husband is a doctor doesn't make her sicker: 'John is a physician and perhaps . . . that is one reason I do not get well faster.' What is interesting about this sort of nearly offhand remark is the way it reveals a knowledge that the narrator knows but on which she cannot act.[25] That is a source of much of the deepest irony in women's writing: understand that you're living inside a corrupt or absurd system without feeling as if anything can be done to change it.

'Wit has truth in it', said Dorothy Parker, but she also added that 'there are things that never have been funny, and never will be'.[26] *The Yellow Wallpaper* falls on the boundary between those two categories, as do a number of other works by women writers.

That boundary, that 'liminal' territory charted by Little, has been a source of energy for those women writers who are not traditionally classified as 'humorous' but whose works are shaped by and filled with irony, satire, wily wryness, and a sense of the ludicrous. We have already seen how Flannery O'Connor, for example, can be read in the light of her humour. Emily Dickinson, too, can be re-read through the lens of her wit and wordplay as a writer of a particularly feminine humour. Novelist Edith Wharton, whose *House of Mirth* is indisputably an American classic, laces her prose with a venomous and pointed humour that makes her both 'unladylike' and emblematic of the woman writer. In other words, Wharton goes far in proving that the woman writer who uses humour isn't a 'lady' because she is committed to the idea of undermining the social conventions that strangle and warp women's lives. A male friend suggests to the heroine Lily that marriage is her vocation. Lily agrees and explains that in terms of marrying, 'a girl must, a man may if he chooses', thereby illustrating her awareness of the absurdity of her life as a woman. She must marry only because she is not permitted the freedom to live her life independently, as a man might. Lily illustrates her point by observing to her friend that

> Your coat's a little shabby – but who cares? It doesn't keep people from asking you to dine. If I were shabby no one would have me: a woman is asked out as much for her clothes as for herself. The clothes are the background, the frame, if you like: they don't make success, but they are part of it. Who wants a dingy woman? We are expected to be pretty and well-dressed till we drop – and if we can't keep it up alone, we have to go into partnership.[27]

The 'partnership' offered to a woman in terms of marriage is an unequal arrangement, given that women 'must' marry when they can offer their assets at their most valuable: when they are young and beautiful.

For Lily, at the turn of the century, few options other than marriage offered themselves if a woman was to remain in the middle or upper classes. Lily is expected to marry the first reasonable man who will have her since, in her late twenties, she is seen as running out of time. She considers her situation with a certain amount of cynicism, such as when she is trying to snag the attention of Percy Gryce. Gryce has come into a fortune 'which the late Mr Gryce has made out of a patent device for excluding fresh air from hotels'. At one point, Lily has 'been bored all the afternoon by Percy Gryce – the mere thought seemed to waken an echo of his droning voice – but she could not ignore him on the morrow'. Lily knows that she must 'follow up her success, must submit to more boredom, must be ready with fresh compliances and adaptabilities, and all on the bare chance that he might ultimately decide to do her the honour of boring her for life'. Wharton's humour is ruthless in exposing the mechanism behind the set-up that would harness the energetic, intelligent and witty Lily to the droning, airless-heir Gryce.

But Lily knows that she shouldn't risk rejecting Gryce if she wants to remain within her chosen social circles. Importantly for Lily, marriage would offer her a way into the community from which, as a single woman with little money, she would otherwise be excluded. She is trapped between the pressures of entering into a domestic life, which is the only way to be accepted, and her own 'political' awareness that the system was developed without her in mind. The personal and the political are braided together in the lives of women, whose lives have historically been governed by men.

In this category I would also put such solid figures as Abigail Smith Adams (1744–1818), wife of statesman John Adams, whose letters to her husband are full of barbed social commentary as well as domestic detail. Consider the letter from Abigail to John written on 31 March 1776, in which she makes explicit her desire that

> you would Remember the Ladies and be more generous and favourable to them than your ancestors. Do not put such unlimited power into the hands of the Husbands. Remember all Men would be tyrants if they could. If particular care and attention is not paid to the Ladies we are determined to foment a Rebellion, and will not hold ourselves bound by any Laws in which we have no voice, or Representation . . . [that] your Sex are Naturally Tyrannical is a

Truth so thoroughly established as to admit of no dispute, but such of you as wish to be happy willingly give up the harsh title of Master for the more tender and endearing one of Friend.

Abigail Adams's pleas for the woman's 'voice' to be heard by the government is one that echoes through over 200 years of American history. The plea has called forth only the most perfunctory responses for the most part. (Her husband's reply, in a letter dated 14 April 1776, complains that her 'Letter was the first Intimation that another Tribe more numerous and powerful than all the rest were grown discontented – this is rather too coarse a Compliment but you are so saucy. I won't blot it out'.[28] In effect, his reply reduces her argument to a 'saucy' bit of feminine nagging.)

We can see that even the more 'canonical' women writers (if that phrase isn't itself a contradiction in terms) use humour, but it should also be stressed that there is a history of women humorists in America as well. Only recently studied by feminist scholars, writers such as Mercy Otis Warren (1728–1814), 'Fanny Fern'/Sara Willis Parton (1811–72), Frances Miriam Berry Whitcher (1814–52), 'Josiah Allen's Wife'/Marietta Holley (1836–1926), Alice Duer Miller (1874–1942), Agnes Repplier (1855–1950), Helen Rowland (1875–1950), and Shirley Jackson (1919–65) should be added to the more contemporary list that would include Erica Jong (*Fear of Flying*), Nora Ephron (*Heartburn*), Rita Mae Brown (*Southern Discomfort*), Ntozake Shange (*For Colored Girls...*), Jane Wagner (*The Search for Signs of Intelligent Life in the Universe*) and Cynthia Heimel (*Sex Tips for Girls*), among others.

Although by no means exhaustive, this discussion of humour, anger and comedy in American women's writing is meant to suggest ways of perceiving those elements characteristic of women's writing which have long been ignored or misread by the critical tradition. Comedy in all its familiar forms – from novels to films, from cartoons to stand-up comedy, from humour in the workplace to humour in intimate relationships – can help women recognize new sources of power within themselves. The productive use of humour is a challenge facing a generation of women who have grown up only half-recognizing the power of their own laughter.

Notes

1. Walker N 1988 *A very serious thing: women's humour and American culture*. University of Minnesota Press, Minneapolis, p 9.
2. Toth E 1988 Female wits. *Massachusetts Review* 22 (4): 783–93.
3. Russ J 1983 Dear colleague, I am not an honorary male. *How to suppress women's writing*. University of Texas Press, Austin.
4. Washington M 1987 *Invented lives: narratives of Black women 1860–1960*. Doubleday, New York, p 5.
5. Baym N 1978 *Women's fiction: a guide to novels by and about women in America*. Cornell University Press, Ithaca and London, p 14.
6. Parker D 1958 Introduction *The most of S. J. Perelman*. Simon & Schuster, New York, p xii.
7. Blyth R 1970 *Humour in English literature: a chronological anthology*. Folcroft Press, Penn, p 14.
8. Hollander N, interviewed by Regina Barreca, 1989.
9. Toth 1988.
10. Apte M 1985 *Humour and laughter: an anthropological approach*. Cornell University Press, Ithaca.
11. Freud S 1960 *Jokes and their relation to the unconscious* trans J Strachey. W W Norton & Co, New York, p 105.
12. Walker 1988 p 118.
13. Ibid p 36.
14. Fitzgerald S (ed) 1979 *The habit of being: letters of Flannery O'Connor*. Farrar, Strous & Giroux, New York, p 79.
15. Dickinson E Consulting summer's clock. In T Johnson (ed) 1960 *The poems of Emily Dickinson*. Harvard University Press, Boston and Toronto, p 697.
16. Dickinson E Tell all the truth but tell it slant. DeRoche J (ed) 1991 *The Heath introduction to poetry*. Heath, Lexington, Ky, p 201.
17. Bradsteet A Prologue. In K. Rogers (ed) 1991 *The Meridian anthology of early American women writers 1650–1865*. Meridian, New York, p 13.
18. Little J 1983 *Comedy and the woman writer: Woolf, Spark, and Feminism*. University of Nebraska Press, Lincoln, p 187.
19. Walker 1988 p 11.
20. Holloway L (ed) 1889 *The woman's story as told by twenty American writers*. J B Alden, New York.
21. Rich A 1979 *On lies, secrets, and silence: selected prose, 1966–1978*. W W Norton & Co, New York, p 13.
22. Loos A 1974 *Kiss Hollywood goodbye*. Viking Press, New York, p 43.

23. Carey G 1988 *Anita Loos: a biography*. Knopf, New York, p 148.
24. Cohen E 1988 Uncommon woman: an interview with Wendy Wasserstein. In Barreca R (ed) 1988 *Last laughs: perspectives on women and humour*. Gordon & Beach, New York, p 259.
25. Gilman C P 1899 The yellow wallpaper. Rpt in Clayton J (ed) 1992 *The Heath introduction to fiction*. Heath, Lexington, Ky, pp 220–34.
26. Plimpton G 1989 *Women writers at work: the Paris review interviews*. Penguin Books, New York, p 115.
27. Wharton E (1905) 1985 *The house of mirth*. Penguin Books, New York, pp. 12, 22, 25.
28. Adams A and J (1982) Letters to each other in *American Families: A Documentary History*, eds D M Scott and B Wishy, Harper and Row, New York, p 106.

4 The two narratives of the Western

Antony Easthope

'the most perfect example of the modern state is North America'
Marx and Engels, *The German Ideology*

George Stevens's film, *Shane* (1953), is an instance of a traditional Hollywood Western plot: the conflict between cattlemen and homesteaders. Its hero (Alan Ladd) finally steps in to settle the conflict by shooting Wilson (Jack Palance), a gunman hired by the Riker brothers to protect their ranching interests. If you listen to the dialogue carefully it is made clear at one point that Sam Grafton, the man who owns both the saloon and the general store, seeks to avoid trouble by restraining the Rikers. He has an interest in the custom of both cattlemen and homesteaders and is the one who will benefit from both in the long run. Yet the attention of the film focuses elsewhere on the confrontation between hero and villain.

Shane, then, can be read according to two different contexts of interpretation which in turn correspond to two competing narratives. One, concentrating on individuals, their reactions to an immediate physical and social environment, and their personal success or failure within that environment, might be called 'the liberal narrative'; the other, concerned with the individual only in so far as he or she is positioned within a history of economic forces, I shall refer to as 'the social narrative'. Both narratives have been drawn on to account for the development of the Western genre, the liberal more often than the social. However, as I shall argue, the social narrative should be understood as a metanarrative in relation to its liberal opponent since it provides grounds for explaining the liberal narrative as a selective and displaced version of itself. But I will begin by considering a feminist narrative about the Western (since all forms of signifying practice are specific, this discussion will concentrate on one, the Western as genre in the American cinema).

In a striking and original essay, 'West of Everything', Jane Tompkins has defined the Western by contrasting it with the nineteenth-century domestic novel, which, she proposes, it answers at every point.[1] While the domestic novel is committed to supernatural Christianity, the domain of feeling, and the portrayal of women, 'the Western is secular, positivist, and antifeminist'.[2] Rejecting the afterlife, the Western shows its hero defeating death by killing adversaries, a game in which survival in this world is everything. When women do appear in the Western they and what they may represent become marginalized, either left behind at the end or, typically, put forward merely as the stake in a masculine enterprise:

> Time after time, the Western hero commits murder, usually multiple murders, in the name of making his town/ranch/mining claim safe for women and children. But the discourse of love and peace which women articulate is never listened to. . . .[3]

I find this account of the generic history of the Western very convincing. But when, in conclusion, a more general historical narrative is offered to explain the social causes for this generic realignment, some problems arise.

For Tompkins the Western 'owes its essential character to the dominance of a women's culture in the nineteenth century and to women's invasion of the public sphere between 1880 and 1920'.[4] The Western, therefore, has nothing to do with the West as such but is rather a masculine counteraction to 'mens fear of losing their hegemony and hence their identity'.[5] This essentially sociological account is only partially convincing, for three reasons in the main. Even granted that women did invade a public sphere traditionally held as a male prerogative, this would still not explain (however self-evident it may seem) *why* and *how* men should fear such invasion (and there is evidence that anxieties about traditional masculinity and the place of the feminine become articulated well before the chosen period). Secondly, there is the question of precisely how lived experience – the invasion of men's public space – could become transposed into a specific mode of fictional representation as a Hollywood genre.

A third, and for my purposes here a more telling objection, would be this. The Western is a version of historical drama, particularly in the cinema, characterized by a detailed and specific representation of landscape, townscape and everyday life at a particular period in the history of the United States between 1865 and 1885. While *The Magnificent Seven* (1960) transposed theme, plot and even characters from *Seven Samurai* (1954) into an American historical setting, the John Sturges film counts as a Western, Kurosawa's does not; Sergio Leone's movies with Clint Eastwood, though subtlely yet distinctly unWestern in tone (mingling sadism with an invitation to male homosexual desire), maintain a careful recreation of place and everyday life and so are recognized as Westerns, albeit qualified as 'spaghetti'. While the Tompkins analysis well explains the Western negatively as a rejection of the domestic novel, it fails to account for it positively. The Western has everything to do with the American frontier, is vividly and seductively marked by its specific connotations. An iconography, a set of typical plots and a particular representation of the hero give the genre an indelible meaning in terms of the history of the United States. But what is the frontier, what is this history? The social and liberal narratives give contrasted explanations of the development of the American West.

'This rising Empire'

Although the Founding Fathers spoke with enthusiasm of 'this rising Empire', it is still unconventional to tell the story of the American West in terms of the colonization of foreign territory, a conquest masked by the continental boundaries. Enshrined in any list of place-names – New Orleans, Albuquerque, Santa Fe, Wichita, Nacogdoches – the magic of the old West derives from the names given to the places by other nations the American Empire drove out: French, Spanish, Mexican, Indian, English. In the social narrative the original thirteen colonies took what is now the United States through a series of territorial acquisitions:

1776: Transappalachia
1803: Louisiana Purchase

1819: Florida
1845: Texas
1846: Oregon Territory
1848: California, Nevada, Utah, New Mexico, Colorado
1854: 'Permanent Indian Territory', i.e. Nebraska, Kansas, the
      Dakotas
1867: Alaska
1898: Cuba, Puerto Rico, Philippines, Hawaii.

As purchased, taken by conquest or 'annexed', each piece of land was rapidly occupied and exploited by a ruthless and unofficial army of settlers. 'America . . . has its growing "colonies" in the far west', said an unnamed Englishman in *Bradstreets* in 1881, his own national experience enabling him to call an empire an empire.[6]

An exemplary version of the social narrative of the expansion west in terms of its social and economic basis is offered by the American historian, William Appleman Williams. In *The Contours of American History* (1961) he divides the growth of empire into three phases. During the first, which Williams calls 'Mercantilism' and dates from 1740 to 1828, the new government sought to control western expansion while the east gained cohesion and strength, a combination that would generate further expansion. With the 1820s and the Monroe Doctrine that time had come. This period of 'Laissez Faire' (1819–96) is epitomized by Daniel Webster, who said in 1824:

> Our age is wholly of a different character, and its legislation takes another turn. Society is full of excitement; competition comes in place of monopoly; and intelligence and industry ask only for fair play and an open field.[7]

The third phase, that of 'Corporation Capitalism', is dated from 1882. In this there is a concentration of ownership, of railways, oil and mining interests for example, in the hands of big businessmen such as J. Pierpont Morgan, John D. Rockefeller and Andrew Carnegie. Granted differences between these stages of development, a single economic and social narrative defines western expansion. It may be analysed as ensuing from the interaction of five factors: (a) land, occupied only by 'inferior' civilizations and full of resources contemporary technology was able to exploit; (b) cheap labour, a huge pool ever replenished by immigration and supplying the planters, trappers, hunters, miners, sodbusters, homesteaders, scouts, soldiers, ranch-hands, together with certain middle-men such as land agents and storekeepers; (c) eastern industrialism, able to manufacture and sell western pioneers everything from Colt revolvers to barbed wire; (d) eastern capital, which found unlimited opportunities for investment and speculative ventures in westward expansion; (e) crucially, a society *already* formed on the basis of capitalism, and which by the Revolution threw off some of the restraints and vested interests that continued to inhibit European societies; a society therefore which already had what Williams christens the market-place conception of reality.

In *The Roots of the Modern American Empire* (1969) Williams argues that the nineteenth-century western empire provided both an economic base and a social habit for international expansion in the twentieth. The end of one frontier implied the need for a new one, for as Representative Joseph Cannon of Illinois said in 1883: 'The time may come when we have fully developed this continent, when we will have to look elsewhere for a market.'[8] Transition from a continental to an international imperialist outlook was anticipated by Henry Cabot Lodge in 1895: 'We have a record of conquest, colonization and expansion unequalled by any people in the Nineteenth Century. We are not to be curbed now.'[9] It is a strength of the narrative in Williams that it can extend so persuasively its account of American development before 1900 to the period after.

The social narrative would be able to trace a connection between everyday life and economic forces, for example in the life of the cowboy. According to the liberal narrative (to anticipate) the cowboy is apparently free-standing, a model of independence and self-reliance, stoically discharging commitments freely undertaken; fair-skinned if suntanned, he rides lonesome with the cattle between the prairie and the sky. The social narrative would work things out differently, stressing, for example, that about a quarter of ranch-hands were Mexicans and many were freed slaves. The gun the cowboy carried was manufactured by Colt Revolvers in Hartford, Connecticut,[10] and the barbed wire he fenced by the American Steel and Wire Company after the patent of Joseph Glidden of 1874. His beans and coffee came to him from the chuck wagon owned by the rancher to whom he was contracted. Ranches in turn were owned by the large ranchers or investors in the east or in Britain. In 1880 a British Parliamentary Report declared that profits of 33⅓ per cent could be made from ranching and in 1881 the Prairie Cattle Company (a Scottish consortium) declared profits of 28 per cent. In the 1890s the Wyoming Stock Growers Association kept a black-list of militant cowboys (something mentioned in Michael Cimino's *Heaven's Gate* (1980)); some ranch-hands in Texas went on strike. According to the social narrative the cowboy is a form of cheap casual labour whose surplus value typically went to enrich a top-hatted Victorian banker in London or in Edinburgh.

'Precipitated by the Wilderness'

While the social narrative of the West is mainly institutionalized as a high cultural and mainly academic discourse, the liberal narrative has a much more embedded purchase on the social formation. If the social narrative is critical and currently subordinate, even marginal, its liberal opponent continues to be official and hegemonic, diversely and pervasively instituted. How it was defined and propagated in the nineteenth century is well chronicled by Henry Nash Smith, who describes three aspects of its generation.[11]

In various biographies of Daniel Boone, in Cooper's *Leatherstocking* novels (1823–41), and in Frémont's accounts of his travels with Kit Carson, the liberal narrative is given a literary high cultural expression. This coincides during the 1850s with its promotion as an ideology in the doctrine of manifest destiny. The slogan 'Go west, young man, go west and grow up with the country' was given currency through Horace Greeley's *New York Tribune* from 1841, and in the significantly named *Mission of the North American People* (1874) the indefatigable William Gilpin defined it as 'the *untransacted* destiny of the American people' to push westwards and 'subdue the continent'.[12] Thereafter a breakthrough into popular culture and a mass audience came with the enterprise of Erasmus Beadle and his dime novels, after 1860.

Nash Smith ends with the dramatic presentation of the narrative by Buffalo Bill Cody, whose Wild West Show toured to the end of the century. Propagation of the myth has continued in the twentieth century with pulp magazines and children's comics, but the main signifying practice for its reproduction has been Hollywood and subsequently television. Already adapted for dramatization, the Western genre was – like so much else of the vaudeville and melodrama tradition – taken up by the cinema; in fact, the first commercial feature film, Porter's *The Great Train Robbery* (1903), is a Western, recounting an exploit of the Wild Bunch. In the wake of Hollywood, television, with *Bonanza*, *High Chapparal*, and *The Virginian*, carried a further mutation of the liberal narrative throughout the English-speaking world so that it is now both international and transhistorical (probably a third of the world's children can play Cowboys and Indians). The liberal narrative of the West has outlasted the official closing of the frontier in 1890 by nearly a century and its *continuing* hegemony and popularity needs to be understood. We may begin with Turner.

In a high cultural mode, the essential outlines of the liberal narrative of western expansion – and further, a claim that it defines American national culture – is provided by F. J. Turner, whose 'The Significance of the Frontier in American History' (1893) narrates a history of western expansion. Denying that American culture was determined by taking its origin from 'European germs', Turner says rather that 'complex European life' was 'precipitated by the wilderness into the simplicity of primitive conditions' and makes the flat assertion that 'the existence of an area of free land, its continuous recession, and the advance of American settlement westward, explain American development'.[13] The frontier accounts for both the Americanization of different immigrant nationalities and ethnic groups as well as for the American democratic tradition: immigrants were Americanized in the 'crucible' of the frontier, frontier individualism 'from the beginning promoted democracy'.[14]

Turner's narrative is couched throughout in firmly physicalist metaphors. Complex life changes into the primitive in the same way as water vapour is precipitated by a drop in temperature to become rain; the frontier unites different nationalities just as intense heat fuses together separate pieces of the same metal.

Western expansion is like the operation of glaciers: the land is 'free' (not occupied by other people) until it recedes in front of an inevitable 'advance'. What for the social narrative was a history of imperialism and exploitation becomes a natural function. In a Darwinian process of 'social evolution' (Turner's phrase)[15] culture is the necessary consequence of interaction between objective 'conditions' and subjective genetic inheritance ('germs'); social relations are equated with a physical environment which the individual subject experiences directly and responds to without mediation.

No discourse can be pure, can avoid imbrication with other discourses which divide it from itself. So it is with Turner. His narrative is of a specific kind in that it intervenes as that of a frontier historian. Frontier historians are something of a rarity but Owen Lattimore in *Studies in Frontier History* (1962) compares and contrasts frontiers. His critique of Turner needs to be cited at length:

> Turner, in fact, was an acute observer; but what he saw so clearly, he saw while standing on his head. In large measure, when he thought he saw what the frontier did to society, he was really seeing what society did to the frontier. That he was standing on his head accounts for the fact that he touches only glancingly on the American frontiers of the French and Spanish. (He does mention that while the British took the land off the Indians and farmed it, the French in adjoining Canada emphasised trade with the Indians.) Yet why was it that the Spanish and French frontiers in America (especially the frontier in Canada, so close geographically to New England) did not create societies more like that of the United States – except, significantly, in Canada west of Quebec, where the settlers were British?[16]

Is Turner standing on his head or is Lattimore? Which can best lay claim to the status of being a metanarrative?

Just as a metalanguage is characterized by its capacity to cite an object language within it (most obviously through the use of quotation marks), a metanarrative may be defined by its ability to include and comprehend another competing narrative. A metanarrative earns its power to cite another narrative by understanding it as it cannot understand itself, and this is evidenced by two effects: it treats of what is recognizably the same material as the other narrative but does so within a perspective which discloses boundaries beyond which the other cannot move – able to 'see' both what the other narrative 'sees' and also what it can't, namely its own boundaries. Accordingly, within the competing narratives of frontier history, Lattimore stands as a metanarrative in relation to Turner. Lattimore contains Turner, in the first place because he does not deny that the American frontier in its local effects was very much as Turner claims. But Lattimore exceeds and comprehends Turner because he is working within a comparative argument able to recognize and set geographical and temporal limits beyond which Turner's narrative cannot hold because it cannot even acknowledge these are its limits. This is very literally the case here, for if Turner's account were to be generalized, extended beyond America in 1890, it would predict that other frontiers, for example in South Africa or Australia, must create similar traditions and institutions to those of the United States. And we would have to imagine that it was the Russian frontier in Siberia, replete with free land and a crucible for many nationalities, that planted a fifth column of American democracy within the Soviet borders and led the advance towards *glasnost*, the collapse of Communism and the rise of a free market economy.[17]

Lattimore's narrative (American history was created not by what the frontier did to society but 'what society did to the frontier') clearly coincides with the social narrative of the West (it is not that the frontier shaped American society but that the market-place conception of reality shaped the frontier) which therefore must be accorded a metanarrative status in relation to the liberal version exemplified by Turner. However, Lattimore is introduced here not simply to argue the metanarrative status of social over liberal but further because his critique of Turner (his error is to invert liberal and social narratives of the frontier) helps to exhibit how the Western works. The Western contains within itself both the social and liberal narratives and lends itself to both readings; but it contains them only in order to promote the liberal over the social version. And it does so according to a logic or structure presaged by Turner.

No doubt all American texts, in so far as they are historical, must depend on features from the social narrative. But the Western relies upon the social narrative in a special way. It seeks, as Turner rightly perceives, to express the epic of American nationality and define a central version of American identity. And it does so by working and reworking a particular situation from the history of the United States, the frontier 1865–85. In this way the Western necessarily trenches upon the social narrative of expansion even while it proposes the liberal version (so *Shane* made sense in terms of both the social and the liberal narrative). Reproducing both narratives, the Western works precisely *by transposing the social into the liberal narrative* in a way which actively denies or disavows the social narrative. Turner's account itself exemplifies this restructuring process. If Turner inverts the principle that social and economic forces determine the American West into the assertion that the frontier environment determines individual action, so does the Western. It seeks to achieve exactly this inversion or conversion or recuperation by eliding the social with the natural environment. It thrusts to the centre of our attention a (William) Jamesian trinity of 'facts', 'action' and 'power' while setting in disregard the social context which gives these value and meaning. Through a variety of narrative and semiological mechanisms we are led to picture the lone cowboy coping pragmatically and heroically with simple dangers and overlook any nexus binding him to the chuck wagon, the ranch owner, and perhaps a banker in London.

In John Ford's *The Man who Shot Liberty Valance* (1961) conflict between ranchers and homesteaders is introduced long enough to demonstrate the hero's good guy sympathies with the 'little people'; thereafter, its function as characterization completed, it is set aside while the rest of the movie follows the hero's successful rise to become Senator and Governor of his state. The text directs our attention towards apparently self-sufficient individuals and the conditions they encounter and away from awareness of historical conflict. Thus in *Liberty Valance* the lawyer (James Stewart) must choose whether to fight oppression with the law or with a gun. When he agrees reluctantly to use a gun, the text encourages us to see this as an inevitable and natural decision in the environment of a gun-toting western township. He could abandon his career and return east, but this is mentioned only to be dismissed. His ambition can only be satisfied at the price of becoming a gunman, however ineffectively (the character played by John Wayne actually shoots the villain, not him). Choice is forced on him by ambition, not simply circumstances. His ambition is assumed as a natural fact in the situation and is not open to question. Without it the Western could not present him as a hero, and it is in terms of the presentation of the heroic individual that the particular kind of reworking and transposition the Western makes between social and liberal narrative can be most vividly illustrated.[18] Elsewhere I have been concerned to analyse the Western hero as a version of a dominant masculinity and complex of drives;[19] here, while underwriting the argument from Jane Tompkins that this is a masculinist genre, I shall give attention to the ideological connotations of the hero.

What a man's gotta do

At the centre of the Western, then, is an individual hero coping pragmatically with a hostile environment. This must be so both negatively, because possible alternative centres of attention are either ignored or attenuated, and positively, because the man alone is foregrounded. Awareness of a full range of domestic, social and historical relations is subsumed into dramatization of the hero and the 'facts' of his situation. Religion also is remarkable by its absence, as Jane Tompkins notes. In surprising contrast to traditional cycles of epic and adventure stories – Homer, Sinbad the Sailor – the Western is an apparently secular myth without magic or supernatural intervention. Positively, in place of such traditional material, there is full presentation of the hero and his attributes. His environment may be hostile because of human or natural forces: gunmen, grizzly bears and Indians are indifferently equated as 'facts'. What matters is that the hero match these with virtues of his own. Not all present in any one hero, they may be summarized as follows.

The hero is a man of *authority*, established by a style of dress, movement and speech. His clothes mark his self-respect: hat, shirt, vest (the English waistcoat), gunbelt, pants, boots. Even if his hat is old he will replace it after a fight. For long periods the hero is in repose but his inertia is a form of activity, a preparation for moments of fierce energy, when, as Lawrence Alloway points out, he becomes intensely psyched up.[20] His speech is characterized by understatement and taciturnity; there is stress on being 'a man' and juxtapositions of the kind, 'I'm not asking, I'm telling'. The hero has *self-control*; he never does anything without a purpose. If he makes love with a woman he will not permit this to influence his decisions; if he drinks he won't get drunk. He is a model therefore of delayed gratification. He shows complete *technical mastery* of his specialized skills: his fists, his horse, the terrain, his gun.[21] He never attempts what he knows he cannot do. In the special situations for which his capacities are developed he will show unerring *perception* of what is possible and what must be done. He doesn't argue – he pronounces. A foolish suggestion, particularly one marked by the self-deceptive narcissism of youth, the hero will hear out and answer with a suitably lapidary and paternal refutation ('We'll chisel that on your tombstone').

Above all the hero is right. Pike Bishop (William Holden), the leader in Peckinpah's *The Wild Bunch* (1969), says at one point, 'Being sure is my business'. In this sense the hero is characterized by his *vocation*, a compulsive inner necessity, a higher obligation that rests on him as 'a man' – as the trope encapsulating the genre says, he does what a man's gotta do, or, somewhat more roundly, as the hero played by Randolph Scott in Budd Boetticher's *Seven Men from Now* (1956) asserts of his need to take revenge on the men who tortured and killed his Indian wife, 'There's some things a man just can't ride around'. But his sense of honour, his duty to himself and his own conscience, is not without reward. For if he does what he knows is right he is certain to succeed.

For the Western the ultimate and determining measure of success is the conflict in which one man tries to kill another with his revolver. Indeed the hero faces death but the narrative guarantees that he will not die. The ritual of the gunfight, while appearing to conform to the positivist and empiricist premises of the Western, in fact introduces a supernatural effect via the mystique of the faster draw. Even in the cinema, a visual medium, the faster draw remains invisible though technically it could easily be shown (in Kurosawa's film the expertise of the most proficient of the samurai is replayed at one point *in slow motion* to show how it works). For the hero the draw is a moment of grace knowable solely by its consequences and vouchsafed exclusively to those with proven vocation. Only villains, like the one who shoots Jesse James, will draw except in conditions of perfect equity. But even when circumstances are weighted against the hero, magically he still wins. Something more than technique is at work, for movies are full of instances in which the temporarily disadvantaged hero kills the technically superior villain, the well-intentioned amateur shoots the evil-minded professional. What counts is purity of heart, not skill in the hand. In a world without an afterlife, as Jane Tompkins says, 'survival is everything',[22] but the limits of this secular materialism are set by what sanctions the hero's victory in the final gunfight: implicitly he is bearer of a *manifest destiny*.

In sum, the hero is single-minded, self-reliant, patient in the mastery of specialized techniques, ruthlessly pragmatic in the application of known means to gain firmly perceived ends, self-controlled in denying himself immediate pleasures for the sake of ultimate gratification. He is in fact an epitome of the virtues of the successful *entrepreneur*, an exemplum of the qualities Andrew Carnegie prescribes for business success. In *The American West* John Hawgood asks: 'Why were Collis Huntington, Leland Stanford, Charles Crocker, John Mackay and Benjamin Holladay so much more important in the making of Western America than Wild Bill Hickok, George Armstrong Custer, Billy the Kid, Jesse James, the Earp Brothers, and even Buffalo Bill?'[23] My argument is that the Western *does* give us a rendering of the attitudes and values of these railroad and transportation entrepreneurs. But it does so according to the logic of transposition with which the genre operates: by means of an individualist-environmental structure the social narrative of the West becomes re-presented as liberal narrative.

From this there are two pay-offs. One is of course that what the social narrative defines as imperialist and exploitative can be effectively marginalized and disregarded (classically, when the Indian nations are treated as part of nature and just another physical hazard). The other is that the prestige and positive connotations of the United States as the world's leading industrial and scientific power along with a dramatization of the entrepreneurial ethic becomes available in the guise of a history of apparently elemental simplicity, the frontier 1865–85. An analysis such as this is needed to explain why the Western narrative has acquired and retains international popularity long after the supposed moment of its historical origin.

I shall conclude by rehearsing briefly the history of the Western in Hollywood because it provides confirmation for my argument. Though it is the work of the Western to foreground the liberal narrative over the social narrative according to the logic of recuperation this essay has outlined, the genre can never escape the possibility that the social narrative will come through nevertheless. If extra-cinematic conditions and a crisis in ideology weaken the general dominance of the liberal narrative and threaten to bring the social narrative *too* much to attention, then the Western becomes temporarily a prohibited genre for Hollywood. This has occurred at two conjunctures.

The modern Western begins effectively with Ford's *The Iron Horse* of 1924 and its epic account of the making of the trans-American railroad. After James Cruze's similar film *The Pony Express* (1925) and Wesley Ruggles's *Cimarron* of 1931, the Western was not able to hold any serious position in the generic ensemble during the Depression years. That conjuncture brought a crisis in ideology which meant that any attempt to make a Western would risk the social narrative disrupting the liberal narrative. In fact – though this is another story – the energies of the Western became largely displaced into the recently invented gangster genre for most of the decade. It survived only as a children's genre and with singing cowboys until *Stagecoach* (1939) marks its confident re-emergence in association with renewed ideologies of nationalism and expansionism. The high plateau of the Western lasts from 1940 through the 1950s when a crucial feature (one always present in the way the narrative structure finds a place for the Mexican as representative of a subject race) is the reworking of ideas around racial prejudice and integration through stories in which Indians play the role of symbolic American blacks, as in Delmer Davies's *Broken Arrow* of 1950.

During the 1960s, responsive to a fresh crisis in imperialist ideologies arising especially around the Vietnam War, the Western becomes increasingly troubled. A series of texts and notably those directed by Sam Peckinpah from *Major Dundee* (1965) to *The Wild Bunch* (1969) show the liberal struggling to contain the social narrative. By 1975, when the war ended, this struggle can no longer be won. Arthur Penn's *The Missouri Breaks* of 1976 subverts almost every aspect of the traditional Western. The cattlerancher's economic interests are explicitly discussed, the woman seeks the hero (Jack Nicholson) mainly to satisfy her own desire and discards him thereafter, the hero (if he is the hero) kills the villain when he's asleep ('You know what woke you up – it's the sound of having your throat cut'). The lawman or Enforcer (Marlon Brando) kills one rustler by deliberate slow drowning, shoots another while he is in a latrine and kills a third by throwing a Ninja star in his eye. Meanwhile he speaks in a variety of affected accents, makes love to his horse and ends up wearing women's clothes, dressed in which he exclaims after a particularly sadistic murder, 'Well, Ol' Granny's getting tired now'. It's a long way from Gary Cooper.

At this point the Western seemed to have become an impossible genre for Hollywood, something the unfortunate Cimino did not know when he undertook *Heaven's Gate* at the end of the 1970s, a film which vividly illustrates the social narrative breaking through and undermining the liberal narrative of the West. Since then there has been nothing except the nervy and incoherent *Silverado* (1985), a (postmodern?) reprise of *Shane* in *Pale Rider* (also 1985) and the so-called Brat pack in *Young Guns* (1988) – nothing, that is, until Costner's extraordinary *Dances with Wolves* in 1990. Far from avoiding what I have called the social narrative, this film works because it takes that as its very basis. Perhaps picking up the baton where it was left by John Ford with *Cheyenne Autumn* in 1964, it succeeds in part because it can see its European hero from the perspective of the Sioux. Previously every portrayal of Native Americans, however sympathetic, saw them from the outside – even if they spoke their own language (instead of broken English), they had to be interpreted by someone in the narrative. In *Dances with Wolves* the Sioux language is not translated by a scout or other intermediary but directly represented in subtitles. Although the film does not have the courage to make Costner's partner a Sioux, it nevertheless breaks with the Western tradition by taking Native Americans as its *collective* hero. It therefore reinstates the frontier landscape and what it connotes in a new form as the Utopian Western, imagining how the history might have been if it

had not followed the imperialist compulsion. To the extent that
the movie confronts a terrible history it aligns itself with some of
the most progressive forces in the United States today which are
trying to do the same thing. *Dances with Wolves* makes the
Western possible again, though possible only with a profound
difference.

Notes

1. Tompkins J 1987 West of everything. *South Atlantic Quarterly* **86**
   (4): 356–77. Although parts of my own essay were drafted before
   this appeared, it has been revised as both a response and a
   supplement to 'West of everything'. I am also glad to acknowledge
   how far my version has been improved by comments from Jane
   Tompkins.
2. Ibid p 361.
3. Ibid p 373.
4. Ibid p 375.
5. Ibid p 376.
6. *Bradstreets*, 25 June 1881. Cited in Williams W A 1969 *The roots
   of the modern American Empire: a study of the growth and shaping
   of social consciousness in a marketplace society*. Random House,
   New York, p 275.
7. Daniel Webster. Cited in Williams W A 1966 *The Contours of
   American History*. Quadrangle Books, Chicago, p 225.
8. Cited in Williams 1969 p 278.
9. Cited in Williams 1966 p 345.
10. Colt manufactured at Paterson, New Jersey, until they went
    bankrupt in 1842 and were re-established in Hartford in 1847. At
    the end of his *American notes* (1842) Charles Dickens includes a set
    of cuttings from contemporary newspapers to illustrate his sense of
    the violence of the new country: among these shootings, straight
    murder predominates (see Dickens C 1972 *American notes*. Penguin,
    Harmondsworth, pp 269–84).
11. See Smith H N 1950 *Virgin land: the American West as symbol and
    myth*. Harvard University Press, Cambridge, Mass.
12. William Gilpin. Cited in Smith 1950 p 37.
13. Turner F J (1893) 1953 The significance of the frontier in American
    history. In Heffner R D (ed) 1953 *A documentary history of the
    United States*. New American Library, New York, pp 183–95, 185,
    183.

14. Heffner 1953 pp 187, 190.
15. Ibid p 186.
16. Lattimore O 1962 *Studies in frontier history*. Oxford University Press, London, pp 490–1.
17. Turner's version of the liberal narrative continues to permeate writing about the West, appearing, for example, in a standard textbook as follows: 'Even the most carping critic will agree that the unusual environment and the continuous rebirth of society in the western wilderness endowed the American people and their institutions with characteristics not shared by the rest of the world' (Billington R A 1949 *Westward expansion*. Macmillan, New York, p 3). In the third edition (1967) Billington removes the first 11 words of this sentence, but retains reference to the moulding effect of this unique environment. The liberal narrative is a commonplace casually repeated, for example, when Jenni Calder says: 'The drama springs from the country itself' (Calder J 1974 *There must be a Lone Ranger: the myth and reality of the American Wild West*. Hamilton, London, p 12).
18. Of course this typical effect of naturalization and dehistoricization is overdetermined by at least three other effects. One arises mainly from the internal economy and force of the genre as it has become established into an exceptionally closed and repetitive structure. The scriptwriter Frank Gruber has claimed there are only seven basic plots in the Western: Cavalrymen and Indians; the big project Union Pacific or Pony Express theme; cattlemen and homesteaders; the dedicated lawman; the outlaw story; the revenge theme; and the Empire story in which a ranch or way of life is threatened with decline (MacCann R D 1962 *Hollywood in transition*. Houghton Mifflin, Boston, pp 175–7). This high degree of repetition has made the genre susceptible to one of the more convincing instances of structuralist analysis: Will Wright's *Sixguns and society* (Wright W 1975 *Sixguns and society: a structuralist study of the Western*. University of California Press). Secondly, there is the powerful tendency of American national culture to abstract and universalize. I have tried to open discussion of this effect in *British post-structuralism since 1968* (Easthope A 1988 *British post-structuralism since 1968*. Routledge, London, pp 194–8). A third factor is that Hollywood's pervasively dominant mode has been realism. This reinforces and supports the Western's commitment to representing the individual subject and his or her immediate environmental conditions, as though these were as empirically perceptible as they may seem to be in contemporary everyday life.

19. See Easthope A 1986 *What a man's gotta do: the masculine myth in popular culture*. Paladin, London.
20. See Alloway L 1971 *Violent America: the movies 1945–64*. Museum of Modern Art, New York.
21. Jane Tompkins notes how far the genre is committed to science and technology (Tompkins 1987 p 367).
22. Ibid p 351.
23. Hawgood J A 1967 *The American West*. Eyre and Spottiswoode, London, p 23.

5 Narratives of the Native American

Robert Burchell

The United States has had a major problem defining its cultural identity. It was created as a nation-state by a series of acts of will: a detailed and proclaimed Declaration of Independence, a revolution, a sustained war of independence and a ratified constitution. Political and economic institutions then grew up informed by shared ideologies of liberalism and capitalism. There may have been debates over details but not over basic political and economic principles. There was, however, far less agreement over whether the new country would be culturally pluralist or uniform.

After 1776, the majority of the nation's elite believed in uniformity. They expected American culture, that is its language, its public and private values and moralities, to become a variant of a reformed, meritocratic Protestant British system, amended to produce attitudes and behaviour proper for a deliberately created, successful republic. But there had been doubts about the relation between German-speakers and Roman Catholics and Protestant British cultural norms even before the Revolution, not to mention, among a minority, a questioning of the places of enslaved African Americans and of the very independently minded, possibly unassimilable, Native Americans.

Debates over the proper form of the American cultural identity grew louder during the nineteenth century as the numbers of non-English-speaking, non-Protestant Europeans arriving rose significantly, while debate over slavery and abolition grew ever more virulent. At the same time, discussions of the future of the Native American became a minor, though far from unimportant, topic.

The reason why debate over the relation of Native Americans to the general culture was comparatively less strident than, say, that over the place of Catholics, slaves or freed African Americans, was not that those who directed society had an answer to the question of how the Native American was to be accommodated. It was largely the result of a series of events that had been occurring since at least the early sixteenth century: briefly, the catastrophic demographic decline of Native American populations as a result of the diseases brought to the New World from the Old.[1] Few whites at any point before the 1930s grasped either the nature or the enormity of the demographic disaster that had hit the original populations of the United States, but most explained the decline in Native American numbers as a sign of a plan of action prepared by Divine Providence whereby Europeans were to replace Native Americans in the Western Hemisphere in general and in the United States in particular. Most white Americans saw the substitution of the Native American cultures by their own as a working out of a general law by which lower cultural forms were superseded by higher, there being little doubt which culture was which.

But not all white Americans were happy with the idea of the entire disappearance of Native Americans and there was much significant debate in the nineteenth century over how the Native American could be saved from extinction and how far Native American cultures had to be modified to ensure this. An implication here was that American culture itself might need adapting to accommodate the original inhabitants. This essay looks at part of that debate as a means of distinguishing and understanding what nineteenth-century white Americans took to be the nature of their culture.

It is undoubtedly difficult to establish what the great majority of the white population felt about the nature of the relationship between themselves and Native Americans. It is, however, possible to identify what books whites bought in large numbers; which novels, biographies, works of history and travel or collections of poetry were most popular; and which plays best attended. The main body of this work will therefore review the images of Native Americans found in a number of genres of bestselling literature of nineteenth-century America, on the assumption that the citizens of the United States were defining their cultural identity through these texts, especially because they were so widely read.[2]

General images of the Native American

Analysts of these nineteenth-century literary and other images of Native Americans have differed fundamentally in their inter-pretations. Some have suggested that images are reflexively undifferentiated, intended to produce little more than hostile, exclusive, condescending, and therefore wrong-headed and incorrect ideas of their subject.[3] Others have argued that it is not as simple as this, that there is no single 'white' view of the Native American, or as Albert Keiser said in his pioneering work pub-lished in 1933: 'In traversing the whole field of Indian literature, the student is struck by the number and diversity of attempts in delineating the red man.'[4] This view would seem to be the more correct, particularly if it is true that the doubts, hesitations, self-contradictions and inconsequences seen in white images of Native Americans are taken as mirroring those present in the debates over white self-images, over what the American way as a whole had been, was and would be.

Despite what some recent analysts have stressed, many nineteenth-century writers did not suggest that there was an impassable cultural gulf between the civilized and the savage. They did not treat their Native American subjects as so unlike whites that there could be no mutual understanding or dialogue, though even the best-intentioned sometimes appeared to despair at the difficulties in the way of accommodation. Some writers explicitly sought ways by which the white and Native American communities might come together and so stressed cultural similarities. A number of solutions to the problem of coexistence were aired. Writers like James Fenimore Cooper, for instance, recognized that whites and Native Americans were bound together by a common humanity, but separated by history and culture. They did not argue that white and Native American cultures were of equal status and viability, but equally they did not argue for the extinction of the Native American, and they were clear that something of value was being lost as the Native American vanished. Their texts show a struggle to think of a way forward that was practicable rather than visionary and if they stressed assimilation through substantial cultural surrender by the Native Americans they did not call for genocide. At the same time, as Native Americans freely adopted horses, guns, and European-made blankets, entered trading relations with white trappers and traders, and accepted, if often from force or from despair, a federal government's obligation to feed them, they showed that it was impossible for them to retain their cultures unadulterated or uninfluenced by white.[5]

One way of sorting the wide variety of white views is to see them as lying along an axis which ran from what can be called frontier to eastern attitudes. The frontier derived from the desire of frontier whites for Native Americans' lands. Frontier attitudes rested on a number of familiar rationalizations: that Native American cultures were of a lower order than white; that the two were not assimilable; that the lower would inevitably give way to the higher, peaceably if possible, violently if not.

At the other end of this axis lay an eastern view that whites and Native Americans were part of a common humanity, that Native Americans could and should adapt to survive and that whites had an obligation to establish the means by which this end could come about. In this view adaptation was a possible alternative to extinction and extinction was unacceptable.

Whites also divided along a second axis that ran from what can be called high-brow to low-brow attitudes. The high-brow tended to be seen in easterners from higher social groups, many influenced by eighteenth-century views of the noble savage. The high-brows often disparaged the low-brows for their prejudices which they saw as reflecting the attitudes of an ill-educated, non-reflecting, unintelligent and illiberal mob. Holders of low-brow views saw the high-brows as impracticably sentimental, ignorant of savage and duplicitous Native American character which would always undermine attempts at accommodation.

By and large, attitudes also changed over time. The position of the Native Americans in 1787, as players in a geopolitical drama, and consequently a seemingly substantial military threat, was not the position in 1887 when they could threaten little more than local disorders. But if eastern attitudes moved west as a result, low-brow views continued to battle high-brow and were re-inforced after the Civil War by dime novels and extravaganzas like Buffalo Bill's Wild West Show. Readers were presented with conflicting visions of the Native American throughout the nineteenth century.[6]

Bestselling novels, 1799–1906

The low-brow, frontier view of the Native American is apparent in the earliest text considered here, *Edgar Huntly* (1799) by Charles Brockden Brown. It assumed that the only relation between white and Native American would be one of violence and that this would end with the supersession of Native Americans by whites; the novel did not consider a future containing both communities. Native Americans do not appear in the work until 180 pages have passed but once introduced they are quickly killed off. By the time the Native Americans enter the story they have but one representative in the region, Old Deb, or Queen Mab, but she has no wish for close relations with whites. The lack of cultural interaction is symbolized by her refusal to speak English. She regards herself as biding her time until she can organize and bring back bands of warriors who will overcome and destroy the English, thus returning the area to the exclusive control of her tribe.[7]

Two further points may be made, however, which modify the picture so far given of a relationship exclusively governed by violence. The eponymous hero needs to explain why he is able to kill Native Americans when he would not dream of killing a white. He does this in a way that is to be seen in a number of other texts by suggesting that he is only retaliating against a prior, heinous and therefore justifying act of the Native Americans, in his case, the massacre of his parents and a sibling and the suspicion that his uncle and two further sisters have also been murdered, leading him to remark: 'Hitherto the death of the savage, whom I had despatched with my hatchet, had not been remembered without some remorse. Now my emotions were totally changed.'[8] Thus the implicit assumption is that relations with Native Americans ought to be governed by the moral code and that readers will expect some moral justification for an essentially immoral act. This further implies that Native Americans have rights which may not be ignored without explanation. They are part of a universal moral community. The newly independent white culture had to take this into account in defining its relationships.

There is little doubt that James Fenimore Cooper did more than any other early nineteenth-century writer to explore white relations with Native Americans. Cooper took his central message, that coexistence was possible, from his reading of the work of the eighteenth-century missionary writer, the Reverend John Heckewelder, who believed that accommodation would come through the Native Americans' adoption of Christianity, for cultural divisions would dwindle once the religious divide was removed. Cooper published the first of his five bestselling novels with western frontier themes, *The Pioneers*, in 1823, the last, *The Deerslayer*, in 1841. The Preface to *The Deerslayer* explicitly attacked those critics who appeared to want him to present all his Native American characters as two-dimensional savages, stressing how inadequate it was 'to suppose that the redman is to be represented only in the squalid misery or in the degraded moral state that certainly more or less belongs to his condition', since that condition was none of his choosing.[9] He also defended himself against the other charge that was frequently made against him, that his 'characters were Indians of the school of Heckewelder, rather than the school of nature', by suggesting in this novel as throughout his work that if there was a school of nature it was one of a common human nature and that there was no impassable gulf between the two which might not, for instance, be crossed by conversion to Christianity, although Cooper did not always think conversion a necessity.[10]

In putting forward Heckewelder's message, however, *The Pioneers* had to confront one of the major contemporary arguments against accommodation between two communities with differing skin colours, that non-white skins represented general incapacity. One character, the ex-sailor Benjamin, suggests the untrustworthiness of such an analysis, saying: 'If-so-be that they took count of the colour of a skin in heaven, why, they might refuse to muster in their books a Christian-born, like myself, just for the matter of a little tan, from cruising in warm latitudes.'[11] In a highly symbolic fashion, however, Cooper suggests that there may be more than one afterlife and therefore more than one religious way when he has the Christian Major Effingham, a member of the gentry class, and Chingachgook, the Native

American warrior-hero, buried in neighbouring graves – this in an age of segregated cemeteries.[12] Cooper's attitudes may sometimes strike late twentieth-century readers as asking for greater cultural accommodation by Native Americans than by whites but they did not mean he saw no value whatever in Native American ways. Reflecting the opposite, the medical man Elnathan Todd says: 'Now in cancers and hydrophoby, they are quite ingenious. . . . A man should never be above learning, even if it be from an Indian.'[13]

The Last of the Mohicans (1826) explicitly attacks the idea of a separate and separating Native American nature. Speaking of a Native American character who later, revealingly, turns out to be a villain, one of the heroines, Cora, asks: 'Should we distrust the man because his manners are not our manners, and that his skin is dark!', while later as she, her sister Alice, and Duncan Hayward, the upper class hero, are discussing Uncas, the last of the Mohicans, Hayward remarks: 'As bright examples of great qualities are but too uncommon among Christians, so are they singular and solitary with the Indians; though, for the honour of our common nature, neither are incapable of producing them.' To this Cora replies: 'Now Major Hayward speaks as Major Hayward should. . . . Who that looks at this creature of nature, remembers the shade of his skin!'[14]

The Prairie (1827) restates many of these themes, explicitly suggesting that whites and Native Americans are divided by culture, not nature. As Leatherstocking puts it: 'It is greatly to be mourned, that colour, and property, and tongue, and l'arning, should make so wide a difference in those who, after all, are but the children of one Father.'[15] Leatherstocking is implying that white colour prejudice divides where it need not, for when the lower class frontiersman, Ishmael Bush, attacks him, saying: 'You have the colour and speech of a Christian, while it seems that your heart is with the red-skin', he replies: 'To me there is little difference in Nations.'[16]

Cooper's villains are not invariably Native Americans but often lower class whites. In *The Prairie* they are white squatters. It is their attitudes which prevent accommodation between whites and Native Americans. The novel ends with the death of Leatherstocking, who is buried by 'his friends' Uncas Middleton, the upper class white, and Hard-Heart, the principal Native

American character.[17] *The Pathfinder* (1840) further restates Leatherstocking's philosophy. Here Cooper admits the difficulties to be faced in cultural accommodation, in that it was impossible for whites and Native Americans to obtain a full knowledge of each other's 'real nature', but he insists that 'each colour has its gifts, and its laws, and its traditions, and one is not to condemn another because he does not exactly comprehend it'.[18]

The Deerslayer, as the remarks from the preface already quoted would suggest, continues the themes outlined above, including that of degraded whites and naturally heroic Native Americans. Two lower class frontiersmen, Henry Marsh and Tom Hutter, reveal their moral nature by approving of scalping, whereas Leatherstocking, here the Deerslayer with his natural humanity, does not. Indeed, one of the climaxes of the novel brings the deaths of Marsh and Hutter who have foolishly gone off on an expedition to scalp. The novel continues to stress the possibility of intimate relations between white and Native American, continuing the friendship between Leatherstocking and Chingachgook.[19] It is no wonder the novels exasperated those who wanted little more than violent and destructive confrontation.

Catharine M. Sedgwick published her *Hope Leslie* in 1827. Here major characters include both whites and Native Americans, living side by side in the Massachusetts of the 1630s. This was a period of tension between whites and Native Americans which the novel uses to provide the main theme. But despite the fact that the Pequod War acts as one point of departure for the plot, the novel scarcely argues that Native Americans and whites are unable to connect culturally. Indeed, the earliest sustained reference to Native Americans has William Fletcher, a major character, say to his wife: 'You surely do not doubt, Martha, that these Indians possess the same faculties that we do? The [Native American] girl just arrived, our friend [John Winthrop] writes me, hath rare gifts of mind, such as few of God's creatures are endowed with.'[20]

This girl, Magawisca, plays a major role in the story and her attempts to discover a proper role for a Native American in a rapidly changing Massachusetts exemplify the problem Native Americans faced as white numbers grew. Magawisca's father, Mononotto, had been a friend of the English but had seen his hopes for a peaceful accommodation between the two communities dashed by the Pequod War, which the novel describes from the Native American point of view. Mononotto wants vengeance for the death of a son but his capture of two whites, Everell Fletcher and Faith Leslie, has the unexpected result of creating strong attractions between Faith and Mononotto's son Oneco, and between Everell and Magawisca. Indeed, the novel ends with Faith and Oneco married and settled in a Native American community, implying that inter-racial marriages were acceptable and that the communities were close enough culturally for a white to pass into a Native American. Admittedly Sedgwick reassures the reader that Faith has not become an animist and somewhat sells the pass by converting her to Roman Catholicism and having the marriage blessed by a Jesuit, but even that is remarkable in the context of early nineteenth-century New England where Protestant nativism was strong.[21]

It is also remarkable that at another point Magawisca is given a speech in which she argues that particular religious differences are unimportant since all men and women share a common humanity. When she tells Hope Leslie that her sister has married Oneco, Hope cries out: 'O, God! restore my sister to the Christian family.' Magawisca's response is to ask: 'Think ye not that the Great Spirit looks down on these sacred spots, where the good and the peaceful rest, with an equal eye? Think ye not their children are His children, whether they are gathered in yonder temple where your people worship, or bow to him before the green boughs of the forest?'[22]

On a number of occasions the novel suggests that there are higher laws and obligations than those imposed by the Christian religion, notably when Hope Leslie persuades the minister, Craddock, to help her assist Magawisca escape from her prison cell. This might suggest a shared ethical basis on which the two communities might have built a shared culture but Sedgwick also knew that this had not happened historically. Ultimately the novel has no answer to the problem of accommodation: Magawisca and her father and brother go west and their story is 'lost in the deep, voiceless obscurity of those unknown regions'.[23] But they were accompanied by Faith Leslie who could see very obvious merits in Native American life and culture.

If it is granted that, among easterners, some northerners and some New Englanders in particular were likely to be more liberal and accommodating in matters of race and culture, as they were in parallel on slavery, it might also be assumed that a southern novelist would reveal a different, more hostile attitude toward Native Americans. William Gilmore Simms's *The Yemassee* (1835), set in seventeenth-century Carolina, shows that even a southern writer who was convinced of the inferiority of the black race had ambivalent feelings about the Native American. Simms ascribes moral and personal traits to some of his Native American characters which he would never have suggested for his African Americans.

Sanutee is a major character who wishes to drive the encroaching English out of Carolina. His nobility is established partly by comparison with the venality of other Native Americans who are too ready to sell land for 'presents and promises'.[24] The main white character, Gabriel Harrison, a Proprietor, and thus an upper class Englishman, fully understands Sanutee's feelings and the unrest to which they would lead: 'The Indians had suffered on all sides from the obtrusive borderers, and had been treated, he felt conscious, with less than respect and justice by the provincial government itself.'[25]

The novel includes a number of incidents which show whites and Native Americans acting according to a common set of values. Both groups show an equal respect for life. One white, Grayson, saves Sanutee's son, the alcoholic Occonestoga, from drowning. Occonestoga in turn saves the heroine Bess Matthews from a rattlesnake. In thanking Occonestoga Gabriel Harrison makes the significant gesture of shaking him by the hand. Sanutee's behaviour on the capture of his son is given the highest praise, being likened to that of the ancient Romans. Simms's treatment of Occonestoga's alcoholism also shows understanding rather than censure.[26]

This is not to say that Simms does not see distinctions between whites and Native Americans. He describes Native American song as uncouth and barbarous. He saw one of the tribes, the Coosaws, dismissively, as having 'diminutive persons, . . . small, quick, sparkling eyes, . . . dusky, but irritably red features, . . . [a] querulous upward turn of the nose – a most distinguishing feature with this clan, showing a feverish quarrelsomeness of disposition, and a want of becoming elevation in purpose'. Overall, however, the novel suggests that virtue is to be found among Native Americans as infamy is among whites.[27]

Robert Montgomery Bird published his *Nick of the Woods* in 1837, particularly, he told his readers, to take issue with the way in which Fenimore Cooper had presented the image of the Native American. As Bird put it in the Preface to the novel: 'The single fact that he wages war – systematic war – upon beings incapable of resistance or defence – upon women and children, whom all other races in the world, no matter how barbarous, consent to spare, has hitherto been, and we suppose to the end of our days will remain, a stumbling-block to our imagination.'[28]

Unflattering references throughout the text to 'red niggurs', to Native Americans as thieves, evil, coarse barbarians and murdering monsters, add weight to this point.[29] But the novelist ties himself up in a knot of his own making in an early passage that begins in logical fashion only to lose its way soon thereafter in discussing one aspect of the Native Americans' supposed savagery. A character suggests that Native Americans scalp 'wives and daughters', but does admit, 'As to their torturing them, that's not so certain, but the brutes are n't a bit too good for it; and I did h'ar of their burning one poor woman at Sandusky.' This remark brings an extraordinary authorial interjection in the form of a footnote which reads: 'The worthy Kentuckian was, perhaps, mistaken. A female captive from Pittsburg was, however, actually bound to the stake near the Sandusky villages, and rescued with difficulty by British traders', thus leaving the reader in some difficulties as to the precise nature of Native American savagery.[30]

Bird's work see-saws between the blanket condemnation of the Native Americans promised in the Preface and descriptions of individual virtues. It continues to stress their savagery as in a passage which ends with a remark on the incompatibility of the races. Communication between them only brings 'misfortune – the destiny in every quarter of the globe of every barbarous race, which contact with a civilized one cannot civilize'.[31] But the novel also contains episodes like the one involving the chief Piankeshaw, who has become an alcoholic. Bird presents his fellow, younger Native Americans as fully capable of judging the chief and finding him wanting. They seize the cask of liquor he is transporting, break it open, and let the contents drain away. The majority of this Native American party were thus not helpless alcoholics, but able to control their desires. Piankeshaw was in the minority, a point emphasized by the fury with which the younger Native Americans react to the chief's drunkenly killing his horse.[32]

Bird also has to confront two moral problems dealt with by other writers, that is, the justification for taking Native American lives, and what was acceptable behaviour thereafter, particularly whether white men could scalp with moral impunity. These questions were connected to the basic one of what rules should govern white behaviour toward non-white, how both should fit into one cultural and moral scheme.

Bird uses the same justification for killing Native Americans as Brown had done nearly 40 years earlier: not that it was generally acceptable because the Native American was an inferior species, to be removed without second thought, but that individual whites could be justified if they had some particular and defensible reason for their behaviour, as Bird's character Nathan the Quaker does. Nathan's conduct is explained as springing from the desire to avenge the deaths of his mother, wife and three children. Roland, the high-born hero of the novel, needs to have the justification explained to him and is given it at length with the coda: 'All murdered, friend! – all – all – all cruelly murdered!'[33]

The question of scalping also offered Bird a moral problem. It is interesting, considering Birds stated view of Fenimore Cooper, that he gives the same answer to it as Cooper. No white from the upper classes would scalp, but regrettably, due to the limited social, economic, educational and moral backgrounds of lower class whites, *they* might. Bird has an episode in which Roland becomes aware of what Nathan would like to do, having recently killed some Native Americans. Nathan knows he should not scalp but his longing is severe. Roland reacts with horror to the suggestion that he might like to take scalps, exclaiming: 'I will kill Indians wherever I can; but no scalping, Nathan, no scalping from me!' Nathan later leaves Roland on a pretext, returns to the scene of the fight and scalps.[34] Roland the officer, educated in the east, and Nathan the backwoodsman have different moral codes which promote the two different reactions to the Native Americans.

The year 1860 was noteworthy not only in seeing the United States slide toward Civil War but also for the production in June of the first 'dime novel'. This, *Malaeska: The Indian Wife of the White Hunter*, by Mrs Ann S. Stephens, perhaps not surprisingly had a Native American theme. Also not surprisingly, considering the readership at which it was aimed, it took an ultimately pessimistic view of the possibilities of cultural accommodation. The novel highlights the question of whether whites and Native Americans could come to some mutually acceptable way forward by examining the predicaments of a marriage between a white and a Native American and of the offspring of such a union. Malaeska is the wife of the hunter William Danforth. They have a child at the opening of the narrative which also makes clear, early on, that though the child 'scarcely bore a tinge of its mother's blood' Danforth was ashamed of it being 'not quite white'.[35]

Danforth is killed by Malaeska's father, the chief of the tribe, in a skirmish resulting from the death of a Native American. Danforth has chosen to ally himself with the white settlers. As he dies he instructs Malaeska to take his son to New York City to his parents. Faced with Malaeska and the young Danforth, the parents, mainly because of the father's feelings about the Native American who has killed his son, solve the problem of what to do by rejecting Malaeska and relegating her to a marginal role in their household and fully adopting their grandson. The young Danforth grows up not knowing Malaeska is his mother and thinking himself the son of two white parents. The novel implicitly proposes that someone like the young Danforth would have no problems adjusting to white life. Nurture would triumph over nature.

Malaeska is driven away after an unsuccessful attempt to take her son back to their original home. Her character contrasts markedly with those of her husband and son. The novel suggests that this was partly the result of having benefited from living in both cultures as she had done, for the experience had led to a combination of 'all that was strong, picturesque, and imaginative in savage life, with the delicacy, sweetness, and refinement which follows in the train of civilization'.[36] Unhappily her son has inherited not her nature but the prejudices of the grandfather, and so strongly as to worry even his fiancée. Inevitably the son discovers the truth. He reacts frenziedly and despite his considerable wealth, education and having passed as fully white for twenty years, cannot foresee a future, and drowns himself.

Dime novels were supposed in part 'to instil a pure and elevating sentiment in the hearts and minds of the people', so *Malaeska* ends with the fiancée, Sarah, 'going back to her useful life, without a murmur against the Providence that had made it so lonely'.[37] It is not clear whether Providence abhorred inter-racial unions or whether the young Danforth dies the victim of his grandfather's prejudices and his own cowardice. It is possible to read the novel as suggesting the tragedy of prejudice producing loss, when gain was very probable.

Seth Jones, by Edward Ellis, was also produced in 1860 and was also a dime novel. Of scarcely any literary merit, it is set in western New York at the end of the Revolutionary War and deals with the abduction of the heroine, Ina Haverland, by the Mohawks, and her recapture by a mixed band of whites. Given the plot there is surprisingly little violence and something of a mixed message on whether whites and Native Americans can coexist peaceably. At one point the author suggests violent confrontation was inevitable, for 'as the tide of emigration has rolled westward, it has ever met that fiery countersurge, and only overcome it by incessant battling and effort'. But as the novel both implicitly and explicitly states, that violence should only occur in military confrontations.[38] At one point the whites have stolen a canoe and find a Native American in it. The frontiersman Haldidge, exhibiting the kind of attitudes already alluded to, wants to 'pitch him overboard' but Seth (whom we later discover to be an educated member of the upper classes in disguise) refuses, saying, 'there ain't no need of it, the poor imp hasn't hurt us; and, for all I detest his whole cowardly race, I don't believe in killing them, except when they've done you some injury or are trying to'.[39] In formulaic fashion Haldidge's feelings are explained as the result of the murder of 'his defenceless wife and child' by Native Americans.[40]

Haldidge's views contrast with the instincts of another character, one of ' "nature's noblemen" ', Alfred Haverland, who explains to Seth Jones that his 'conduct toward the Indians has ever been characterized by honesty and good-will upon my part, and they have ever evinced a friendly feeling toward me and my helpless ones'. Continuing, he says, 'I place great reliance upon this state of feeling – in fact my only reliance'. The disguised Jones takes the frontier view, replying: 'Just so; but I tell you, it won't do to trust an Injin. They're obstropertous. Go to put your finger on them, and they ain't thar.'[41] There the matter rests.

Elsewhere the author stresses inequalities between whites and Native Americans. When the hero Everard Graham attempts to escape pursuing Native Americans, Ellis interjects: 'When the Anglo-Saxon's body is pitted against that of the North American Indian, it sometimes yields; but when his mind takes the place of contestant, it *never* loses.'[42] Native Americans are depicted as cruel and barbarous, cruel to other Native Americans as well as to whites; cowardly, in the sense that they attempt to avoid a fight in the open; cunning but no match for the white intellect. The overt message is that they have little in common with whites but that they do have rights as human beings. They might thus take up a position in white society, probably an inferior one.

Twelve years later, though, the message of Helen Hunt Jackson's *Ramona* was quite different. This novel suggests that religion, in this case Roman Catholicism, can bridge the gap between the whites and Native Americans, also that the attitudes and behaviour of the incoming Americans were highly destructive morally and culturally and needed replacing.[43] The heroine is a part of the suggested bridge, being part-Scot and part-Native American. She is brought up in a California household with a foster brother Felipe whose family has been in California since before the American conquest. Ramona marries Alessandro, a Native American, but he is killed by a lower class, prejudiced white. She falls ill but is rescued by Felipe who eventually, disgusted by what he sees as Anglo-Saxon corruption of California, takes Ramona to Mexico where they marry.

Alessandro, his father Pablo and the other Native Americans who appear in the novel are humane and unprejudiced. Alessandro and Pablo have adopted white religion, language, music and are literate. They work, save and want their own land. Jackson's message, as befitted a supporter of severalty, is that Native Americans are able to share much of white culture, though it is at least interesting that they do not choose Protestantism. Some modern readers may think that Jackson is a little too careful to stress that Alessandro's skin colour 'was not a shade darker than Felipe's' and that Ramona 'had just enough of olive tint in her complexion to underlie and enrich her skin without making it swarthy', but taking *Ramona* together with Jackson's other major work, *A Century of Dishonour*, there is no doubt that the author intends to suggest that it is disgraceful white behaviour which is preventing accommodation and that sufficient acculturation had already occurred for there to be the hope of some degree of peaceful coexistence if whites would moderate extreme ethnocentric stances.[44]

There are a number of reasons why a study of nineteenth-century attitudes on the place of the Native American might be based on a comparison of Robert Montgomery Bird's *Nick of the Woods* and Zane Grey's *The Spirit of the Border*, published in 1906, not the least being the close similarity of the plots. Grey, who was notorious for his borrowing, seems to have embellished Bird's plot rather than bothered to invent his own, with the frontiersman Wetzel paralleling Nick of the Woods in scalping foes, in his reason for hating Native Americans immoderately (both had seen their families killed), and in character.[45]

But the great difference is Grey's message that even before the nineteenth century began there was a great desire on the part of some Native Americans to change some aspects of their lives and adopt aspects of white culture, in this case the Christian religion. Furthermore, hostility and tensions between the whites and Native Americans were not inevitable but the responsibility of either British Machiavellianism or renegade whites. The Grey family ancestor Colonel Zane had married a Native American and both Zane Grey and his brother were proud of the fact.[46] The ancestor appears in the novel and sums up its central tragedy, the massacre of Christian Native Americans by an alliance of Tories, led by the infamous Simon Girty, and other non-Christian Native Americans, in saying: 'The beautiful Valley of Peace owes its ruin to the renegades.'[47] Grey describes Girty in language Bird would have reserved for Native Americans: the forehead was narrow and sloped backward from 'the brow, denoting animal instincts'. The eyes were 'close together, yellowish-brown in colour', and had 'a peculiar vibrating movement', as though they were 'hung on a pivot, like a compass-needle'. The nose was 'long and hooked', and the mouth set in a 'thin, cruel line'. There was in the man's aspect an extraordinary 'combination of ignorance, vanity, cunning and ferocity'.[48]

By contrast, Native Americans possessed 'wonderful sagacity'; if rebellious, they were so partly because pioneers were seizing lands without paying for them.[49] The Christian Native Americans were massacred because white frontiersmen refused to help them. Grey suggests in the way that the Christians go to their death how fully they have accepted the Christian message, that is how fully they are able to accommodate culturally. The point is not whether Grey's assumptions were pernicious in suggesting that Native Americans give up their traditional beliefs, but that they were worlds apart from Bird's in that, as Grey put it referring to Native American children, they were as 'good, pure, innocent' as white.[50]

Other bestselling literature

There were other kinds of bestselling literature in the nineteenth century dealing with Native American themes whose study would lead to similar conclusions to those outlined above, that there were a variety of white attitudes to the original inhabitants and that these were seldom uniformly and exclusively hostile. James E. Seaver's *A Narrative of the Life of Mrs Mary Jemison* (1824) was compiled 'from her own words'. Mary Jemison had been 'taken by the Indians, in the year 1755, when only about twelve years of age', and had 'continued to reside amongst them to the present time'.[51] As this suggests, readers might receive at least three very distinct impressions from this work: first, that Native American communities continued to exist; second, that there was sufficient common cultural ground for successful adaptation to Native American ways by a white; and third, that a white could prefer certain aspects of Native American culture to the point of refusing to return to white society when offered the opportunity. All these three points undermined the idea of the inescapable supersession of Native American by superior white culture.

Further, the fact that her grandson Jack Jemison attended Dartmouth for two years and later thought of studying medicine suggests that the family did not object to members passing into white society either temporarily or permanently and that they accepted that this was culturally possible.[52] Thus, far from implying that cultural interrelations had inevitably to be hostile and mutually exclusive, the *Narrative* suggests at many points a complex cultural pluralism already at work by the 1820s. Interestingly, in light of the post-Civil War view that individual land-ownership could form the basis on which Native Americans could construct lives within the American republic, Mrs Jemison had been given a land grant by her tribe shortly after the Revolutionary War ended and she improved it partly by letting or leasing some of it 'to white people to till on shares'.[53]

The best-attended play and the most popular poem on Native American subjects were almost indistinguishable in the treatment of their themes. John Augustus Stone's *Metamora*, which was so popular that it was offered to the Philadelphia public in 23 of the 25 consecutive seasons after its appearance in 1825, and Longfellow's *Hiawatha* stressed the nobility of their heroic subjects but also that they were doomed to disappear in the face of white expansion.[54] Longfellow suggested that the Native American was capable of religious conversion and that that might have bridged the gap between two cultures. But the end of the poem shows Longfellow without any solution to the problem of mutual accommodation, as he sends Hiawatha 'Westward! westward!' and suggests a like and dismal fate for all his people. Hiawatha's 'darker, drearier vision' beheld his nation scattered:

> Saw the remnants of our people
> Sweeping westward, wild and woeful,
> Like the cloud-rack of a tempest,
> Like the withered leaves of Autumn![55]

Hiawatha's counsel had been to hail the whites as 'friends and brothers' and his remarks implied that the failure to do so explained the threatening disaster. Longfellow intimated that the failure to convert to Christianity, to move toward an accommodation with white culture, was crucial.[56] Native American culture was too weak to resist the white invaders, for all the glories of the pre-Contact life so minutely detailed.

Both heroes, Metamora and Hiawatha, symbolized the vanishing Native American, whose disappearance provided one solution to the problem of cultural accommodation. By the

1830s, however, interest in historical Native American figures was so strong that it produced two bestsellers, Benjamin Thatcher's *Indian Biography* (1832) and Benjamin Drake's *The Life and Adventures of Black Hawk* (1838). Thatcher's intentions were revealed in the subtitle to his work, which he defined as 'An historical account of those individuals who have been distinguished among the North American Natives as Orators, Warriors, Statesmen, and other remarkable characters'. This suggested a level of talent among Native Americans which could easily have befited them for a multicultural community.

Drake's sympathies were revealed in his remark on the Black Hawk War of 1838 as one 'which had its origins in avarice and political ambition, which was prosecuted in bad faith and closed in dishonour'.[57] He further believed that the federal government had to pursue a vigorous role in order to provide the means through which cultural accommodation could be worked out.

Not surprisingly, Drake took explicit exception to Timothy Flint's views of Native Americans, evident in Flint's *Memoir of Daniel Boone* (1834).[58] It portrayed Native Americans as cruel and uncaring savages who were as 'unsparing and unrelenting as tigers' in battle. They tortured captives with relish and dashed 'the tomahawk with merciless indifference into the cloven skulls of mothers and infants', though, Flint had to admit, 'they are universally seen to treat captive women with a decorous forbearance'.[59]

A similar low-brow frontier view was also to be seen in David Crockett's *Autobiography* (1833), but there it lay beside others that allowed Crockett to have good personal relations with individual Native Americans, work with Native American allies and vote against Andrew Jackson's 'infamous' Removal Bill which sent the Five Civilized Tribes from Georgia to Oklahoma.[60]

Francis Parkman's *The Oregon Trail* appeared in 1849. This sometimes incoherent and self-contradictory work illustrates much of the contemporary prejudice and also the tensions that emerged when writing about Native Americans. In reflective mode Parkman could argue that the Native American was destined to disappear as the buffalo died out, whisky took its toll, and 'awed by military posts' they lost the will to resist.[61] There was thus no need to define their place in the wider American culture. Travelling in the West, however, Parkman had seen and recorded sights that seemed to contradict this conclusion, as he came across 'half-civilized Shawanoes', who appeared to be adjusting to new lives with some success. He described their settlement in glowing terms. 'Every field and meadow bespoke the exuberant fertility of the soil. The maize stood rustling in the wind, ripe and dry, its shining yellow ears thrust out between the gaping husks. Squashes and huge yellow pumpkins lay basking in the sun in the midst of their brown and shrivelled leaves.'[62] Whatever else, this passage surely suggested some approximation to the white agrarian ideal, as did an earlier reference to Shawanoe slave-holding.

Indeed, though Parkman spoke elsewhere of the 'unfortunate and self-abandoned Kickapoos' and of the Pawnee as 'a treacherous, cowardly banditti, who, by a thousand acts of pillage and murder, have deserved chastisement at the hands of government', in a telling passage, writing of the Pueblo, he remarked with no evident sense of irony or paradox, 'The human race in this part of the world is separated into three divisions, arranged in the order of their merits: white men, Indians, and Mexicans; to the latter of whom the honourable title of "whites" is by no means conceded.'[63] He wrote elsewhere of 'swarthy ignoble Mexicans' with 'brutish faces', a description strikingly at odds with the following of a Native American: 'He was a young fellow, of no note in his nation; yet in his person and equipments he was a good specimen of a Dacotah warrior in his ordinary travelling dress. Like most of his people, he was nearly six feet high; lithely and gracefully, yet strongly proportioned; and with a skin singularly clear and delicate.'[64]

Albert D. Richardson travelled more widely than Parkman in the trans-Mississippi West and produced a more complex picture of the state of white–Native American relations there in his *Beyond the Mississippi*. Richardson, unlike Parkman, did not expect the Native American to die out – indeed, he took up the point that Parkman made of the Shawanoe that a number of Native American groups had made significant strides toward an accommodation. According to Richardson, the Shawnees and Wyandottes had acculturated to the point that they now voted.[65] Richardson's remarks on the Choctaws and Cherokees introduced an aspect of cultural contact seldom dealt with in polite literature

– sexual relations. Speaking of Governor Walker of the Choctaws, Richardson described him as 'educated in Kentucky, intelligent and agreeable; nearly as white as myself, with no betrayal of Indian origin in speech or features'. As for the Cherokees, they 'lead in civilization. They are largely tinctured with white blood. In their most populous sections one may travel all day without seeing a person of unmixed Indian extraction.' Generalizing from these two communities to all the Native American inhabitants of what was to become Oklahoma, he continued: 'Before seeing [them] . . . I was skeptical about the possibility of civilizing Indians. But these once cruel and barbarous tribes were now governing themselves, educating their children, protecting life and property far better than adjacent Arkansas and Texas, and rapidly assuming the habits of enlightened man.'[66]

Disease, alcoholism and cultural disruptions, however, characterized the position of other tribes. He saw little hope for the Arapahoe, the Cheyenne, the 'Diggers' of Utah, or the Native Americans of Washington State whom he thought were particularly unlikely to adapt and survive.[67] But his work suggested the complicated pattern of inter-cultural relations now present in the West in remarks on two tribes that remained relatively untouched and continued to resist acculturation in their separate ways. One was the Comanches, 'the destroying angels of our frontier'; the other was the Pueblo, who also stood apart: 'They never intermarry with whites, and their women (almost the solitary exception to Indian tribes in general) are reputed inflexibly chaste.'[68]

Richardson also distanced himself from the frontier idea of the Native American, saying, 'I should sympathize more with the general frontier feeling that the Indians ought to be exterminated, had I not known many cases of . . . lamentable "mistakes" [that is atrocities by whites], to say nothing of gross and premeditated barbarities. . . . The Indian is cruel, bloodthirsty and treacherous; but he often behaves quite as well as the Pale-face.'[69]

Mark Twain's view of the Goshute Indians of Utah is well known, and puts him firmly into the camp of those who saw no possibility of cultural accommodation. It should be said, however, that the passage on the Goshutes contains the only extended mention of Native Americans in *Roughing It* (1872).[70]

Twain's racism and his love of words led him to unreflecting attitudes and extravagant phrases. But he undoubtedly helped perpetuate the idea that cultural distances were so vast that there was no hope of traversing or narrowing them for a future accommodation.

The purpose of this survey of the bestselling texts of the nineteenth century with Native American themes has been to show how they grappled with the question of what should be the relationship between white and Native American and how American culture should be constructed to accommodate both. White writers exhibit a range of attitudes and provide a number of answers to the problem as well as suggesting on occasion that there is no answer. Readers should not be surprised at this, for American government and society were also simultaneously tacking between policies. The problem of how a diminishing number of original inhabitants should react to and be reacted against by an increasingly disproportionate number of incomers presented problems to which the century had no answer. It has, however, been a strength of American culture that some Americans have always argued for the value of constituent parts and have tried to see how interrelationships could be best arranged. Many of the texts described above show the struggle to understand cultural differences and to define similarities, others the effects of prejudice and wishful thinking; all represent the continuing struggle to define the totality of American culture.

Notes

1. For a recent set of discussions on the subject and on the difficulties in trying to estimate the size of the pre-Contact population, see Verano J W and Ubelaker D H 1992 *Disease and demography in the Americas*. Smithsonian Institute Press, Washington, DC.
2. The work that established the canon of bestsellers in the United States was Mott F L 1947 *Golden multitudes: the story of best sellers in the United States*. Macmillan, New York. This used a sliding scale which required a bestseller to have had a total sale equal to 1 per cent of the population of the continental United States for the decade in which it was published (see p 303). Thus the required sale in the 1790s would have been 40,000 copies, in the

1850s 225,000 and in the 1900s 750,000 (see pp 305, 307, 312). The texts discussed in this piece with their Native American themes were drawn from the list of titles on pp 303–23.

3. Writing in this vein began with Pearce R H 1953 *The savages of America: a study of the Indian and the idea of civilisation.* John Hopkins Press, Baltimore. Rpt as Pearce R H 1988 *Savagism and civilisation; a study of the Indian and the American mind.* University of California Press, Berkeley and London. Works influenced by Pearce include Barrett L K 1975 *American literary racism, 1790–1890.* Westport, Conn; Berkhofer R F Jr 1978 *The white man's Indian.* Knopf, New York; Drinnon R 1980 *Facing West: the metaphysics of Indian-hating and empire-building.* University of Minneapolis Press, Minneapolis; Fiedler L 1968 *The return of the vanishing American.* Paladin, London; Rogin R P 1975 *Fathers and children: Andrew Jackson and the subjugation of the American Indian.* Knopf, New York; Turner F W 1980 *Beyond geography: the western spirit against the wilderness.* Viking, New Brunswick; Washburn W E 1971 *Red man's land/white man's law: a study of the past and present state of the American Indian.* Scribner, New York. For an argument for the importance of the Native American to nineteenth-century American literature see Maddox L 1991 *Removals: nineteenth-century American literature and the politics of Indian affairs.* Oxford University Press, New York.

4. Keiser A 1933 *The Indian in American literature.* Oxford University Press, New York, p 298.

5. Miles G 1992 To hear an old voice: rediscovering Native Americans and American history. In Cronon W *et al* (eds) 1992 *Under an open sky: rethinking America's western past.* W W Norton, New York, pp 54–6.

6. Burchell R A 1988 The American West as a cultural fount: high brow meets low brow. In Kroes R (ed) 1988 *High brow meets low brow: American culture as an intellectual concern.* Free University Press, Amsterdam, pp 172–86. See also Mitchell L C 1981 *Witnesses to a vanishing America: The nineteenth-century response.* Princeton University Press, Princeton, NJ, esp pp xiv–xvi; and for an argument that white women were able to empathize with Native Americans, Riley G 1988 *The female frontier: a comparative view of women on the prairie and the plains.* University of Kansas Press, Lawrence, pp 45, 78, 125–7, 182–3.

7. Clark D L (ed) 1928 *Edgar Huntly or memoirs of a sleep-walker* by Charles Brockden Brown (1799). Macmillan, New York, pp 216–21.

8. Clark 1928 pp 181, 187, 196.

9. Cooper J F *The Deerslayer or the First War-Path*. G P Putnam's Sons, New York, p vii. For Heckewelder's influence on Cooper and its results, see Slotkin R 1973 *Regeneration through violence: The mythology of the American frontier, 1600–1860*. Wesleyan University Press, Middletown, Conn, pp 357–8.
10. Cooper *Deerslayer* p vi.
11. Cooper J F 1832 *The Pioneers: a descriptive tale*. Colburn and Bentley, London, p 86. See also p 142.
12. Cooper *The Pioneers* p 454.
13. Ibid p 79.
14. Cooper J F (1826) 1962 *The Last of the Mohicans: a narrative of 1757*. Collier Books, New York, pp 24, 62.
15. Cooper J F (1827) 1987 *The Prairie*. Penguin Books, New York, p 58.
16. Ibid p 76.
17. Ibid p 385.
18. Cooper J F (1840) *The Pathfinder or The Inland Sea*. Frederick Warne & Co, London, pp 18, 347.
19. Cooper *Deerslayer* pp 7–16, 35–7, 56–7, 73, 266, 364–74.
20. Sedgwick C M 1827 *Hope Leslie: or, Early Times in the Massachusetts* (2 vols). Harper & Brothers, New York, vol 1 p 24.
21. Ibid vol 2 pp 13–14.
22. Ibid vol 2 p 13.
23. Ibid vol 2 p 243.
24. Simms W G 1882 *The Yemassee: A Romance of Carolina* rev edn. A L Armstrong & Sons, New York, pp 90–102, esp p 98.
25. Ibid p 249.
26. Ibid pp 167, 176, 183, 195, 209.
27. Ibid p 175. For remarks on Simms's high opinion of the Indians as a race see Cowie A 1962 Introduction. *The Yemassee*. Hafner Publishing Co, New York, pp xxvii–xxix.
28. Bird R M (1837) nd *Nick of the Woods: A Story of the Early Settlers in Kentucky*. A L Burt Company, New York, p v.
29. Ibid pp 12, 14, 23, 122, 216.
30. Ibid p 23.
31. Ibid p 200.
32. Ibid pp 213–14.
33. Ibid p 240.
34. Ibid pp 245–6.
35. Stephens A S (1860) 1971 *Malaeska: The Indian Wife of the White Hunter*. B Blom, New York, pp 32–3.
36. Ibid pp 158–9.
37. Ibid pp [v], 254.

38. Ellis E (1860) 1966 *Seth Jones; or The Captives of the Frontier.* Odyssey Press, New York, p 6.
39. Ibid pp 84–5.
40. Ibid pp 38–9.
41. Ibid p 5.
42. Ibid p 27.
43. Jackson H H 1929 *Ramona.* Little, Brown, Boston, pp 21–7, 43, 58–60.
44. Ibid pp 45, 60–2, 89.
45. Grey Z 1920 *The Spirit of the Border.* T Werner Laurie, London, pp 4, 72. In 1930 Grey was sued for plagiarism by Charles A Maddux, who charged that much of *The Thundering Herd* was stolen from his *The Border and the Buffalo.* See Scott K W 1979 *Zane Grey: born to the West: a reference guide.* G K Hall, Boston, Mass, pp 88, 94.
46. Jackson C 1973 *Zane Grey.* Twayne, New York, p 18.
47. Grey *The Spirit of the Border* p 264.
48. Ibid pp 44–5.
49. Ibid pp 51, 80–1.
50. Ibid pp 84–5, 234–5.
51. Seaver J E 1826 *A Narrative of the Life of Mrs Mary Jemison.* Howden, London, frontispiece.
52. Ibid p 97.
53. Ibid pp 91–2.
54. For the text of *Metamora* see Page E R (ed) 1965 *America's lost plays reissued* vol 14 *Metamora and other plays* by John Augustus Stone. Princeton University Press, Princeton, NJ.
55. Longfellow H W nd *Longfellow's poetical works.* Oxford University Press, Oxford, p 269.
56. Ibid pp 269, 271–2.
57. Drake B 1841 *The Life and Adventures of Black Hawk: with sketches of Keokuk, the Sac and Fox Indians and the late Black Hawk war* 6th edn. G Conclin, Cincinnati, Ohio, p 199.
58. Ibid pp 264–72, esp pp 268–9.
59. Flint T 1845 *Biographical Memoir of Daniel Boone, the first settler of Kentucky, interspersed with incidents in the early annals of the country.* G Conclin, Cincinnati, Ohio, p 86.
60. Shackford J A and Folmsbee S J (eds) 1973 *A Narrative of the Life of David Crockett of the State of Tennessee.* University of Tennessee Press, Knoxville, pp 106, 108, 109–10, 129, 205–6.
61. Parkman F (1849) 1949 *The Oregon Trail.* Penguin Books, Harmondsworth, p 176. The tone of Parkman's journals often contrasts with that of his published work. See Lee R E 1966 *From*

West to East: studies in the literature of the American West. University of Illinois Press, Urbana, ch 4; also Fender S 1981 *Plotting the Golden West: American literature and the rhetoric of the California Trail.* Cambridge University Press, Cambridge, p 163.

62. *The Oregon Trail* p 344.
63. Ibid pp 28, 60, 280.
64. Ibid pp 69, 86.
65. Richardson A D 1867 *Beyond the Mississippi; from the great river to the great ocean. Life and adventures on the prairies, mountains, and Pacific coast.* American Publishing Co, Hartford, Conn, p 95.
66. Ibid pp 219, 220, 224.
67. Ibid pp 163, 173, 189, 200, 412.
68. Ibid pp 230, 264.
69. Ibid p 367.
70. Twain M (1872) 1924 *Roughing It.* Harper & Brothers, New York, pp 131–2.

6 African American song in New Orleans: the voice of the people

Mary Ellison

Since the days when slavery dominated the South, African American music in the United States has fulfilled at least two vital functions. It has been an expressive and empowering conduit of African American responses to oppression and aspirations for freedom and equality. It has also provided the nation with its most distinctive and influential cultural form. To Amiri Baraka, a remarkable black poet and musical analyst, any study of African American people has to begin with the music 'because it is the basic national voice' of those who are of African origin, and 'there is no American culture without African-American culture'.[1] Within and alongside these two functions, it is also a positive force for change. William McLendon, a black academic and musician, has argued that 'in those few areas where white barriers erected against blacks have partially fallen . . . black music helped open the way'.[2]

The city that has longest nurtured and shaped the many-branched tree of African American music is undoubtedly New Orleans. Founded by the French in 1718 it was to become, claims colonial historian Gwendolyn Midlo Hall, the 'vital stream feeding the formation of American society and culture'.[3] It has also been acknowledged as the 'primary source of black music in the United States, with all genres of black music having at least some of their roots in that city'.[4] The polyrhythmic complexity of the African-based songs of New Orleans offered a multi-layered, pluralistic approach to cultural forms and communal problems. It was in this city that African-rooted blues were to provide the strong trunk from which jazz and rhythm and blues would eventually grow and flourish. Baraka is convinced that:

> New Orleans was where all the cycles of culture had linked up, sweeping out the countryside from the plantations, the Native American villages, settlements of English, French, Spanish (Jelly Roll's Spanish tinge), Italian, Portuguese, all the various cultures, and the African base, African-American collective whatever-you-got-I-need-logic.[5]

New Orleans has always been simultaneously the most African and most European of American cities. The cultural links with Africa were maintained more strongly than anywhere else in the South by slaves in New Orleans, and the fusion of cultures that is at the essence of America was perfected in the crescent city. Perhaps more importantly, it was here that African music was retained, acculturated and developed to a degree where uniquely American forms such as blues, jazz, rhythm and blues and rock and roll could be created. Nowhere else did the African heritage fuse so selectively with European elements in an American environment to create such nationally distinctive sounds.

Slaves had originally arrived in New Orleans from a variety of African countries but the largest number knew their origins were in Senegambia and resolutely continued to play the music of their homeland. Others were from Dahomey and brought with them an allegiance to voodoo that rapidly became syncretized with the Catholicism that dominated French- and Spanish-controlled Louisiana to create an African-influenced, musically altered and inspired form of Christianity. This was reinforced by the continuous influx of Africans who had spent a transitional time in the Caribbean with its assertive African-dominated culture. It is hardly surprising that the early music played by the slaves of New Orleans had a distinctive African character and was almost always associated with dancing. Eye-witness reports make it clear that drums and a plethora of percussive instruments were alive and pounding in slave New Orleans.[6] Laws against drumming were neither enforced nor effective in Louisiana and slaves used drums liberally as they sang and danced in Congo Square in the centre of New Orleans, as well as in less formalized meetings on sugar and cotton plantations on the outskirts of the city. Where

Christianity was adopted and adapted, the songs that were sung in church had African rhythmic and harmonic patterns. Frequently the melodies were also of African origin. Dancing, shouting, handclapping and percussive instruments accompanied the lyrics that spoke of freedom in a form that was poetic in structure and multi-layered in meaning.

There seems to be a scholarly consensus about the dominant influence of Senegambia on African American music. What is surprising is how independently different scholars have arrived at such similar conclusions. Gwendolyn Midlo Hall in 1992 published a meticulously researched study of the colonial period in Louisiana which demonstrated just how close were the cultural links between Senegambia and New Orleans.[7] She comes to these convictions without having read the more musicologically orientated work of Michael Coolen, who had been researching musical connections between Senegambia and New Orleans since 1975 and has no doubt about the Senegambia roots of American music.[8]

Hall has emphasized that two-thirds of the slaves who came into New Orleans through the French slave trade were from Senegambia. As George Washington Cable had also noted a century earlier, it was the Bambara slaves from this region who played a preponderant role in the formation of New Orleans culture. Cultural continuity was secured by the music which enshrined belief systems as well as coping mechanisms. In Louisiana, reinforced by their music, 'the Bambara maintained an organized language community, formed alliance with Indian nations who were in revolt against the French, and conspired to take over the colony'. Alliances of a communal and personal nature were to be a hallmark of Indian and African American relationships in the New Orleans area.[9] Their songs were a source of independence and strength as well as a repository of their collective memory.

For African Americans themselves the retention of African musical traditions and instruments was symbolic of their ability to maintain a certain autonomy within the constraints of slavery.[10] In his unpublished manuscript for a 'Black History of Louisiana', Marcus Christian identifies clear African characteristics in the work songs that rang out from buildings and fields in and around New Orleans. He finds ample evidence that 'the slaves brought with them their native music, and their masters, quick to sense the advantages to be gained . . . encouraged this talent'.[11] That they could replicate their African instruments in a New Orleans setting is borne out by contemporary witnesses. Benjamin Latrobe, the architect who redesigned much of New Orleans after the 1812 war, describes the dancing and singing he witnessed in Place Congo on 21 February 1819 as perpetuating 'here those of Africa among its inhabitants'. The singer used 'some African language' and was backed by women stretching, bending and holding single notes. There was also a great deal of call and response. The singing was accompanied by two drums beaten with the edge of the hand and with the fingers which made 'an incredible noise', and by a

> most curious instrument . . . a stringed instrument which no doubt was imported from Africa. On the top of the finger board was the rude figure of a man in a sitting position, and two pegs behind him to which strings were fastened. The body was a calabash. It was played upon by a very little old man, apparently 80 or 90 years old.[12]

The music kept pace with the varied rhythms of the dancers who moved in circles around a further small calabash while using more unusual instruments including a square drum and other African percussive instruments. Ring dances were essentially African and are mentioned as occurring regularly in New Orleans throughout and beyond slavery. Dancing 'Calinda', for instance, is referred to by Le Page du Pratz in 1758 and by Charles Warner in 1775.[13] The style and intensity of these dances underlines the therapeutic functionality of African culture in the lives of black New Orleanians.

Black clubs where music was accompanied by alcohol abounded in New Orleans in the *ante bellum* years. The white community feared that such places would provide stimulus and opportunity for slave insurrections. According to one New Orleanian journalist, at these music venues 'mobs and caucuses of our slaves nightly assemble at their orgies, to influence the brains with copious libations, and preach rebellions against their white masters'.[14] A New Orleans editor went further: 'should a servile outbreak ever occur in the City of New Orleans', he said, 'we shall have to thank the keepers of those negro cabarets and club houses for it, within the precincts of whose damned halls, at the dead hour of midnight, heaven knows what plots are hatched against our peace'.[15] Speakeasies were generally perceived as providing the perfect environment for those plotting to destroy the entire structure of bondage. Freedom to spend time in music venues was uniquely available in New Orleans – the only city where a slave's free time was unconstrained.

Music sung and played in churches could be equally dangerous. It was often at church services that slaves were allowed to gather in large numbers and spirituals alluding to freedom were sung. Spirits would be nurtured by songs about escape and liberty, and flight was often arranged in churches. Preachers were arrested as abolitionists likely to foment discontent and lead to running away or rebellion. To the editor of the New Orleans *Bee* these 'psalm singing chaps are Abolitionists in disguise, and of the most dangerous kind'.[16] It certainly seems likely that insurrectionary fervour would have been stirred by such call and response spirituals as

Broders don't you hear the horn?
Yes, Lord, I hear the horn;
The horn sounds in jubilee.

or the more veiled allusions to combating harsh and evil masters in

Hip and thigh, we'll pull him down,
Let us pull him down,
Let us pull old Satan down.[17]

The impact of such songs was reinforced when they were followed 'by sermons, the subject of which was of the most inflammatory character'.[18]

Fear of revolts was not unfounded. There was much revolutionary agitation among slaves in New Orleans in the 1790s. According to Marcus Christian, insurrections were 'common' and 'the slaves' unquenchable desire for freedom gave birth to many plots and uprisings'. One instance of this stretched beyond the boundaries of the city to the plantation of Julian Poydras, over 100 miles from New Orleans. A plot was hatched whereby on 14 April 1795 an army of slaves was to march from the Poydras plantation to New Orleans, killing white masters on the way. The conspiracy was discovered and 25 slaves were killed. A further 23 were hung one by one along the route they had planned to take to New Orleans. There were threats and fears of uprisings in the next decade or so, with 1804 and 1805 being years of virulent rumours and suspicion, the most conflagrationary being the 1805 plot to burn New Orleans.[19] To Eugene Genovese the 1811 rebellion in New Orleans was 'probably the greatest in the history of the slave South'.[20] It alone was comparable in size to risings in the Caribbean – it involved around 500 slaves who marched into the city with axes, hoes, pikes and drums. Some 66 of the rebels were killed and sixteen leaders were tried and beheaded.[21]

The African origins of the spirituals sung in New Orleans have been documented and analysed by an impressive range of modern musicologists as well as contemporary observers. The most popular spirituals have been identified as having closely similar rhythmic, harmonic and melodic structures to those found in songs sung by the Ashanti, or by those who lived in Dahomey or the Gold Coast: the complex characteristics of polyphony and polyrhythm; antiphony; overlap; repetition of short phrases for the purpose of arousing ecstasy; call-and-response; part-singing; recurrent incremental lines and the principle of incremental repetition; and, more often than not, syncopation. All these characteristics have been carefully developed by dozens of musical writers, and double meaning was as intrinsic a characteristic of African song as of the spirituals that disguised lyrics of rebellion as affirmations of religious aspirations. Signifying and codification were techniques used naturally in African song that proved immensely functional in the face of American racism.[22]

In the half-century leading to the Civil War, New Orleans produced Creole composers whose genius earned European as well as American admiration.[23] New Orleans was the first American city to have its own opera company and the city was full of European and light-coloured Creole musicians, many of whom taught free black students. Early in the nineteenth century there were several black orchestras that played in a style that combined European and African traditions. Using fiddles, flutes, pipes, drums, tambourines, clarinets and triangles, they played for dances as well as in a concert setting, suffusing the overall sound with African rhythms.

It seems appropriate that integration on a white public stage occurred for the first time in the United States in a New Orleans theatre when a black singer appeared at the St Charles in 1837. It was also a tradition in the *ante bellum* period for white musicians to play with the Negro Philharmonic Symphony Orchestra.[24] Creole songs were also written as a pertinent and often witty commentary on aspects of Creole life. Joseph Beaument, a free 'Creole of Color' in New Orleans in 1820, wrote a witty song about mulatto Creoles who attempted to pass for white and deny their African heritage:

Ná pas pas-se tanto
(You haven't passed that much)
Tou-con-ton,
(Tou-con-ton)
Yé con-nin vous,
(They know you)
Vous est ein Morico!
(You are a black-a-moor!)
Na pas sa-van,
(There is no soap)
Qu as-sez blanc,
(White enough)
Pou blan-chez to lapo.
(To bleach your skin)[25]

Other topical songs were written and sung in French by enslaved Creoles. This 'escape' song was collected from an ex-slave aged 100 in 1934:

Misère qui mene neg-là dans bois
(Misery led this black to the woods)
Dis mo maitre mo mouri dans bois
(Tell my master that I died in the woods)

Another song collected by Irene Therese Whitfield uses the threat of running away to bargain for better treatment:

C'est pas jordi modans moune,
(It's not today I'm in the world)

Si yé fait ben avec moin, mo resté,
(If you treat me well, I'll stay)
Si yé fait mo mal, má-chap-pé
(If you treat me bad, I'll escape)

The legendary bravery of yet another New Orleans runaway was enshrined in 'The Ballad of St. Malo'.[26] Creole musicians played classical, dance and Creole folk songs that had positive French lyrics with compulsive rhythms as well as parade music that ranged from purely European to the decidedly African influenced.[27] The sounds of Congo square were never as distant or as alien as they seemed. They were to become more richly blended during and after the whirlpool of the Civil War.

It was an earlier war that made possible the parade element in this musical *mélange*. Free black musicians fought in the war of 1812. It was the start of the New Orleans brass band tradition. Jordan B. Noble of New Orleans was a Creole of Color who won a reputation as a superb drummer for the Seventh Regiment of Infantry. It was Jordon B. Noble who drummed the Americans into line at the Battle of New Orleans and as a group New Orleans Creoles of Color rapidly became famous for certain special war songs. 'En Avan Grenadie' was a Creole rallying song used in the Battle of New Orleans. Black brass bands became common in the *ante bellum* period. Playing in a brass band was not only popular, it was a means of obtaining a musical education. As early as 1820, the New Orleans Independent Rifle Company advertised for 'two young men of color' and offered to teach them to play and provide them with instruments, uniforms and a monthly salary.[28] More often the young men acquired a conventional musical education and played professionally in orchestras and in parades as members of a brass band, singing topical songs whenever the occasion seemed appropriate.

Even in the *ante bellum* period, parade bands were fulfilling the vital function of ritualizing joy and sorrow. Weddings and feast days were as much occasions for a parade band to play and sing topical songs as funerals. When festivities were not specifically focused on one event, topical songs often commented on shifting circumstances, and the segregation that crept into areas as diverse as theatres and graveyards was sung about with humour and style.[29] The music strengthened the spirit of the people and toughened resilience and determination.

The tension generated by abolitionism and sectional differences in the build-up to the Civil War reverberated adversely for free black people and slaves with almost equal intensity. Slaves and free men lost jobs on the docks and the riverboats and in every area where black people were employed. Work songs that had accompanied daily tasks acquired a slower, more mournful tempo and the words changed with circumstances. Work songs and hollers sung in New Orleans contained the flatted thirds and sevenths, the elision, the call and response, and sometimes even the A–A–B structure that were to mark fully fledged blues in the period after the war.

There were moments when folk songs would sooth discontent, but more often they expressed communal and individual anger. For African American New Orleanians the Civil War was essentially a fight for liberty. As armed conflict became a likelihood that loomed ever closer, their songs took on a more insistent tone in their demands for freedom and equality. New Orleans slaves and free Creoles of Color were always better informed and more aware of emergent political attitudes and action than those elsewhere in the Deep South. The illusion of the satisfied Sambo was shattered by tens of thousands of slaves.[30] Encoded spirituals rang through the streets:

Didn't my Lord deliver Daniel.
Deliver, Daniel, deliver.
They sang joyfully
We have no massa now, we free
Hallelujah
We have the Yankees, who set us free
Hallelujah

New Orleans rang with freedom songs like 'Many thousands go' or

Slavery chain done broke at last!
Broke at last! Broke at last!
Slavery chain broke at last!
Gonna praise God till I die!

or even more specifically

Hurrah, hurrah for freedom!
It makes de head spin 'roun

De nigga' in de saddle
An' de white man on de ground![31]

George Cable stresses the lighthearted jubilation with which
African Americans in New Orleans greeted Farragut's victory in
April 1862 in a song of remarkable length and mockery that
includes the lines:

An-hé!
Qui ça qui rivé
C'est Ferraguitt et pi Botlair,
Qui rivé.

Other songs, like the Creole slave musical witticism 'Neg Pas
Capa Marche', were repeated and adapted as the war advanced.
Similarly, 'Criole Candjo' with its flirtatious sexual innuendo was
turned into a celebration with the lines

But Creole tek' sem road, and try
All time, all time to meck free

The escape song 'Dé Zab', with what Cable assumes was Congo
phrasing but more reasonably seems influenced by Senegambian
dialect, was sung as a song of triumph ending with the rousing
'Rozah, rozah, rozah a-a mom-zah'.[32]

Other songs by Creoles of Color were very different in their
air of resentment and determination to foil the efforts of the
Union troops. 'Chaque Colonel' was a parody of a marching
song that was obviously indicative of free New Orleans suspicion
of the Union:

Chaque coronel n'ont pas, n'ont pas (de) soldats (2)
(Each colonel has no, has no soldiers)
Nous fais-ye galoper (3)
(We make them gallop)
Jusqù à la Rue Canal.
(Up to Canal Street.)
Nous preñ ferry, nous traversons à l'autre bord (2)
(We take a ferry, we cross to the other side)
Nous fais – yé galoper (3)
(We make them gallop)
Jusqù à la Rue Canal.
(Up to Canal Street.)[33]

Yet when the Confiscation Act of 17 July 1862 declared all the slaves of those in rebellion to be free, songs like

I free, I free!
I free as a frog
I free till I fool
Glory Alleluia!

resounded through the streets of New Orleans alongside such rousing choruses as

It's stomp down freedom today
Stomp it down![34]

Now freedom was within grasp it had become 'a song itself'. The revolutionary impulse to transform life on this earth that coursed through the spirituals seemed to have attained its primary goal with emancipation and at last there could be 'a great camp meeting in the Promised Land'. In New Orleans the battle for freedom was literally fought and won 'Down by the riverside':

We will end this war, brethren
Down by the river,
End this war,
Down by the riverside.

Armed uprisings were put down, ringleaders were hanged and lesser conspirators were whipped. There was serious talk of 'servile war' when a large group of plantation slaves came pouring into New Orleans in 1862 'armed with clubs and cane knives'. Other observers just noticed the menacing atmosphere, the insults and the refusal to work. Slave reaction to Confederate defeat and the Union victory was either to compound the damage to property or to celebrate as if 'jubilee' had come.[35] Their freedom was celebrated in songs and songs inspired their battle for freedom. The 'Runaways Song' had been heard in New Orleans since Spanish colonial times but was reborn as a song of defiance during the Civil War. The historic core of the song was retained and with adapted verses could be heard on streets throughout the crescent city in the early stages of the conflict:

O General Florido!
Indeed fo' true dey can't catch me
Dey got one schooner out to sea
Indeed fo' true dey can't catch me.[36]

Some spirituals began to abandon the dual implications of immorality and mortal gain that had been their hallmark during enslavement. Now the lyrics could be unambivalent:

Slavery chains, Slavery chains,
Thank God Almighty, I'm free at last,
Free at last, free at last,
Thank God Almighty, I'm free at last.

or

We'll fight for liberty
When de Lord will call us home.

Others among what W. E. B. DuBois called those 'weird old songs in which the soul of the black slave spoke' and 'the most beautiful expression of human experience born this side the seas' rejoiced in the ending of so many depredations and deprivations:

No more driver's lash for me,
No more driver's lash for me,
No more driver's lash for me,
Many thousand go.

Similar relief was expressed in songs like 'Babylon is Fallen', 'Bobolishion's Comin' and 'De Massa Run', or 'Done wid massa's hollerin' ':

Done wid massa's hollerin'
Done wid massa's hollerin'
Roll, Jordan, roll.

These are all spirituals that possess, as James Weldon Johnson noted, 'a striking rhythmic quality, and show a marked similarity to African songs in form and intervallic structure'. The lyrical sophistication was matched only by their 'harmonic development'.[37] Once the Union army had taken over New Orleans the melodic patterns of the spirituals became more powerfully positive and insistent and the demand for full freedom reverberated more loudly in the words as the need for 'coded meaning' diminished. The father of the great clarinet and saxophone master, Sidney Bechet, recalled a swift mood change in New Orleans songs once emancipation was announced. The persistent demand for freedom had at last won through. According to Bechet, 'a different feeling had got started'. For years they had been singing 'Go down Moses', when

> suddenly there was a different way of singing it. You could feel a new way of happiness in the lines. All that waiting, all that time when that song was far-off music, suffering music; and all at once it was there, it had arrived. It was joy music now. It was Free Day . . . Emancipation.
>
> And New Orleans just bust wide open. A real time was had. They heard the music, and the music told them about it. They heard music from bands marching up and down the streets and they knew what music it was . . . That music, it wasn't spirituals or blues or ragtime, but everything all at once, each one putting something over on the other . . . Some of those people didn't even know what Emancipation was; they just knew there was a hell of a parade going on, a whole lot of laughing and singing, a whole lot of music being happier than the music had ever been before.[38]

New Orleans was the city where 'Daddy' Thomas Rice had sung and danced 'Jump Jim Crow' in the 1830s, almost certainly adapting it from a song by 'Old Corn Meal', a New Orleans African American reformer whose repertoire was used by the early minstrel clown George Nichols. Corn Meal had been acknowledged in the local press as unusually talented and politically aware for a 'Negro street peddler'. His obituary in the conservative *Bee* in 1842 had mourned the passing of 'his double-toned voice – never again shall his corn meal melodies, now grumbled in a bass – now squeaked in a treble, vibrate on the ear. He was a public spirited politician'. His political acumen and performing power of expression had made it quite evident that he was using the stage to attack discrimination against all black people in New Orleans. It was in New Orleans during the war years that a song often attributed to a later period could be heard reinforcing black demands for an end to segregation as well as servitude:

No more Jim Crow. No more Jim Crow.
No more Jim Crow over me.
And before I'll be a slave,
I'll be buried in my grave
And go home to my lord and be free.

Other songs published in New Orleans were fairly obviously intended to be sung by white minstrels in blackface. In 'Nigger Will Be Nigger', black men are painted as cowardly:

I got down to New Orleans, ole Massa was forgotten
As sojer man he cum along, an' sot me rollin cotton
At night I axed him for de pay, he tole me take my lip in,
He tuck me to de Calaboose, an' dar I cotch a whippin.

Similarly 'The Happy Contraband', about a slave who had been transported to New Orleans from Virginia and is supposed to prefer slavery to freedom:

Then away with 'mancipation, give me back the old plantation,
'Tis the best place in the world for the nigger
That's the idea of the Happy Contraband.

There were times, of course, when African American minstrels would sing these songs with such sarcasm and wit that their meaning would be totally subverted. Even 'I Wish I was in Dixie', which was first published in New Orleans (by Philip Werlein), had its words altered and its meaning turned around by genuinely black New Orleans minstrels.[39]

There now seems little doubt that the blues were born as slavery ended and attempts were made to reconstruct the way in which black and white southerners related to each other. A plethora of scholarly studies place embryonic blues in the period but few sum up the gestation more succinctly than musicologist Edna Edet:

For the first time, the Freedmen were able to sing out loud about their misery in secular song, without religious disguises. For the first time, they had the hope of a better life – a hope quickly extinguished. The dichotomy between their hopes and desires and their actual experiences was enough to give birth to the blues.[40]

Early forms of blues evolved in the crescent city when plantation slaves poured into New Orleans to escape their masters and join the Union army. They brought with them their hollers and work songs, their shouts and spirituals and adapted them to their new circumstances and urban surroundings. Songs shifted and changed their patterns while emphasizing the flatted notes and topical content. Typical of embryonic blues was

> Don't you see the lightning flashing in the cane breaks, (2)
> Looks like we gonna have a storm.
> Oh no, you're mistaken, it's the Yankee soldiers (3)
> Goin' to fight for Uncle Sam.

Just as popular was an 'enlistment' song formed in a more traditional mode:

> I've listed and I mean to fight,
> Yes, my lord,
> Till every foe is put to flight,
> Yes, my lord.[41]

Obviously much of New Orleans life centred around the Mississippi and river songs or chanteys were sung by black boatmen. One of the most popular in New Orleans was 'Sally Brown', who was apparently a part black, part Indian 'Creole lady' who married a 'Negro soldier' who fought in the Civil War. Other New Orleans chanteys and spirituals were defiantly anti-Confederate and pro-Union. Some ended 'Dis Union Forever'. Stonewall Jackson was the focus of the improvised street chant 'Stood Wall Jackson' popular during the war among Creoles in the city and sung for generations afterwards by rivermen.[42]

The most important socio-musical phenomenon fostered in New Orleans during the Civil War was the brass band. Throughout the war, black musicians formed and joined brass bands that were more numerous and more inventive than in other American cities.[43] Bands such as the St Bernard Band and Kelly's Band were splendid in their musical expertise and diversity. They captured the spirit of funerals and dances with equal precision. They were there as a regular accompaniment to every important stage and occasion of life in this most alive of cities. The Excelsior Brass Band began in the 1860s and was to become experienced enough to make a stirring and varied contribution to the New Orleans Cotton States Exposition of 1885. They and most of the Civil War era New Orleans brass bands were as at ease with syncopation and improvisation as they were with the more conventionally structured marches. That these bands were well-established in New Orleans during the Civil War and Reconstruction, rather than emerging in the 1890s, as has often been suggested, is clear from contemporary accounts. James Monroe Trotter's analysis of New Orleans music included brass bands and was published in 1878.[44] Just before the Civil War, the instruments used by brass bands had become more sophisticated and adaptable. In 1840 Adolphe Sax had invented the saxophone and from then on piston-valve instruments of conical bore were seen in most band ensembles. During the war itself the need for economy of movement helped to refine the instrument and the clumsy, backward-pointing saxhorn was replaced by the forward-aimed soprano, alto, tenor and baritone saxophones as well as helicons or tubas. Throughout the Civil War, New Orleans was exposed to both southern and northern military brass bands. Quartered in the city at different times in the war, such bands held parades and gave concerts that whipped up enthusiasm for their opposed causes. Every public ritual, ceremony or mere occurrence was usually accompanied by a brass band. Instruments proliferated and became more available in the poorer as well as the Creole black areas of the city. By the end of the Civil War 'a brass-band tradition was firmly rooted in the black community'.[45] Along with that tradition went one of the quintessential hallmarks of New Orleans music – the 'second line'. Just as alternative rhythms were set up by those who followed the mourners and the official band at a funeral, so musical youths followed the army bands and established harmoniously discordant second-line rhythms of their own.

Those roots went deepest into the culture of those free Creoles who had grown up playing classical instruments, either professionally or as a diverting accomplishment, and adapting them to the needs of emergent local brass bands. These were the men who played in marching bands and who volunteered for the Native Guard. But by 1863 there were also ex-slave bands and minstrel shows that incorporated a dominant brass band element and provided a humorous and musically eloquent commentary on the war. Smallwood's Great Contraband Minstrels and Brass Band had formed in New Orleans during Union occupation and by the end of the war had become a Louisiana template for other bands. Like other aspects of New Orleans music, 'self aware comedy and dignity' combined in such bands to evoke deep political and emotional feelings with words that were as masked and multi-layered as the second-line music:

> Freedman sat on a pile of bricks,
> As the rain was pattering down,
> His shoes were worn and his coat was torn,
> And his hat was without a crown,
> He viewed the clouds and he viewed himself
> And he shook the wet from his head,
> And a tear dimm'd his eye as he saw go by,
> A boy with a loaf of bread,
> And he raised his voice in a doleful tone
> That sounded like a gong,
> While the rain came down on his happy crown
> And he sang to himself this song.[46]

In the best African tradition, New Orleans was 'a city where music accompanied every moment of life, from the cradle to the grave, and musically underlining most of those moments was the brass band'.[47]

Once the war was over in 1865, African American efforts to gain land, education and the vote intensified. Frustrated by the return to power of the former Confederates, with their restricting Black Codes, black people began to organize. When a group of ex-slaves, 'preceded by a brass band', marched to a rally at the Mechanics Institute in July 1866, a riot broke out when the police opened fire wildly into the marchers. Thirty-four black men and three whites were killed. Sorrowful and angry songs were sung in the streets as they were laid to rest. The US army moved back in under the 1867 Reconstruction Act, and black voters were registered. The battle for political rights and socio-economic desegregation was spearheaded by the Creoles of Color.

Despite the election of many astute and able Creoles of Color and ex-slaves, including Oscar Dunn, the Lieutenant Governor, and P. B. S. Pinchback, who was acting Governor in 1872–73, few rights were advanced and segregation increasingly impinged on the personal freedom of anyone with any African ancestry whatsoever. The division between those with French or Spanish wealth and education behind them, and those who had been slaves, eroded, and both groups met to blend and transform their talents into urban blues and jazz. Increasingly denied a role in government and steadily disenfranchised, they found a fresh voice in music. This voice was enriched by those who poured into the city from the country both during and after the war, doubling its black population, and bringing with them many songs that combined the musical characteristics of both hollers and work songs, like Robert Williams's 'Levee. Camp Blues'.[48] Early blues began to emerge out of the turmoil and frustration of Reconstruction.

Sung on the river and in the streets of New Orleans, these introspective songs attempted to define the new parameters of life. Sidney Bechet recalls his father talking about the mood in the city at the start of Reconstruction:

> Seems like there was always music around New Orleans in those days. All those people who had been slaves, they needed the music more than ever now; it was like they were trying to find out in this music what they were supposed to do with this freedom: playing the music and listening to it – waiting for it to express what they needed to learn, once they had learned it wasn't just white people the music had to reach to, nor even to their own people, but straight out to life and to what a man does with his life when it is finally his.[49]

Bechet, the legendary Buddy Bolden, Jelly Roll Morton, Louis Armstrong and many other influential crescent city jazzmen, sang as well as played the blues while they built up the city's reputation as the birthplace of jazz. They all made it clear that blues had laid the foundation for jazz, and that those flatted notes and the A–A–B structure of the honest, life-encompassing lyrics were more important than European instrumentation and classical training. The structure of the holler had combined with 'the common harmonic accompaniment patterns of the blues ballad' to create a new form of immense strength and lasting power.[50]

The segregation laws that crept in during and after Reconstruction were given Supreme Court approval in a decision involving a very light-skinned New Orleanian, Homer Plessy. Poet and historian Marcus Christian was to grow up living with the consequences in the crescent city and considered that the Court's ruling in the case of *Plessy v. Ferguson* so reduced the rights of Creoles of Color as well as ex-slaves that it 'practically made them aliens in the land of their birth, wholly subject to the petty tyrannies of state legislators whose salaries were paid in part from the pockets of their Negro victims'.[51] Creoles of Color became more excluded, and opportunities became increasingly unequal. A branch of the National Association for the Advancement of Colored People was organized in New Orleans in 1915, but was neither particularly aggressive nor effective. Blues singers attracted far more interest and attention.

It became increasingly obvious that, to white society, those with a classical musical training were as unacceptable as self-taught bluesmen. As Amiri Baraka points out in *Blues People*, this created 'a brilliant amalgam of diverse influences', since a black New Orleanian 'could not participate in the dominant tenor of the white man's culture. It was at this juncture that he had to make use of other resources, whether African, subcultural or hermetic. And it was this boundary, this no-man's land, that provided the logic and beauty of his music.'[52] These diverse influences obviously included the songs that emerged from the sugar – and cotton – plantations on the periphery of New Orleans. The 'hypnotic, one-chord drone blues, with darkly insistent vamping, violent treble-string punctuations, and songs that filled both traditional and improvised lyrics into a loose, chant-like structure' became characteristic of Louisiana bluesmen and were to influence not only New Orleans singers but also those with Louisiana roots like John Lee Hooker, whose stepfather was from the Pelican State, and Buddy Guy, who was born in Baton Rouge.[53]

In a city like New Orleans it is hardly surprising that among the earliest and the best blues singers were the most influential jazzmen. Jelly Roll Morton grew up listening to the blues. He had a clear memory of Mamie Desdoumes singing a blues about poverty in 1902.

Can't give me a dollar, give me a lousy dime,
Just to feed that hungry man of mine.

According to Morton, 'Music was pouring into the streets from every house. Women were standing in the doorways, singing or chanting some kind of blues – some very happy, some very sad'.[54] Four years earlier, Ophelia Simpson sang a prison blues:

> I ain't got not a friend in dis town (2)
> Cause my New Orleans partner done turned me down.
>
> Po'gal wishin for dat jail-house key, (2)
> To open up de door and let herself go free.
>
> Stony Lonesome no place for a dog (2)
> Not even if itten for a razor-backed hog.
>
> High Sheriff said "Gal don't be so blue, (2)
> Cause dat jail-house keeper goin' to be good to you."[55]

Another song that Mamie Desdoumes popularized on the streets and in the bars where she accompanied herself on the piano became 'Mamie's Blues' and juxtaposed poverty and sex – sex, moreover, with a toy boy or 'kid man':

> I like the way he cooks my cabbage for me (2)
> Looks like he sets my natural soul free.[56]

The linkage of sex with freedom in these early lyrics is typical of the codification inherent in the blues. References to physical and emotional relationships were sometimes perfectly straight-forward, but more frequently were used to mask allusions to socio-economic conditions. Supported by the impossible-to-notate music, the lyrics frequently 'slipped the yoke' and 'changed the joke' and defied accurate interpretation by many listeners. Blues could be enjoyed by all but understood most clearly by the African American community. In New Orleans, blues that focused on trouble between men and women frequently repre-sented resentment over the lack of equal opportunities in employment, education and politics. The encoding had an innate logic in that any family so deprived was likely to be unhappy.

The last decade of the nineteenth century was a fertile time of change and adaption as well as disillusionment. The burgeoning black population found solidarity in the proliferation of clubs and benevolent societies. Their social functions were as important as their political roles and local brass bands played for them on every feasible occasion. Some societies formed in 1860 like the Eureka Benevolent Association had their own bands. The same bands and jazz-orientated groups played for Italian social functions and Italians frequently contributed to the music.[57] In the 1890s the West Side of the French Quarter, Storyville, became a centre of prostitution and employment for jazzmen and women. Jelly Roll Morton himself frequently played and sang blues at Lulu White's Mahogany Blues Hall.[58] Until it was shut down by a Navy directive in 1917, blues and jazz of sophistication and raw energy reverberated through the quarter. Lizzie Green sang 'Good Time Flat Blues' about her loss of livelihood when Storyville was closed down.

> I can't keep open, I'm gonna close up shack.
> The chief of police done tore my playhouse down,
> No use in grievin, I'm gonna leave this town.[59]

Improvisation and duple and triple time became characteristic of the city's blues as well as its blues-based jazz. As Baraka has highlighted,

> New Orleans became famous because it was the city where the blues country impulse could remix with open African expression (Congo Square drum sessions) and come in contact as well with the urbane, even international flavor of French, Spanish, English and Native American influences. Jazz incorporates blues, not just as a specific form, but as a cultural insistence, a tonal memory . . . Blues is the national consciousness of jazz – its truthfulness in a lie world, its insistence that it is itself, its identification as the life expression of a specific people, the African-American nation.[60]

Given the prevalence of the misconception that blues resonates only with misery or anger, it seems appropriate that the first recording by a male blues artist should have been full of tongue-in-cheek humour. In July 1924, New Orleanian 'Papa' Charlie Jackson recorded 'Papa's Lawdy Lawdy Blues', which he followed with 77 other recordings, including 'Salty Dog Blues', in which he gave his own version of the Buddy Bolden classic:

> Funniest thing I ever saw in my life
> Uncle Bud came home and caught me kissin' his wife.
> Salty Dog, oh, yes, you Salty Dog.[61]

His sophisticated, joyous style took the country by storm. He seemed to encapsulate the expectations and optimism of black people in his warm voice, complicated banjo-picking and free sense of rhythm. He also sang duets with Ma Rainey and offset his humorous and bawdy songs with those like 'Ma and Pa Poorhouse Blues', which focused on poverty.[62]

More typically New Orleanian in his ability to blend blues and jazz into a seamless whole was Lonnie Johnson, one of the most powerful and popular artists of the twenties. Between 1924 and 1932 he cut dozens of singles and then went on to be a seminal influence on the blues for over 40 years, making many remarkable albums. He toured with Bessie Smith and cut singles with Louis Armstrong, Duke Ellington and King Oliver. He filled perfectly the bluesman's archetypal role of community articulator of common fears and aspirations, not only for his native New Orleans, but for St Louis, where he later met and settled with his wife. The thoughtful complexity of the encoded lyrics of 'Death Valley is Just Half-Way to My Home' went beyond what many black southerners might have said to touch the essence of what they subconsciously feared.

> There's no train to my home town,
> Ain't but no one way to go, (2)
> Mile after mile travellin that muddy road,
> Ain't but one thing that worries me both night and day, (2)
> Death valley is just half way to my home.

In songs like 'Men, Be Wise to Yourself', acerbic cautioning is underpinned by wit. Yet the tragedy of failed aspirations and of hopes doomed by an inequitable system subsumed Johnson's spirit as early as 1924, when he recorded 'You Don't See Into These Blues Like Me':

> People, I've stood these blues 'bout as long as I can.
> I walked all night with these blues, we both joined hand in hand.
> And they travelled my heart through, just like a natural man.[63]

A few years later he believed he could override this despair even though

> The blues are round my bed
> And round the foot of my door.

Ralph Ellison said of the blues that they simultaneously express 'both the agony of life and the possibility of conquering it through sheer toughness of spirit'.[64] The blues make sense of the 'frustrated complexities' of life and behind so many blues lines is a hidden allusion to grief at the destruction of communal values.[65] The allusions frequently go further and centre on the unconquerable determination to rise above, laugh at or turn into positive action the setbacks so unjustly encountered. Johnson is considered by Paul Oliver to be one of the greatest composers of affecting and appropriate blues songs written and sung to sustain and encourage.[66]

The Depression coincided with the gubernatorial regime of Huey Long and after his election in 1928 it was hoped that more black people would be allowed to vote. In actuality, black voting and educational opportunities decreased during Long's twelve years in office, and music became an even more important outlet for discontent.[67] That discontent became more intense as poverty escalated. Johnson's early years playing on the streets of New Orleans with other members of his musical family were filled with deprivation and hardship. In his case this was exacerbated when his family died during his teens. To him the Depression seemed the norm, and to cause no more than a slight deterioration in his circumstances. Tragedy apart, this was just as true for a large proportion of the black community. In 'Hard Times Ain't Gone Nowhere' Johnson was a spokesman for his people:

> People is raisin' 'bout hard times,
> Tell me what it's all about,
> People is hollerin' 'bout hard times,
> Tell me what it's all about,
> Hard times don't worry me,
> I was broke when it first started out.
>
> People ravin' 'bout hard times,
> I don't know why they should,

People ravin' 'bout hard times,
I don't know why they should,
If some people was like me,
They didn't have no money when times was good.[68]

Contemporary jazzmen such as Lee Collins from New Orleans considered Johnson 'one of the greats'. Pops Foster remembered that 'Lonnie Johnson and his daddy and his brother used to go all over New Orleans playing on street corners. Lonnie played guitar, and his daddy and his brother played violin. Lonnie was the only guy we had around New Orleans who could play jazz guitar'.[69] There is indeed a consensus that 'Johnson's guitar style set the standard for urban blues guitarists for decades to come'.[70] He was considered unique for his diversity of experience and his ability to transmit a vast range of emotions and responses in fresh, multi-layered yet accessible lyrics that were imbued with a poetic spirit. His words and music could reintegrate and make sense of contradictory and disturbing experiences. He simultaneously healed and inspired.

Arguably less influential, but no less prominent, was Champion Jack Dupree. Born to a Cherokee mother in New Orleans in 1910, he was orphaned two years later, and grew up in the same Colored Waifs Home for Boys that had provided Louis Armstrong's early environment. His technique as a blues pianist and singer was not learned there, however, but from a barrel-house piano player called 'Drive Em Down'. Before he was out of his teens, Dupree could express the dull, painful ache of deprivation and loss with his voice and his fingers. Yet Dupree always lightened anguish with humour, and his lyrics joked wryly about poverty. His 'Warehouseman Blues', a huge seller in the Depression, was typically sardonic.

My grandma left this morning
with her basket in her hand,
She's goin' down to the warehouse
to see the warehouse man.
She got down to the warehouse,
them white folks say it ain't no use,
For the government ain't givin' away nothing
but that canned grape fruit juice.
Its a low, low down dirty shame.[71]

In the 1920s Little Brother Montgomery also sang about the pervasiveness of the blues ethic during his early years in New Orleans before, like many of the city's musicians, he moved to Chicago. There was a rare poignancy in songs like 'Crescent City Blues', and menace in 'The First Time I Met You'. Montgomery accompanied himself with the most distinctive boogie piano playing. He used the 4/4 time of the ostinato left hand with consummate, impassioned skill.[72]

Even Mahalia Jackson grew up singing blues and jazz alongside the spirituals that she performed in church. Long before Georgia Tom Dorsey 'invented' gospel by fusing these genres, Mahalia Jackson was creating that same sound in the churches of New Orleans, before she too left the poverty of her native city for the promises held out by Chicago.[73] But her style was always a product of the crescent city and her voice was given an edge by the tough upbringing it had provided.

Among the lesser known blues singers of the 1920s and 1930s were other New Orleanian women like Ann Cook, Blanche Thomas and Lizzie Miles, whose self-penned 'He's Red Hot to Me' was a vaudeville sensation. Greater longevity was shown by Blue Lu Barker who quipped that 'I'm too wise for you to jive' in the 1920s, and was still singing cryptic blues in the 1980s.[74] Equally enduring was Cousin Joe Pleasant (Pleasant Joseph) who wrote and sang gritty songs like 'Barefoot Boy' and 'Railroad Avenue', and cynical lyrics like 'I didn't build this world, But I sure can tear it down'. Playing fine blues piano and singing in New Orleans in the 1920s with Sidney Bechet, he continued recording and touring into the 1970s.

Other younger bluesmen emerged in the forties and were to play rhythm and blues as expertly as the more straightforward urban blues. Roy Brown had enormous national success between 1948 and 1951 with his moving blues-shouting style in such songs as 'Hard Luck Blues', 'Rainy Weather Blues' and 'Good Rockin' Tonight'. 'Good Rockin' Tonight' was covered by Elvis Presley some years later, and 'Hard Luck Blues' became one of the most recorded blues classics, but few versions could match the despair in Brown's voice when he moaned of being so troubled he could throw himself on his mother's grave and die:

I've got so much trouble
Sometimes I sit and cry.
I've got so much trouble
Sometimes I sit and cry.
But I'm gonna find my momma's grave
Fall on the tombstone and die.[75]

One of Brown's contemporaries called him 'a blues singer's blues singer' who infused every rendition with emotion and humour. He has been described as 'one of the great blues lyricists of all time'.[76] The desperation that wailed out from songs like 'Hard Luck Blues' could be taken as a reaction to a statement made a few years earlier by Louisiana Senator John Overton: 'we let the negroes understand – and they do understand – that here in Louisiana we have a white man's government, run by white men. Here in Louisiana we permit neither social nor political equality.'[77] It was enough to drive local poet, activist and historian Marcus Christian to write his 'Segregation Blues' in which he determined to walk until he wore out his shoes.[78]

The assertive, rhythmically complicated yet catchy songs of Smiley Lewis, Huey 'Piano' Smith, Allen Toussaint, Dave Bartholomew, Lee Dorsey, Sugar Boy Crawford and James Booker were among those that danced their way through attitudes and laws that diminished and restricted the rights and freedom of black New Orleanians. This was music that was so positive and life-enhancing that a new mood was created regardless of whether the lyrics were explicitly political.

The sound of rhythm and blues and rock and roll has extended a cultural language that stemmed from the diverse musical heritage of New Orleans. It has indeed been called 'the oldest, richest and most influential tradition of rock-and-roll'.[79] Of its essence it was a powerful force for integration. It united the white and black youth of America and gave them a common voice. When the rhythm and blues of New Orleans was relabelled 'rock and roll' it became a national agency of change. Before the *Brown* v. *the Board of Education* decision ordered the desegregation of southern schools in May 1954, New Orleans rhythm and blues was desegregating the entertainment patterns of America's youth.

Fats Domino was a formative force in the translation of

rhythm and blues into rock and roll, which was to become the national music of youth. This shy Catholic from New Orleans Ninth Ward combined his talents with those of band leader Dave Bartholomew to produce major crossover hits. In 1955 the punchy 'Ain't That a Shame' not only made the Billboard Top 100 but was voted 'best song' by American disc jockeys. 'I'm Walking' reached number five in the Top 100 charts in 1957 and simultaneously became New Orleans' R & B anthem. Its parade-beat rhythm and simple lyrics greatly appealed to a country where moving on was a national pastime. 'Walking to New Orleans' continued the theme in 1960 and reached number six. Fats Domino's bluesy piano and dynamic vocals were filled with energy and excitement and he has had more than 70 hits in the Billboard Top 100. Charlie Gillet attempted to explain his extra-ordinary appeal a few years ago: 'Domino's complete trans-formation into a rock 'n' roll singer was possible because he sang with a plaintive tone which did not seem so adult and alien as did the tone of most of his contemporary rhythm and blues singers. He seemed to be singing about experiences equivalent to those his white listeners knew about.'[80]

Yet, perhaps even more than Fats Domino, Professor Longhair (Henry Byrd) epitomized the New Orleans sound with his multi-rhythmic, second-lining piano playing and his celebratory lyrics. Mardi Gras is central to New Orleans' unique character just as rhythm and blues was the foundation of that most American of musics – rock and roll. Longhair fused them all in his pounding, funky Spanish inflected piano playing on numbers like 'Go to the Mardi Gras'. Bob Trick has pointed out that Longhair 'was probably the first musician in the R & B field to use the Latin based beat which is now an almost inescapable part of any Rock or Soul performance'.[81] He was a genuine innovator who built on Jelly Roll Morton's 'latin tinge' to create a rhumba sixteen style pulse over which he frequently superimposed sixteen to the bar accents and dramatic right-hand breaks. He created a densely layered driving sound that provided the perfect background for his expressive vocals.

During almost the same period Guitar Slim (Eddie Jones) reached number one in the R & B charts with 'Things I Used to Do'. The line 'the things I used to do, I ain't gonna do no more' expressed a universal regret in a voice resonating like a cry from a weeping heart. A strong follow-up, 'The Story of my life', was fatally prescient. Guitar Slim died in 1959 at the age of 32.[82]

Other slightly younger musicians were to keep the blues torch alight. Guitarist singer songwriters like Snooks Eaglin (Fird Eaglin) and Earl King started out in New Orleans in the 1950s and are still powerful performers in the 1990s. When interviewed in June 1990, Eaglin stressed his debt to Lonnie Johnson and Guitar Slim and his belief in the primacy of blues in New Orleans and all American music. He remembered that as he grew up he 'loved all kinds of music, but especially the blues because the blues tells it like it is and don't have no short cuts'. He feels that this is his heritage: 'I was born with the blues and what I play is the blues, you can call it what you want. I've been called a folk musician, an R & B musician and a rock and roll musician but what I play is the blues.'[83] Born in 1936 in New Orleans, Eaglin had become a legend by the early 1950s for his relaxed guitar style and elliptical, moody lyrics. In the 1980s he won international acclaim for albums like *Baby, You Can Get Your Gun* (1987) and *Out of Nowhere* (1989).

Earl King, with whom Eaglin has oftened played, has been even more prolific. King is as historically astute as he is musically gifted and has asserted that music made a positive difference to race relations in New Orleans. For King blues not only articulates fear and anger but can catalyse action. He said in 1990 that he hoped to write a concentrated group of song lyrics addressing contemporary problems. 'Music', he said, 'can create a fresh consciousness, can help people learn to get over their problem. Racism is the problem of those who are ignorant. It is my contention that politicians sometimes have used racism to create fear so that they can wield power.' King feels it is particularly necessary for lyrics to raise awareness about poverty since few politicians seem to have sufficient concern for 'the hungry and homeless you see on the street. When you don't try and remove that poverty thing you got some monsters that will come out of the urban jungle.'[84] Consequently, his 1973 'Let's Make a Better World' portrayed the national predilection for selfish acquisitiveness and consumerism and argued for equality, care and concern.[85]

King, Eaglin and Longhair all took part in a uniquely rich New Orleans musical tradition that centred on topical songs.

This heritage includes a powerful American Indian element. Some of the Indian tribes who had originally lived in the area that became New Orleans had been absorbed by slavery or wiped out by disease and warfare. Among those who survived were groups of Natchez, Cherokee, Choctaw and Chickasaw who aided and harboured slaves who rebelled or escaped. Contemporary scholarship stresses that intermarriage between native Americans and black Louisianians was prevalent during Louisiana's early history. The traditions of Mardi Gras Indians, or 'Black Indians', began the founding of the Louisiana Territory. Many slaves of African origin escaped then and later to live with Indian tribes. In some cases, African Americans joined the Indian tribes in their resistance against French colonialists and against US authority. Intimations of modern Carnival in the early nineteenth century flowered in 1884 when blacks masked as Indians on Mardi Gras. The leaders, or First Chiefs, of the early Mardi Gras Indian tribes were either Native Americans or their descendants. The songs, dances, drumming, elaborate feathered and beaded costumes, the secret, ceremonial 'practices' became a unique New Orleans native and African American mode of expression.[86]

Almost every black New Orleanian masking as an 'Indian' in the late twentieth century has not only distant but also recent Indian ancestry. These range from young members of new tribes like Pete Hardy of the Golden Star Hunters, whose 'grandmother was a Cherokee', and Clarence Dalcour, the Chief of the Creole Osceolas, whose Seminole lineage is a source of pride and inspiration, to Chief Allison 'Tuddy' Montana of the oldest tribe, the Yellow Pocahontas, who claims 'we had the Indian blood mixed in' on both sides of his family.[87] These days most tribes have women prominently featured, not only as queens, but in several newly invented roles. Their songs are a call and response dialogue that comments on the politics and events of the moment. They are filled with wit and disquiet as well as a consciousness of their Indian ancestry. The Creole Osceolas are named after Osceola, the Seminole chief who fought against the United States army to protect the freedom of African American slaves who had escaped and found refuge with the Seminoles. He is especially esteemed among the Creole Osceolas 'as the only Indian chief who never signed the treaty with the United States'. Several of the Osceolas have Seminole ancestors while others have Cherokee parents or grandparents. Members of the tribe are convinced that 'the Africans and the Indians really had a strong connection'. Led by Big Chief Clarence Dalcour, they generate a keen historical awareness and a sharp appreciation of the organic relationship between music, masking and socio-political comment.[88]

To Big Chief Larry Bannock of the Golden Star Hunters, the Mardi Gras Indians exist as 'a way of paying homage to Indians in the past who aided black people. Masking is a mark of respect.' He wants others to realize that

> Indians were the only ones to harbor slaves and see the whole slavery thing from a black perspective. The Seminoles, Creeks and occasionally the Choctaw and the Cherokee were natural allies and defenders but they were not normally fighting Indians. We chose the image of the Sioux as our model for masking because they symbolise the greatest fighting spirit manifested by Indians who, like black people, were attacked by whites.[89]

Larry Bannock himself is as proud of his own Indian ancestry as he is of his black parentage, and feels these two traditions meet in a uniquely powerful and artistically effective way in the masking and music of the Mardi Gras Indians.

There are a few albums, such as those by the Wild Magnolias and the Wild Tchoupitoulas, that capture the magical rhythmic and lyrical interweaving of all the disparate strands that make up the Mardi Gras tradition. The Wild Tchoupitoulas' album had the immense advantage of the Neville Brothers band providing backing music which combined originality with traditional elements. As Charles Neville points out, the brothers 'grew up with Mardi Gras, our uncle, George Landry, was Big Chief Jolly of the Wild Tchoupitoulas and he made us aware of the importance of the Indians in a traditional and a spiritual sense'.[90] The young Nevilles were surrounded by Catholicism, voodoo and a respect for the existence of an Indian spirit world. The album brought together traditional songs and arrangements with numbers such as Cyril Neville's 'Brother John' and 'Hey Hey' as well as the already popular 'Hey Pocky A-Way'. The album was produced by the inventive master of New Orleans piano and production, Allen Toussaint, and arranged and co-produced by

Charles and Art Neville. Charles explained that the album tried to capture the 'sense of pride generated by the collective experience of black and Indian people that had its roots in slavery times and was expressed in the memories and mood of the songs and chants'. To Charles the 'spiritual unity' was as important as the political solidarity that many of the lyrics referred to. It was this that 'the music set out to capture'. The record has been seen as something of a landmark because the 'African percussive tradition, submerged since the denouement of Congo Square and voodoo, surfaced eloquently in Charles Neville's hand percussions and Cyril Neville's conga drumming on *The Wild Tchoupitoulas*'.[91] This is not to suggest that African percussion had ever ceased to be a force in New Orleans music, but that this strong surfacing made it obvious that Mardi Gras Indian music was a major and original example of that branch of African derived urban dance music that expressed its ethos in spiritually and politically significant lyrics.

The Nevilles have performed consistently and spectacularly as a band since *The Wild Tchoupitoulas* was cut in a New Orleans studio in 1976. They have made critically praised but little known records like *Fiyou on the Bayou*, yet it was not until 1989 that the Neville Brothers as a unit were to find worldwide acclaim as the most fascinating of New Orleans bands. The popularity of the album *Yellow Moon* involved unprecedented touring and exposure for the Neville Brothers and the concerns that fire their music. The single 'Sister Rosa', taken off the album, is a reminder of the crucial role played by Rosa Parks in catalysing the desegregation of buses.[92] On 'Wild Injuns' the Mardi Gras Indians are saluted in appropriate style, welding Indian Chief delivery and Caribbean rhythms with a backing redolent of New Orleans brass bands. The lyrics on this album have been called 'investigative poetry of the highest order'.[93]

'Brother Blood', the opening track on the Neville Brothers' album *Brothers Keeper* (1990), has 'voodoo influenced' tenor sax solos from Charles Neville and he elaborated on his inspiration in his vocals: 'I've got drums of the jungle, drums of the street, drums of the Spirit.' Earlier in this same number, Art and Aaron Neville stress the role of music in the struggle to cross political oceans and climb 'impossible mountains'. More obviously political issues, from Angola to the Ayatollah, appear on 'Sons and Daughters', where there is stress on evasion of responsibility: 'you have freedom of speech as long as you don't say too much . . . we are all running thinking we can hide – but sooner or later we're going to realise we are going to meet up with the truth face to face'. Cutting through politicians' rhetoric to the truth is the Nevilles' aim on this record. While not pretending to provide all the answers, they stimulate a search for the right questions and generate a mood of disquiet that could lead to change.

Charles has described their music as 'New Orleans rhythm and blues with a mixture of other elements including funk, reggae, African and voodoo'. Blues he saw as 'fundamental', and voodoo as an especially New Orleans African survival. He believes that 'it is specific use of voodoo rhythms associated with dancing and laughter that give the Neville brothers their infectious quality and get even the most staid audiences on their feet'. He went further and said that 'the rhythms we play express our love of life, our love of people and our love of music. What we play is not contrived. We play it from our hearts'.[94]

Just as rooted in New Orleans multi-stranded musical tradition are singers like Irma Thomas, Wanda Rouzan and Lillian Boutté who link the past with the present and move easily from blues to jazz and from rhythm and blues to soul. 'I have been singing since I was two years old', says Irma Thomas, but she had to wait until she was a teenager to have her first hit with a punchy blues called 'Don't Mess With My Man'. She began to work with the 'inspirational' Allen Toussaint and had a succession of blues, ballads, rhythm and blues and soul numbers that climbed national charts. ' "Wish someone would care" was the song that meant the most to me – it was the story of my life.'[95] It was the authentic story of a life full of deprivation but never without hope.

Wanda Rouzan is equally adventurous, and creates a fresh fusion of all the musical influences she absorbed as a Creole who 'grew up second lining in the Seventh Ward'. Her dark, sinewy voice sounds just as effective on her self-penned anti-Vietnam 1960s hit 'Men of War' as it does on the jazz-inflected numbers she sings in the nineties at Marie Laveau's on Decatur St. She believes that: 'New Orleans music is such a gumbo – it's not just any one sound – it's a combination of jazz, blues, gospel and rhythm and blues. *You cant find that beat, that particular backbeat anywhere else in the world.* It's got you on your toes. It's just something that's very special.'[96]

Lillian Boutté comes from a long line of Creole New Orleanians who can trace their ancestry through thirteen generations to African, American Indian and European roots. She is proud of the complexity of the lineage from which she springs as well as the music that is an intrinsic part of New Orleans' political life. As Louis Armstrong's successor to the official title of New Orleans Ambassador of Jazz, she sees music as a force for peace and harmony. She believes that music is capable of 'promoting positive feelings that can lead to change'. She is convinced that music can lift individuals and whole groups of people out of a mood of despair and empower them to resist prejudice.[97]

Perhaps the most politically orientated of all the contemporary women singing in New Orleans is Charles Neville's daughter, Charmaine. Charmaine has a wide vocal range and uses it brilliantly to project a free-ranging variety of emotions and ideas. When interviewed about the interaction of politics and music she was very positive that 'music and politics definitely go together because that's the only way that you can sometimes get your message across and try to help people. If you say what you mean in a song, because it's a universal thing, people will listen whereas not everyone will listen to you make a speech.' She went on to say that America 'should stop trying to tell other countries what to do and . . . take care of what's happening here'. She is 'sickened' by the kind of interference which kills indigenous culture and feels it is up to people within the US to persuade the government to run their energies into 'feeding the children'. She hopes 'music' can 'be the healer' and knows it can at least raise awareness and help people confront problems. 'Music touches everyone's lives and is the one thing that cannot be totally controlled.' Using her extraordinary vocal range, she can scat, growl, imitate instruments (or Louis Armstrong) with startling facility. She bends and stretches notes with original and resonating flair. She suffuses her songs with commitment and passion. Her concern about people and politics fires her music with an incandescent urgency. She wrote a song in 1991 juxtaposing the Gulf War with the scandalous level of poverty and homelessness within the US. The recurring phrase 'Tell Me

What You Feel' refers to the insensitivity of a TV reporter questioning a newly bereaved Iraqi child. It is a number that raises vital issues and provokes a positive response without giving facile answers. When interviewed in March 1991, Charmaine expressed the hope that music could change the world.[98]

A rap band run by her teenage sons, Def Generation, wrote and recorded a strongly anti-Duke song. When David Duke, the ex-Ku Klux Klansman, was in the Louisiana legislature and threatening to run for Governor, opposition in the city did indeed centre on song as well as political activity. On 9 June 1990, the New Orleans African American newspaper *The Louisiana Weekly* published 'Kajun Ku Klux Klan', written by 'various artists':

> You niggers listen now
> I'm gonna tell you how
> To keep from getting tortured when the Klan is on the loose.
>
> Stay at home at night and lock your doors up tight
> Don't go outside or else you'll find those crosses burn
> Now, I know you won't believe it,
> So I'm gonna tell you why the Kajun Ku Klux Klan
> Is gonna get you by and by,
> I'm warning you that when I'm through,
> You're gonna change your tune.

The song goes on to describe how Duke threatens those who fight segregation 'since they passed the Civil Rights'.[99] Humour once more allied itself with anger to oppose racism through song in New Orleans.

Referring to a much earlier manifestation of racism, Gerri Hirshey has pointed out that 'it is in the city with one of the most infamous auction blocks in American history, New Orleans, that more kinds of black music, soul among them, survive, intact and undisturbed by the vagaries of marketing and record charts' than anywhere else in the United States.[100] From its African origins New Orleans developed a range of music wide enough to accompany and comment on every aspect of life. The songs reached out and profoundly affected the entire nation. Written and sung by African Americans from New Orleans, they encoded the diversity and common cultural core that united America as a whole.

Notes

1. Baraka A (LeRoi Jones) and Baraka I 1987 *The music: reflections on jazz and blues*. William Morrow & Co, New York, pp 262, 280.
2. McClendon W H 1976 Black music: sound and feeling for Black liberation. *Black Scholar* 7 (5): 20.
3. Hall G M 1992 *Africans in colonial Louisiana: the development of Afro-Creole culture in the eighteenth century*. Louisiana State University Press, Baton Rouge, p 413.
4. Floyd Jr S 1988 The wellspring of black music: New Orleans, Louisiana. *Black Music Research Journal* 8 (1): 1.
5. Baraka 1987 p 277.
6. Cable G W The dance in Place Congo. Rpt in Katz B (ed) 1969 *The social implications of early Negro music in the United States*. Arno Press, New York, p 37; Latrobe B A 1951 *Impressions respecting New Orleans: diary and sketches 1818–1820*, ed Samuel Wilson Jr. Columbia University Press, New York, pp 49–51; Fortier A 1888 Customs and superstitions in Louisiana. *Journal of American Folklore* 1 (July): 136–7.
7. Hall 1992.
8. Coolen M T 1991 Senegambian influences on Afro-American musical culture. *Black Music Research Journal* 11 (1): 1–18.
9. Hall 1992 pp 43, 118.
10. Epstein D 1977 *Sinful tunes and spirituals: Black folk music to the Civil War* (3 vols). University of Illinois Press, Urbana, vol 3 p 90.
11. Christian M 1980 A Black history of Louisiana p 2. Unpublished addition to typescript, Marcus Christian Papers, Archives and Manuscript Division, Earl K. Long Library, University of New Orleans, Lakefront, New Orleans.
12. Latrobe 1951 pp 49–51.
13. du Pratz L 1774 *The history of Louisiana or of the western parts of Virginia and Carolina*. T. Becket, London, pp 380, 384, 387; Warner C W 1904 *Studies in the south and west with comments on Canada*. American Publishing Co, Hartford, Conn, pp 75–82; Epstein 1977 pp 91–5.
14. Wade R 1964 *Slavery in the cities: the south 1820–1860*. Oxford University Press, New York, p 158.
15. *New Orleans Daily Delta*. 10 Sept 1854; Johnson J 1991 New Orleans Congo Square: an urban setting for early Afro-American culture formation. *Louisiana History* 22 (Spring): 124.
16. New Orleans *Bee*. 2 May 1850.
17. Epstein 1977 pp 228, 220.
18. *New Orleans Daily Delta*. 12 June 1846.

19. Christian 1980 pp 319–22.
20. Genovese E 1975 *Roll Jordan Roll: the world the slaves made.* Andre Deutsch, London, p 411.
21. Christian 1980 pp 323–4; Bracey Jr J H, Meier A, Rudwick E (eds) 1971 *American slavery: the question of resistance.* Wadsworth Publishing Co, Belmont, Ca, p 31.
22. Southern E 1981 African intentions in Afro-American Music. In Heartz D, Wadee B (eds) 1981 *Report of the 12th Berkeley Congress 1977.* American Musicological Society, Barenreiter Kasel, pp 53–98; Oliver P 1970 *Savannah syncopators: African retentions in the blues.* Studio Vista, London, pp 10–101; Roberts J S 1973 *Black music of two worlds.* Allen Lane, London, pp 3–15, 21–2, 145–91; Chernoff J M 1980 *African rhythm and African sensibility: aesthetics and social action in African musical idiom.* University of Chicago Press, Chicago, pp 27–39; Lovell Jr J 1972 *Black song: the forge and the home: the story of how the Afro-American spiritual was hammered out.* Macmillan, New York, pp 66, 42–3, 46; Evans D 1987 The origins of the blues and its relationship to African music. In Droixhe D, Keifer K (eds) 1987 *Images african de l'antiquité au xxe siècle.* Lange, Frankfurt, pp 129–41.
23. Creole was used originally to describe anyone born in Louisiana, whether of French, Spanish or African ancestry or intermixture. Gradually the word assumed connotations of colonial French or Spanish genealogy and those with African roots were defined as 'Creoles of Color'. In the twentieth century Creole is most often used to denote a mixture of French or Spanish and African. In the slave city Creoles of Color were considered to be the elite of free black society. Many were slaveowners and they collectively owned more slaves than free black people in any other American city. The society of Creoles of Color was complex and culturally creative but their family structure was precluded from being exclusive by a similar imbalance of the sexes to that which characterized New Orleans slaves. The effect of this imbalance was compounded by a reverse pattern in white society: while Creoles of Color had an excess of women, white society had an excess of men. The likelihood that light-skinned Creole women would have relationships or even marriages with white men became a reality between 1790 and 1865. Although theoretically illegal, marriages between black and white did take place in *ante bellum* New Orleans. It was nonetheless more common for the wealthier white man to have a Creole mistress than a Creole wife. Under a system that came to be known as 'placage', white young men would attend the quadroon balls and select a young female Creole of Color whom he established in a home of her own.

24. Southern E 1971 *The music of Black Americans: a history*. W W Norton & Co, New York, pp 79–82, 141.
25. Rousseve C B 1937 *The negro in Louisiana: aspects of its history and literature*. Xavier University Press, New Orleans, p 66.
26. Whitfield I T 1969 *Louisiana French folk songs* 2nd edn. Dover, New York, pp 140–2; Borders F E 1988 Researching Creole and Cajun music in New Orleans. *Black Music Research Journal* **8** (1): 18.
27. Sullivan L 1988 Composers of Color of nineteenth century New Orleans: the history behind the music. *Black Music Research Journal* **8** (1): 54–66; Le Jeune E 1919 Creole folk songs. *Louisiana Historical Quarterly* **2** (3): 454–7.
28. Southern 1971 pp 77, 139.
29. New Orleans *Louisiana Advertiser*. 3 May 1822.
30. Boles J B 1984 *Black Southerners 1619–1869*. University Press of Kentucky, Lexington, p 185.
31. Jackson G 1991 The way we do: a preliminary investigation of the African roots of African American performance. *Black American Literature Forum* **25** (1): 15–16; Silber I (ed) 1964 *Soldier songs and home-front ballads of the Civil War*. Oak Publications, New York, p 41; Jackson B (ed) 1967 *The negro and his folklore in nineteenth century periodicals*. University of Texas Press, Austin, p 71.
32. Cable G W 1886 Creole slave songs. *The Century Magazine* **31** (February): 816, 814, 816–18.
33. Spitzer N 1976 *Zodico: Louisiana creole music*. Rounder Somerville, Mass, p 9.
34. Blassingame J 1973 *The negro in New Orleans*. University of Chicago Press, Chicago, p 25.
35. Lovell 1972 pp 116, 147, 390–1, 312; Nancy Willard to Micajah Wilkinson, 28 May 1861. Micajah Wilkinson Papers, Louisiana State University, Baton Rouge; L.C. Causey to R.J. Causey, 19 Nov 1863. Causey Papers, Louisiana State University, Baton Rouge; Messner W E 1975 Black violence and white response: Louisiana 1862. *Journal of Southern History* **61**: 22–3; Sitterson J C 1953 *Sugar country. The cane sugar industry in the South 1753–1950*. University Press of Kentucky, Lexington, p 22.
36. Cuney-Hare M 1974 *Negro musicians and their music*. Da Capo Press, New York, p 267.
37. Fisher M M 1983 *Negro slave songs in the United States*. Cornell University Press, Ithaca, NY, pp 47–173; Allen W F, Pickard C, Garrison L M 1929 *Slave songs of the United States*. Peter Smith, New York, passim; Higginson T W 1867 Negro spirituals. *Atlantic Monthly* **19** (June): 685–94; Barton W E 1898 Old plantation

hymns. *New England Magazine* **19** (December): 669–78; Barton W E 1899 Hymns of the slave and the freedman. *New England Magazine* **20** (January): 706–13; Johnson J W, Johnson J R 1926 *The book of American negro spirituals.* Viking Press, New York, pp 10–26.

38. Bechet S 1960 *Treat it gentle.* Cassell, London, pp 47–8.

39. Sheet music of songs mainly published by A.E. Blackmar, 167 Canal Street, New Orleans and collected in the Sheet Music Folio Collection of the Chicago Historical Society; Spaeth S 1948 *A history of popular music in America.* Random House, New York, pp 138–52; New Orleans *Daily Picayune.* 22 May 1842; New Orleans *Bee.* 23 May 1842; Wittke C 1930 *Tambo and bones: a history of the American minstrel stage.* University of North Carolina Press, Durham, pp 17–18; Mathews B 1915 The rise and fall of negro minstrelsy. *Scribners Magazine* **57** (June): 755.

40. Edet E 1976 One hundred years of Black protest music. *Black Scholar* (July-Aug): 42; Walker W T 1979 *Somebody's calling my name: Black sacred music and social change.* Judson Press, Valley Forge, Pa, pp 58–60; Edet 1976 p 39.

41. Kmen H 1966 *Music in New Orleans.* Louisiana State University Press, Baton Rouge, p 226; Cuney-Hare 1974 p 266.

42. Cuney-Hare 1974 pp 81–2, 267; Barton W E 1969 Hymns of the slave and the freedom. In Katz 1969 p 101.

43. Winters J D 1963 *The Civil War in Louisiana.* Louisiana State University Press, Baton Rouge, pp 209–312; Rousseve C B 1937 *The negro in Louisiana: aspects of his history and literature.* Xavier University Press, New Orleans, pp 103–47.

44. Trotter J M 1878 *Music and some highly musical people.* Lee and Shepard, Boston, pp 50–338.

45. Schaeffer W J, Allen R B 1977 *Brass bands and New Orleans jazz.* Louisiana State University Press, Baton Rouge, pp 9–12.

46. The freedman's song. Published by A.E. Blackmar, 167 Canal Street, New Orleans, 1866. Sheet Music Folio Collection Chicago Historical Association.

47. Spedale Jr R 1984 *Jazz New Orleans: a guide to jazz in New Orleans.* Hope Publications, New Orleans, p 125.

48. Oster H 1975 *Living country blues.* Minerva Press, New York, pp 12–13.

49. Bechet 1960 p 50.

50. Evans D 1982 *Big road blues: tradition and creativity in the folk blues.* University of California Press, Berkeley, p 44; Oliver P 1984 *Songsters and saints: vocal traditions on race records.* Cambridge University Press, Cambridge, p 257; Marquis D 1978 *In Search of Buddy Bolden.* Da Capo, New York, pp 109–11.

51. Christian Mend The historic case of *Plessy* v. *Ferguson.* Marcus Christian Papers.
52. Baraka A (LeRoi Jones) 1963 *Blues people.* William Morrow & Co, New York, p 80.
53. Palmer R 1981 *Deep blues.* Macmillan, London, p 242; John Lee Hooker, interviewed by Mary Ellison, 10 July 1988; Buddy Guy, interviewed by Mary Ellison, 19 March 1987.
54. Lomax A 1952 *Mister Jelly Roll: the fortunes of Jelly Roll Morton, New Orleans creole and 'inventor of jazz'.* Cassell, London, pp 53–5, 29, 33.
55. Oliver 1984 p 260.
56. Shapiro N, Hentoff N 1955 *Hear me talkin to ya: the story of jazz by the men who made it.* Holt, Rinehart & Winston, New York, p 19; Lomax 1952 pp 269–91.
57. Shaeffer 1977 p 55.
58. Barlow W 1989 *Looking up at down: the emergence of blues culture.* Temple University Press, Philadelphia, p 184.
59. Ramsey Jr F, Smith C E (eds) 1957 *Jazzmen.* Sidgwick and Jackson, London, p 37.
60. Baraka 1987 p 263.
61. Tirro F 1977 *Jazz: a history.* W W Norton & Co, New York, pp 125–6.
62. Oakley G 1976 *The Devil's music: a history of the blues.* BBC, London, p 125.
63. Johnson L *Historical recordings 1924–1932* (2 vols). Matchbox MS.
64. Ellison R 1972 *Shadow and act.* Random House, New York, pp 94, 257.
65. Benston K 1975 Tragic aspects of the blues. *Phylon* **36** (2): 170–1.
66. Oliver P, Harrison M, Bolcom W 1986 *The new grove gospel, blues and jazz.* Macmillan, London, p 143.
67. Jeansonne G 1992 Huey Long and racism. *Louisiana History* **33** (3): 265–82.
68. Oliver P 1990 *Blues fell this morning: meaning in the blues.* Cambridge University Press, Cambridge, p 35.
69. Collins L 1989 *Oh! didn't he ramble: the life story of Lee Collins* ed Gillis F J, Miller J W. University of Illinois Press, Urbana, p 61; Foster P, Stoddard T 1971 *The autobiography of Pops Foster.* University of California Press, Berkeley, pp 15–16, 92.
70. Barlow 1989 p 260.
71. Oliver 1990 p 296.
72. Gert zur Heide K 1970 *Deep South piano: the story of Little Brother Montgomery.* Studio Vista, London, pp 10–27.
73. Goreau L 1975 *Just Mahalia, baby.* Word Books, Waco, Texas, pp 3–56.

74. *Mean Mothers: Independent Women's Blues.* Rosetta Records RRI 300.
75. Roy Brown *Hard Luck Blues.* Gusto K3-1130.
76. Hannusch J 1985 *I hear you knockin': the sound of New Orleans rhythm and blues.* Swallow, Ville Platte, La, p 71.
77. Overton J H 1942 Radio Address, 28 August. Box 1819, Ellender Papers, Tulane University, New Orleans.
78. Segregation Blues. Marcus Christian Papers.
79. Winner L The sound of New Orleans. In Miller J (ed) 1980 *Rolling Stone illustrated history of rock and roll.* Rolling Stone, New York, p 35.
80. Gillet C 1983 *Sound of the city: the rise of rock and roll.* Souvenir Press, London, p 139.
81. Trick B 1972 Second line jump. *Jazz and Blues* 2 (6): 13.
82. Berry J, Foose J, Jones T 1986 *Up from the cradle of jazz: New Orleans music since World War II.* University of Georgia Press, Athens, pp 90–1.
83. Snooks Eaglin, interviewed by Mary Ellison, 23 June 1990.
84. Earl King, interviewed by Mary Ellison, 23 June 1990.
85. Berry 1986 p 134; Broven J 1977 *Walking to New Orleans: the story of New Orleans rhythm and blues.* Flyright, Bexhill-on-Sea, pp 116–19, 174–6.
86. Martinez M 1983 Black Indians: their heritage is rooted in New Orleans. *National Leader* (24 March): 18–20; Bryan V H 1987 Evocations of place and culture. *Louisiana Literature* 4 (2): 51.
87. Pete Hardy, interviewed by Mary Ellison, 29 July 1988; Tuddy Montana, interviewed by Jason Berry, 13 March 1982. New Orleans Ethnic Music Research Project, Hogan Jazz Archive, Tulane University, New Orleans.
88. Clarence Dalcour and Lolet Boutté, interviewed by Mary Ellison, 24 April 1987.
89. Larry Bannock, interviewed by Mary Ellison, 29 July 1988.
90. Charles Neville, interviewed by Mary Ellison, 7 Aug 1988; *The Wild Magnolias*, Barclay 80529; *The Wild Tchoupitoulas*, Antilles TM/Island AN-7052.
91. Berry 1986 p 236.
92. Neville Brothers *Yellow Moon*, A & M SP 5240.
93. Sinclair J 1988 The Nevilles come home. *Wavelength* (May): 43.
94. Charles Neville, interviewed by Mary Ellison, 7 Aug 1988.
95. Irma Thomas, interviewed by Mary Ellison, 4 July 1989.
96. Wanda Rouzan, interviewed by Mary Ellison, 24 April 1987.
97. Lillian Boutté, interviewed by Mary Ellison, 1 Aug 1990.
98. Charmaine Neville, interviewed by Mary Ellison, 20 Sept 1990; 29–30 March 1991.

99. Def Generation *Medicine*, Endangered Species ES1701-4. Various Artists 1990 Kajun Ku Klux Klan. *Louisiana Weekly* **64** (41): 1.
100. Hirshey G 1984 *Nowhere to run: the story of soul music.* Macmillan, London, p 352.

7 Writing history: Frederick Jackson Turner and the deconstruction of American history

Alun Munslow

The cultural critic Fredric Jameson once claimed historians while they were writing must think 'self-consciously about their own thought', to be both 'conscious and self-conscious' at one and the same time.[1] Although historians have always been aware that their reconstruction of the past can serve social, ideological and state ends, it is the nature of the discipline to which Jameson refers.[2] The philosopher of history Hayden White has also argued that historians must deal with the relationship between the form and content of history.[3] While every written history contains within itself a philosophy of history, the latter foregrounds its conceptual apparatus, whereas history proper conceals it within its own narrative structure.[4] White, following the French cultural critic Michel Foucault, also suggests that the act of writing history helps create social structures of power and group awareness. If we accept that in acquiring their conception of the world individuals always belong to a particular grouping which, as Antonio Gramsci says, 'share the same mode of thinking and acting',[5] then the reconstruction of the past, like every cultural practice, is an ideological act that is socially produced, and it follows that the act of writing a history is central to the process of cultural formation.[6]

In describing the culturally formative role of the historian, Gramsci argues that 'creating a new culture does not mean one's own individual "original" discoveries', rather it ' ... means the diffusion in a critical form of truths already discovered, their "socialisation" as it were, and even making them the basis of . . . intellectual and moral order'.[7] It follows that if a popular historian's attempt to constitute a shared sense of community originates with the dominant social formation, written history may reconstruct a popularly understood past for consumption in the present through the historical narrative.[8]

American history writing came of age in the late nineteenth century at a time when a new business order was being established. It was a new order rooted in a fully articulated set of enterprise values based on individualism, the free market, the gospels of wealth and success, the scientism of evolution, and the philosophy of pragmatism. The new group of professional American historians that emerged in the years from the 1890s to the First World War – the so-called Progressive era – set about meeting the demand for the creation of a new and national American identity.[9] Accepting the argument that every national culture requires a history, even one that is untrue or mythological, the leading professional historian of the era, Frederick Jackson Turner, produced an interpretation of American cultural formation which confounds the ideal that history as it happened, and as it is written, can ever match.[10] Turner took the myth of the American garden and turned it into a useful bourgeois history that would account for both the rise of the new order and explain American exceptionalism.[11] From a practical point of view, in order to be acceptable to his peers his history had to be conceptualized in the form of the newest historical methods. Turner readily accepted the fashion for the scientific reconstruction of the past, claiming that history in general was a social science, and his history of the American frontier experience in particular was occupied with the organization, control and measurement of space.[12]

Space and time

Turner's re-formation of the American historical imagination is significant insofar as he did not accept that Americans could only locate themselves in time.[13] Instead he described America's historical development by reference to the exceptional and culturally determining power of its frontier experience. In this way he offered America a new nationalizing historical and social theory. In the words of postmodernist geographer Edward Soja, he rejected a 'subordination of space to time that obscures geographical interpretations of the changeability of the social world and intrudes upon every level of theoretical discourse'.[14] Through his definition of western space he created an American nationality that would serve to sustain the power of the emergent industrial bourgeois classes.

In his reassessment of space and time Turner imagined space constructed as a lived experience and therefore socially produced.[15] He believed space gave a particular form to social activities and ideology.[16] From 1892 to 1910 Turner was professor of American history at Wisconsin and right at the start of his career was invited to present a paper at the special meeting of the American Historical Association's Chicago World's Fair convention in 1893. The 33-year-old Turner put together an essay on 'The Significance of the Frontier in American History', a paper which made him one of the most celebrated of American historians. His simple yet potent hypothesis was that the 'free land' of the West and the process of its settlement explained American development.[17]

Turner's conception of the West connected the determining force of space to American economic development and its institutions.[18] As he said in his 1893 lecture, 'Behind institutions, behind constitutional forms and modifications, lie the vital forces that call these organs into life and shape them to meet changing conditions.' Consequently the West, but particularly the frontier experience, was 'a form of society', rather than just a place.[19] This argument is found more recently in Michel Foucault's treatment of the spatial imagination. Foucault claims that a certain kind of external space in which we live, and which he calls a heterotopia, 'draws us out of ourselves' and erodes not only 'our lives, our time and our history' but in the process constitutes us as subject individuals.[20]

For Foucault, space is defined as a site or intersection of power relationships. Thus defined, there are two types of space. First there are the imaginary sites, which are analogous to the real yet contradict reality. Utopias are examples of such spaces. They represent society in its perfect form, or society turned upside down. The second site of power relations is again constituted as a counter-site where all other sites in a given culture are simultaneously represented, but are spaces that actually exist. These are Foucault's heterotopias – real places that exert a powerful and direct interpellative influence over the individual, constituting him or her as a subject.

The systematic process of reading society for these sites of power Foucault calls heterotopology. The first principle of heterotopology is that all cultures create heterotopias. The second is that heterotopias can simultaneously possess several different cultural significations and functions. For Turner initially it was the American frontier, and later American sections that were heterotopias. At first it was the frontier that was a site of new relationships but not by any means a utopia. As a heterotopia it was a real place and socially produced, a created space for the exercise of power.[21] It was clear to Turner, as it was later to Foucault, that space, knowledge and power are connected. 'A whole history remains to be written of spaces', said Foucault in 1980, 'which would at the same time be the history of powers . . . from the great strategies of geopolitics to the little tactics of the habitat'.[22] In effect the most substantial contribution to this history had already been made by Turner almost a century earlier. How, then, did Turner actually constitute the frontier experience as a heterotopia in order to create a new sense of nationhood in American historiography and the popular imagination?

In his search for a relevant past upon which to build a popular national culture Turner created a spatial discourse which matched his preferred vision of America as an exceptional historical creation.[23] Turner supported his thesis by a narrative explanation that had two aspects, namely the role of the pioneer, and the peculiar determining power of the frontier itself.[24] Given the unambiguously literary turn of his 1893 historical narrative, Turner's plot is established by reference to a series of past events made understandable as a kind of story, recounted through the culturally provided myth of the West.[25]

Myth and American history

In seeking an explanation for American exceptionalism Turner's historical narrative fits Robert Scholes and Robert Kellog's

definition of myth narrative as 'a traditional story', in effect 'a
traditional plot' which can be transmitted from epoch to epoch.[26]
The most cogent analysis of modern myth is that provided by
Roland Barthes who finds myth to be a process whereby the
figurative, iconic or metaphoric intersects with the social context,
acting as a way of containing social conflict. For Barthes a
historical myth is built from pre-existing semiological chains
equivalent to pre-existing chains of cultural meaning. Consequently it operates at a deep structural level working within a
semiological system. Barthes's interpretation builds on Gaston
Bachelard's distinction between image and ideology.[27] As Barthes
says, a 'second-order sign system' or 'metalanguage' works via
the process of 'hide and seek' simultaneously to reveal and
conceal its signifying function within the total sign system.[28] That
which is a sign in the first system becomes a signifier in the
second level. So there are two semiological systems in a staggered
relationship, the first a linguistic system, and the second a mythic
(ideological) system produced by it. This second or metalanguage
level is the one in which nationalist historians like Turner speak
mythically about the first. The arbitrary relationship between the
signifier and the signified in the Frontier Thesis is the essence of
the frontier as heterotopia and is drawn from America's cultural
well of the frontier myth. In effect Turner takes the signifier 'the
West' to be signified as 'free land', producing the arbitrary sign
'Frontier'. 'The West' as signifier is taken then to be synonymous
with America's unique experience of freedom signified as 'free
land' – Turner's assumption operating at the semiological or
second-order metalanguage level.

At this mythic or second-order metalanguage level the sign of
the first linguistic system, 'the Frontier', now becomes the
signifier of the second order-sign system, with its Turnerian
signification being 'the Frontier Thesis'. The second-order or
metalanguage sign is the bourgeois nationalizing myth of
American exceptionalism. As Turner argues from the outset,
because of frontier 'free land' America possessed a 'perennial
rebirth' and was continually reinventing itself.[29] The laws of
'social evolution' or 'social development' that Turner appealed to
in his lecture are to be viewed as simple but potent myths
constructed at the metalanguage level of the American social and
political imagination.

The role of the pioneer-hero

By utilizing his social science training Turner determined to discover both the true character of the American pioneer and thereby describe American national development. In pursuit of these aims, however, his pioneer is immediately placed in an ambivalent position because of the Frontier Thesis's central proposition stated at the beginning of the 1893 lecture: 'The existence of an area of free land, its continuous recession and the advance of American settlement westward explain American development.'[30] In giving America's national origins in the 'free land' of the West, Turner invested such land with the power not only to shape America's political, economic and cultural institutions, but also to create Turner's pioneer-hero.[31]

Operating as a socially constructed and ideologically inter-pellative space, at the metalanguage level the heterotopic frontier constituted 'the forces dominating American character'.[32] The boldness of this narrative vision lay in his claim that 'American social development has been continually beginning over again on the frontier' simply because of the signification of the West as 'free land'.[33] Turner's deconstruction of the American past meant rejecting the European-biased Teutonic origins theory dominating American history, offering instead 'a steady growth of independence on American lines' which directly related the 'free land' of the frontier and the exceptional character of American nationality. This imaginary relationship was ultimately anthropo-morphized in the pioneer-hero.

> The frontier is the line of most rapid and effective Americanisation.
> The wilderness masters the colonist. It finds him a European in dress, industries, tools, modes of travel and thought. It takes him from the railroad car and puts him in the birch canoe. It strips off the garments of civilisation and arrays him in the hunting shirt and the moccasin. It puts him in the log cabin of the Cherokee and Iroquois . . . In short, at the frontier the environment is at first too strong for the man. He must accept the conditions which it furnishes, or perish. [But] Little by little he transforms the wilderness, but the outcome is not the old Europe, not simply the development of Germanic germs . . . The fact is, that here is a new product that is American . . . Thus the advance of the frontier has meant a steady movement away from the influence of Europe, a steady growth of independence on American lines.[34]

Turner's geographical determinism is modified here, however, by the power of the pioneer-hero. Turner finds himself with a nationalizing frontier, but is driven by the dominant contemporary ideology of individualism to create a pioneer-hero who transcends his world of experience.

The pioneer-hero had perforce to become the archetypal American because it was on the frontier that the new race of Americans was created. A distinctive set of national personality traits, as befits an exceptional nation, were thus endowed. Turner delineates them as

> That coarseness and strength combined with acuteness and inquisitiveness; that practical, inventive turn of mind, quick to find expedients; that masterful grasp of material things, lacking in the artistic but powerful to effect great ends; that restless, nervous energy; that dominant individualism, working for good and for evil, and withal that buoyancy and exuberance which comes with freedom – these are the traits of the frontier, or traits called out elsewhere because of the existence of the frontier.[35]

This original pioneer conception as it appeared in the 1893 lecture constantly re-emerged in his later works, like 'The Problem of the West' published in an 1896 issue of *Atlantic Monthly*. Here he again emphasized the imperative of the frontier to constitute the pioneer-hero as a subject while offering a constant rebirth to the nation. The West signified through its 'free land' thus created a 'new political species' because it was itself 'a phase of social organisation' which as it 'passed across the continent' successfully 'transmitted frontier traits and ideals' to the Americans on the Atlantic coast. As he said: 'The forest clearings have been the seed plots of American character.'[36]

By 1904 Turner had located 'the forces by which the composite nationality of the United States has been created'.[37] With this belief firmly in mind in his 1910 presidential address to the American Historical Association Turner re-emphasized America's frontier-inspired individualism, claiming it created America's unique democracy, produced wealth, and established an 'imperial republic with dependencies and protectorates . . . a new world power, with a potential voice in the problems of Europe, Asia and Africa'.[38] However, looking back from the vantage point of 1910 he had to acknowledge that 'the old pioneer individualism is disappearing', noting 'the forces of social combination are manifesting themselves as never before'. He recognized that the self-made man had become 'in popular speech, the coal baron, the steel king, the oil king, the cattle king, the railroad magnate, the master of high finance, the monarch of the trusts'. All this had 'come out of the individualist pioneer democracy of America in the course of competitive evolution'. While the frontier had created the pioneer-hero, in Turner's mythic history the pioneer had been transmuted into the entrepreneur-hero. Just as the pioneer-hero had been mastered by the wilderness and created over, so the new industrial pioneer was in his turn recreated by corporate forces.[39]

Although loath to admit that the inevitable consequence of the individualistic pioneer-hero was unbridled corporate capitalism, Turner nevertheless saw the robber barons as still frontiersmen 'compelled by the constructive fever in their veins . . . to seek new avenues of action and power, to chop new clearings, to find new trails, to expand the horizon of the nation's activity, and to extend the scope of their dominion'.[40] As a progressive Turner viewed this development with alarm and then with a resignation that had grown with the power of the enterprise class, and had been expressed in his 1896 *Atlantic Monthly* article when he said: 'The striking and peculiar characteristic of American society is that it is not so much a democracy as a huge commercial company for the discovery, cultivation, and capitalisation of its enormous territory.' Turner claimed the 'free land' of the West meant 'America is like a vast work-shop, over the door of which is printed in blazing characters "No admittance here except on business" '.[41] This was the contemporary essence of American exceptionalism.

Written history and American nationalism

Like all modern myths, the ultimate function of this frontier-inspired myth-history is ideological, a means to contain the tragedies and tensions of the new order, notably imperialism, racism, monopoly and economic inequality. This containment was achieved through Turner's integration of pioneer-hero traits into those of national character – an 'inventive turn of mind', 'restless, nervous energy', 'coarseness and strength' and 'masterful grasp of material things' – which Turner accepted were inevitably translated into the gospels of success and wealth. The Frontier Thesis thus attempted to create an ahistorical uniqueness for America which contradicted the commonly accepted notion that history is created as a process of contemporary social change. While Turner might at one level there disapprove of the robber baronage, they were, he had to admit, the transhistorical sons of the frontier, possessing its spirit and experience. It was this determining power of the frontier which constituted the second important aspect of his myth-history and which revealed the conservative nature of his theory of slow-paced social change.

For Turner, the determining power of the frontier ensured American nationality and American exceptionalism. Because Turner believed in 'the peculiar importance of American history' as a mode of contemporary social investigation which could reveal 'processes of social development'[42] he was sure he had discovered the laws of social change in his connection of space and time in his power/knowledge equation.[43]

That American nationality as determined by the heterotopic frontier experience was the site of cultural power-struggle is evidenced among other things in the causes of the Civil War, which for Turner was 'a conflict between the Lake and Prairie plainsmen, on the one side, and the Gulf plainsmen, on the other, for the control of the Mississippi Valley'.[44] His social theory was thus also predicated on the complex relationship of the pioneer-hero in struggle with the frontier but which was this time transmuted into a sectional conflict. But again this was taken by Turner as further evidence for his composite American national character. Turner's nationalist teleology derived, ultimately, from his combination of time and space, frontier and section.

> We need to investigate the forces by which the composite nationality of the United States has been created, the process by which these different sections have been welded into such a degree of likeness that the United States now constitutes a measurably homogeneous people in certain important respects. We need to study the rise and growth of the intellectual character of the people, as shown in their literature and art, in connection with the social and economic conditions of the various periods of our history. In short we need a natural history of the American spirit.[45]

The central argument underpinning this statement of the American national spirit was, of course, his constant iteration of the determining power of 'the free lands of the United States' which he insisted 'have been the most important single factor in explaining our development'.[46]

Because in the end the Frontier Thesis is reductionist – reduced to its essence 'the existence of an area of free land'[47] – the 'free land' of the frontier invented not just the personality of the pioneer, but also American democracy, values, and national institutions. Turner's social theory emerging from the organic nature of the frontier experience chimed well with the dominant evolutionary biologism of the age. Turner's evolutionism produced a particular ideological inflection in his work that actually undermined his apparent progressive radicalism. In the 1893 lecture the tone for the slow and evolutionary opening of the frontier was set with his use of an extended simile: 'The United States lies like a huge page in the history of society. Line by line as we read this continental page from West to East we find the record of social evolution.'[48]

The tenor of evolutionary change is amplified with his overblown description of the growth of civilization in America akin to a bizarre process which is at once a wave-like development and also geologic, biologic and organic:

> Thus civilisation in America has followed the arteries made by geology, pouring an ever richer tide through them ... It is like the steady growth of a complex nervous system for the originally simple, inert continent. If one would understand why we are today one nation, rather than a collection of isolated states, he must study this economic and social consolidation of the country. In this progress from savage conditions lie topics for the evolutionist.[49]

The evolutionary explanation of frontier-inspired change in the 1893 lecture and 1896 article matured in later years as he translated his mythic laws of historical change into laws of social evolution, at the same time moving his emphasis away from the individual and toward a more corporate view of American culture but a view still constrained by the heterotopic frontier.[50]

Later in his career this corporatism enabled him to emphasize further the unique nature of American nationality through the relationship between sections. The section eventually came to replace the frontier as another heterotopia. Talking of sections he exclaimed: 'We should study their economic evolution, their peculiar psychological traits ... their relations with other sections. Such a treatment would illuminate the history of the formation and character of the American people.'[51] He felt the next generation of historians must attempt to explain 'the evolution of the social structure' of the various sections in order to understand the social forces operating to create America.[52] While his presidential address in 1910 to the American Historical Association spoke of the broad issues of social and ideological forces in America, the overall ideo-cultural implications of his general position can already be seen from his earliest reference to the closure of the frontier in the 1893 lecture. In it he claimed the closure of the frontier witnessed the ending of a stage in American history, but a stage which revealed America's exceptional national and racial identity. With the frontier gone a new phase of American cultural development had to be explained.[53] The tenor of Turner's bourgeois evolutionist explanation is evidenced in the manner in which his myth-ideological system of Western frontier history was later transmuted into a sectional rather than a class analysis.

National history and subordinate cultures

Turner's ideological commitment to explaining the rise of national institutions as an inevitable evolutionary process meant he had to isolate subordinate and potentially oppositional cultural/class formations. Even his apparently favoured producer groups were lost in the heterotopia of the West. Certainly immigrant and race groups, as well as women, were nationalized through their assimilation or marginalization. Immigrants, on one occasion described as 'dull brains', became subject to the cultural imperative of the heterotopic frontier. With a rare touch of whimsy he claimed that 'in the crucible of the frontier the immigrants were Americanised, liberated, and fused into a mixed race, English in neither nationality nor characteristics'.[54] The strong likelihood that the majority of immigrants were not being moved to go west but staying in the cities was an inconvenient fact Turner could not afford to address directly. It did not sit well with his overall image of either the interpellative frontier or of the secondary importance of the foreign-born.

Although acknowledged constantly throughout the 1893 lecture, Native Americans are cast as peripheral historical agents, usually as guides or even obstacles to be overcome in the push west. 'The Indian was a common danger, demanding united action', and each wave of frontier expansion 'was won by a series of Indian wars'.[55] Turner agreed with Theodore Roosevelt that Indians had to be regulated and controlled.[56] Moreover, as Martin Ridge argues, because Turner developed his ideas around job functions he tended to overlook the role of women in opening up the West.[57] In providing a useful history for the emergent bourgeois-industrial social formation he embraced the dominant prejudices against women, effectively interpellating them by either hiding them from history or placing them in the gender-defined, subject position of motherhood. In the 1893 lecture, for example, women only appear as the wives and mothers of pioneer-heroes, noting in passing that 'Kit Carson's mother was a Boone'.[58]

In a 1903 article, while he argued that 'the question of Socialism' was a core issue of the day, he said that should 'legislation [take the place] of the free lands as the means of preserving the ideal of democracy' it would endanger 'the other pioneer ideal of creative and competitive individualism'. While 'we can understand the reaction against individualism . . . in favour of a drastic assertion of the powers of government', it 'would be a grave misfortune if [Americans] . . . so rich in experience, in self-confidence and aspiration, in creative genius, should turn to some Old World discipline of socialism or plutocracy, or despotic rule, whether by class or dictator'.[59] This was one of Turner's clearest statements of what was an anti-European, but much more importantly a dominant American, evolutionary conservatism.

In his 1910 presidential address Turner spoke directly to the contemporary conflicts and contradictions in America, concluding that among other progressive demands, socialism was an inevitable consequence of the end of 'free land':

The present finds itself engaged in the task of re-adjusting its old ideals to new conditions ... It is not surprising that socialism shows noteworthy gains as elections continue [and that] the demand for primary elections ... popular choice of senators, initiative, referendum, and recall is spreading ... They are efforts to find substitutes for that former safeguard of democracy, the disappearing free lands.[60]

In his Commencement Address that same year to the University of Indiana, Turner again spoke of class and its conflictual character. Because of the closure of the frontier, or as he said, an America 'without her former safety valve of abundant resources', classes were 'becoming alarmingly distinct'. While not favouring the robber baronage's solution of absolute power 'unvexed by politicians and people', he could not support the ideas of 'an inharmonious group of reformers', among whom he put the Granger and Populist 'prophets' and 'Mr. Bryan's Democracy and Mr. Debs' Socialism'. Later in the speech Turner praised 'University men', perhaps with historians in mind who

shall disinterestedly and intelligently mediate between contending interests. When the words 'capitalist classes' and 'the proletariat' can be used and understood in America it is surely time to develop such men, with the ideal of service to the State, who may help to break the force of these collisions, to find common grounds between the contestants and to possess the confidence and respect of all parties which are genuinely loyal to the best American ideals.[61]

The process of cultural formation, described by Turner as the constitution of 'memories, traditions, an inherited attitude toward life', thus clearly depends upon the intellectual's mediation of the great Western experience rather than the material force of class.

A unique history – an exceptional nation

Turner's historio-spatial imagination with its evolutionary inclination required him then to reject economic class as an agent of rapid cultural change or national identity formation. In spite of his pragmatism, it is not surprising he agreed with America's foremost idealist philosopher Josiah Royce and his argument that men are defined by their loyalty to a cause or region. Turner agreed with Royce that a region's 'true consciousness of its own ideals and customs' is the prerequisite to any check on 'mob psychology on a national scale'.[62] Although he accepted that physical geography alone could not explain how men gather into 'political groupings', neither equally could 'economic interests'. The only real explanation lay in accepting that there were also 'the factors of ideals and psychology, the inherited intellectual habits, derived from the stock from which the voters sprang'.[63] Ultimately then Turner rejected the danger of class as an explanation of social change in favour of the organization of space. In a remarkable anticipation of Foucault Turner said: 'Habit rather than reasoning is the fundamental factor in determining political affiliation of the mass of voters, and there is a geography, a habitat, of political habit.'[64] This was the essential interpellative and mythic power of the frontier heterotopia.

It is at this ideo-cultural level of history as myth that Turner's deconstruction of America's past became a powerful nationalistic force. As a bourgeois intellectual his historical deconstruction in seeking to distil American exceptionalism had to contend with the problems and contradictions found in contemporary America. The political and cultural implications of the swift emergence of metropolitanism, industrialism and cosmopolitanism were vast, producing slums, municipal corruption, the vilest conditions of factory life, racism and the trust. Despite his complex geography of culture these evils which accompanied the rise of corporate America made it increasingly difficult to grasp industrial progress in terms of the unqualified success of individualism or even sections, and consequently the powerful interdependence of the pioneer and frontier could only be handled as a past event.

The pressures experienced by America with the declining producer culture and the conflicts in the industrial cities during the Progressive era demanded a set of modern myths, operating as objective history. Turner, the bourgeois historian, summarized his understanding of the culturally formative role of his version of American history in his 1910 presidential address to the American Historical Association when he exclaimed that 'a just public opinion and a statesmanlike treatment of present problems demand that they be seen in their historic relations in order that history may hold the lamp for conservative reform'.[65] The fact that Turner provided no actual reformist solutions for the cultural conflicts which stained the Progressive era arises from the central contradiction of his work, his creation of a frontier-inspired, potentially radical democracy, but one which carried with it the ideological freight of militant economic and political conservatism.

Turner's written history then has a double status both as a modern myth and as the historical narrative it claims to be. The Turner Thesis as a signifier collapses both meaning and form, its first-order linguistic meaning extant as a narrative explanation of American history, its second-order mythic dimension acting to contain the class and industrial contradictions introduced into the bourgeois culture of the new order. Myth, as Barthes says, 'is defined . . . by the way it utters the message'.[66] The same can be said for Turner's unique history for an exceptional nation.

Notes

1. Fredric Jameson quoted in Introduction to T.W. Adorno. Boyars R (ed) 1972 *The legacy of refugee German intellectuals*. Schocken, New York, p 141.

2. William E. Leuchtenburg, in his 1992 American Historical Association presidential address of 28 December 1991, maintains that this awareness has formed one of the central traditions of the American historical profession. Leuchtenburg W E 1992 The historian and the public realm. *American Historical Review* 97 (1): 1.

3. White H 1973 *Metahistory, the historical imagination in the nineteenth century*. John Hopkins University Press, Baltimore; White H 1978 *Tropics of discourse: essays in cultural criticism*. John Hopkins University Press, Baltimore; White H 1987 *The content of the form: narrative discourse and historical representation*. John Hopkins University Press, Baltimore. For discussions of the nature of history within the American context see Munslow A 1992 *Discourse and culture: the creation of America*. Routledge pp 68–86. For an introduction to the recent debates on the epistemological basis of history as a separate discipline see Novick P 1988 *That noble dream: the objectivity question and the American historical profession*. Cambridge University Press, New York; and the flurry of responses and debates in recent issues of the *American Historical Review*: 1989, 94 (3): 581–698; 1991, 96 (3): 675–708; 1992, 97 (2): 405–39. In addition see Chartier R 1988 *Cultural history* trans

Cochrane L G. Cornell University Press, Ithaca, NY; Hunt L (ed) 1989 *The new cultural history*. University of California Press, Berkeley and Los Angeles; Weinstein F 1990 *History and theory after the fall*. University of Chicago Press, Chicago; Young R 1990 *White mythologies: writing history and the west*. Routledge, New York; Marshall B K 1992 *Teaching the postmodern: fiction and theory*. Routledge, New York; Stanford M 1994 *A companion to the study of history*. Blackwell, Oxford; Goldstein J (ed) 1994 *Foucault and the writing of history*. Blackwell.

4. White 1978 p 127.

5. Hoare Q, Nowell Smith G 1972 *The prison notebooks* by Antonio Gramsci. Lawrence and Wishart, London, p 324.

6. White H 1974 Structuralism and popular culture. *Journal of Popular Culture* 7: 759–75; White 1978 pp 230–60.

7. White 1978 p 325.

8. Ibid pp 323–77.

9. Hofstadter R (1968) 1970 *The progressive historians: Turner, Beard, Parrington*. Vintage Books, New York, pp 3–4.

10. Ibid p 3.

11. A study of Turner as a myth-maker is to be found in Susman W I 1984 History and the American intellectual: the uses of a usable past; The frontier thesis and the American intellectual. Both in *Culture as history: the transformation of American society in the twentieth century*. Pantheon, New York, pp 7–26, 27–38.

12. Susman 1984 p 25.

13. Wright Mills C 1959 *The sociological imagination*. Oxford University Press, New York, p 12.

14. Soja E 1989 *Postmodern geographies: the reassertion of space in critical social theory*. Verso, p 15. For a critique of Soja, and of Harvey D 1989 *The condition of postmodernity*. Blackwell, who both utilize this notion of the spatial adjunct to the historical imagination, see Pinkney T 1990 Space: the final frontier. *News From Nowhere* 8 (Autumn): 10–27.

15. He would probably have agreed with the sociologist Anthony Giddens, that space involves not just the distribution of activities, but their co-ordination with features of the locales within which these activities are carried on: Giddens A 1987 *Social theory and modern sociology*. Stanford University Press, Stanford, p 144. See also Munslow 1992 pp 69–70.

16. Quoted in Jacobs W R 1968 *The historical world of Frederick Jackson Turner with selections from his correspondence*. Yale University Press, New Haven, Conn, p 10.

17. Turner F J (1906) 1935 *Rise of the new west, 1819–1829* with an

introduction by Avery Craven. Henry Holt, New York; Turner F J (1920) 1962 *The frontier in American history*. Holt, Rinehart and Winston, New York; Turner F J 1932 *The significance of sections in American history*. Henry Holt, New York.

18. Every generation produces fresh commentaries on Turner. See for example Benson L 1960 *Turner and Beard: American historical writing reconsidered*. Free Press, New York; Billington R A (ed) 1966 *The frontier thesis: valid interpretation of American history?* Holt, Rinehart and Winston, New York; Billington R A 1966 *America's frontier heritage*. Holt, Rinehart and Winston, New York; Susman W I 1963 The useless past: American intellectuals and the frontier thesis, 1910–1930. *Bucknell Review* **11** (2): 1–20. Noble D W 1965 *Historians against history: the frontier thesis and the national covenant in American historical writing since 1830*. University of Minnesota Press, Minneapolis, argued that Turner was a new political philosopher for the 1890s. Ronald H. Carpenter examines the rhetoric of the Turner *oeuvre* in Carpenter R H 1983 *The eloquence of Frederick Jackson Turner*. The Huntingdon Library, San Marino, California. A sound survey of the commentaries on Turner is Mattson V E, Marion W E 1985 *Frederick Jackson Turner: a reference guide*. G K Hall, Boston, Mass; Ellis R J, Munslow A 1986 Narrative, myth and the Turner thesis. *Journal of American Culture* **9** (2): 9–16; Ridge M 1988 Frederick Jackson Turner, Ray Allen Billington, and Frontier History. *Western Historical Quarterly* **19** (Jan): 5–20. Several recent texts have offered appreciations of the role of nature in the American cultural imagination of the nineteenth century: Miller D C 1989 *Dark Eden: the swamp in nineteenth century American culture*. Cambridge University Press, New York; Gidley M, Peebles R L (eds) 1990 *Views of American landscapes*. Cambridge University Press, Cambridge; Wyatt D 1991 *The fall into Eden: landscape and imagination in California*. Cambridge University Press, New York; Stoneley P 1994 Signifying frontiers, borderlines. *Studies in American Culture* **1** (3): 237–53.

19. Turner 1920 p 1.

20. Foucault M 1986 Of other spaces trans Jay Miskowiec. *Diacritics* **16**: 22–7.

21. Ibid p 24. For an introduction to Foucault's spatial imagination see Rabinow P 1984 Space, knowledge and power. In *The Foucault reader*. Pantheon, New York, pp 239–56; Foucault M 1980 Questions on geography. In *Power/Knowledge: selected interviews and other writings, 1972–1977* ed C Gordon. Harvester, Brighton, pp 63–77. See also Soja 1989 pp 16–21.

22. Foucault 1980 p 149.
23. White 1973 p ix.
24. Walsh M 1981 *The American frontier revisited*. Macmillan, London, pp 11–13, describes Turner's approach as being 'analytical . . . which stressed socio-economic development rather than a romantic narrative endowed with colourful incidents and folk heroes and that he wrote . . . within the framework of the historical facts'.
25. Only a brief examination of earlier narrative accounts of America's Western regions or the American wilderness is required to substantiate this referential-mythic procedure. In Whitman and Thoreau as well as the accounts of early annalists and explorers are many examples of the shaping influence of contact with the frontier. In 1782 for example J. Hector St John de Crevecoeur expressed this mythic narrative in his *Letters from an American farmer*.
26. Scholes R, Kellogg R 1966 *The nature of narrative*. Oxford University Press, Oxford, p 12; Ellis and Munslow 1986 pp 13–15. The analysis of myth offered here is indebted to this article.
27. Gaston Bachelard, *The poetics of space*. Ref Miller 1989 p 5.
28. Barthes R 1972 *Mythologies*. Cape, London, pp 115, 118.
29. Turner 1920 p 38.
30. Ibid p 1.
31. Ross D 1984 Historical consciousness in nineteenth century America. *American Historical Review* 89(4): 909–28.
32. Turner 1920 pp 2–3.
33. Ibid pp 2–3.
34. Ibid pp 3–4.
35. Ibid p 37. In his 1896 article Turner extended the idea of a pioneer capable of transforming America, claiming that the Western man believed in the manifest destiny of his country.
36. Ibid p 206.
37. Turner 1932 p 16.
38. Turner 1920 pp 312–15.
39. Ibid pp 318–19.
40. Ibid p 319.
41. Ibid p 211.
42. Turner 1932 p 5.
43. 'The factor of time in American history is insignificant when compared with the factors of space and social evolution . . . the history of America offers a rich new field for the scientific study of social development [and] it is important to conceive of American history . . . as peculiarly rich in problems arising from the study of evolution of society.' Ibid pp 6–7.
44. Ibid p 15.

45. Ibid p 16.
46. Ibid p 17.
47. Turner 1920 p 1.
48. Ibid p 11.
49. Ibid p 15.
50. Turner 1932 pp 7–8.
51. Ibid pp 9–10.
52. Ibid pp 13–14.
53. Turner 1920 p 37.
54. Ibid pp 278, 317, 23.
55. Ibid pp 9, 10, 15, 17.
56. Slotkin R 1981 Nostalgia and progress: Theodore Roosevelt's myth of the frontier. *American Quarterly* 33(Winter): 618–19.
57. Ridge 1988 p 8.
58. Turner 1920 p 19.
59. Ibid p 246; The West and American Ideals, delivered as the Commencement Address, University of Washington, 17 June 1914, ibid p 307.
60. Ibid p 321.
61. Ibid pp 281, 285.
62. Ibid p 45.
63. Ibid p 48.
64. Ibid p 49.
65. Ibid pp 323–4.
66. Barthes 1972 p 110.

8 Hawthorne, *James and history*

David Timms

In a letter of 26 February 1879, James wrote to his sister Alice that he was 'busy with the little book upon Hawthorne'. It was to be a critical sketch in the Macmillan series 'English Men of Letters', edited by John Morley. By this time James's relationship with the house of Macmillan was well consolidated, and it must have seemed quite natural to ask the young American with the recent success of *Daisy Miller* to his credit, and whose family had known Hawthorne, to write this volume, the first on an American in the series. From the outset, though, James was dubious about the work, and complained to Alice that he had been 'diverted' into it, away from the fiction he would otherwise have been writing, for financial reasons. After the book's appearance, and its very hostile reception in America, James's doubts increased. His 'poor little *Hawthorne*', he twice called it, in letters to T. S. Perry and Charles Eliot Norton. He had confided to Perry even before the book was finished that he had found the writing difficult owing to 'the slenderness of the subject', and to Grace Norton he had said that it was written 'against my will'.[1]

As he confesses at the beginning of the book, he had not engaged in any great labours of original research for it, relying on the *Notebooks* that had been published piecemeal by Hawthorne's widow, the biography of Hawthorne by his son-in-law George Parsons Lathrop, and to a very limited extent on personal information given to him by Julian Hawthorne, who had recently moved to England with his young wife, and was living at Hastings. In writing his own memoirs, Hawthorne's son recalled this time, and in particular a conversation he had with James during a walk along the sea-front. The remarks made by James to Julian suggest that he found the task of writing the sketch more engaging than he revealed to friends and relatives:

'I don't want to do it,' he said again and again. 'I'm not competent: and yet, if I don't, some Englishman will do it worse than I would. Your father was the greatest imaginative writer we had, and yet, I feel his principle was wrong; there is no more powerful and beautifully written book than "The Scarlet Letter", and yet I believe the whole conception of it was wrong! Imagination is out of place; only the strictest realism can be right. But how can a barely known scribbler like me offer criticism on him?'[2]

Of course, Julian's memoirs appeared as late as 1938, in the knowledge of James's eventual stature. Hawthorne's son had an interest in portraying 'The Master' as at one time pupil to his own father. Clearly too, in view of what James wrote at the time in letters to friends, the valuation of Hawthorne expressed here, even if Julian's memory of it is accurate, may be seen in part as social grace.

However, the exact grounds of James's exasperation are instructive. He had recently published *French Poets and Novelists* (1878), largely taken up with meditations on European realists. Here was the other side of the equation, an American romancer undergoing similar scrutiny.

James's realism

The conventional view is that a major shift occurs in James's fiction after *Portrait of a Lady* (1881), and that it finds its full expression in *The Bostonians* (1886). Lyall Powers, for instance, claims that '*The Portrait of a Lady* . . . marks the end of James's first period; his second may properly be said to begin with the publication of his critical essay "The Art of Fiction" in 1884'.[3] Powers defines the difference between these periods in terms of James's 'influences'. Up till 1881 his chief model was Hawthorne, and after 1884 Zola, Turgenev, Daudet and Maupassant.

The changes this shift effected in James's fiction are easy to demonstrate. Take *Washington Square* (1880). Though it is clear that James has Balzac's *Eugénie Grandet* in mind as his model, we will scour James's novel in vain for the kind of contextualizing concrete detail we find in Balzac's book: neither the house in *Washington Square* nor indeed the Square itself are described in any realizable detail. Edward Stone claims that even in James's earliest tales 'the pictorial realism he admires in Balzac is already in evidence';[4] but this is surely not true. Cornelia Pulsifer Kelley makes it clear that the James of *Washington Square* lacked something evident in Balzac: 'James named his novel after a place, thus implying that he was "doing" Washington Square. Adequately done as a background, it is most inadequately done in itself.' This was 'an error of which Balzac was never guilty', according to Kelley.[5] But how different is the New York of *The Bostonians* (1886)!

> Basil Ransom lived in New York, rather far to the eastward, and in the upper reaches of the town; he occupied two small shabby rooms in a somewhat decayed mansion which stood next to the corner of the Second Avenue. The corner itself was formed by a considerable grocer's shop, the near neighbourhood of which was fatal to any pretension Ransom and his fellow-lodgers might have had in regard to gentility of situation. The house had a red, rusty face, and faded green shutters, of which the slats were limp and at variance with each other. In one of the lower windows was suspended a fly-blown card, with the words 'Table Board' affixed in letters cut (not very neatly) out of coloured paper, of graduated tints, and surrounded with a small band of stamped gilt.[6]

The denseness of recorded detail, the 'solidity of specification' of this passage describing the area where Basil Ransom lives has no equivalent in earlier James. Werner Berthoff says of *The Bostonians* and *The Princess Casamassima* (1886), the long fictions that follow *Portrait of a Lady*, that 'with their weight and brilliance of composed detail, it is not to local colour writing but to the great nineteenth-century masters of metropolitan realism that comparisons are relevant'.[7] Lyall Powers is more specific. Of *The Bostonians*, Powers claims that in its attempt to portray a convincing 'here and now', in its full and accurate description of character and setting, in its authorial reticence and objectivity, and in its understanding of heredity as a mainspring of characters' actions, the book may be said to be 'naturalist' without equivocation.[8]

Long before *Portrait of a Lady*, however, James, and others, *thought* that what he was writing was in the realist vein. *The American* offers an excellent example of this. When he revalued the book for the 'New York' edition James described it as 'consistently, consummately – and I would fain really make bold to say charmingly – romantic'. But he noted that he 'had been plotting arch-romance *without knowing it*' (my emphasis).[9] In fact, what he thought he was doing when he wrote the novel was writing a work of realism. He defended his 'unhappy' ending to Howells in 1877: he couldn't have Newman marry Claire, for 'I should have felt as if I were throwing a rather vulgar sop to readers who don't really know the world and who don't measure the merit of a novel by its correspondence with the same'.[10] Contemporary readers too saw it as realism, though they did not always feel this to be a virtue. English reviewers consistently compared the book with the works of the major French realists. *The Saturday Review* claimed that 'Mr James's method is, if internal evidence goes for anything, founded on that of Mr Mérimée and his disciple Mr Tourguenef',[11] and *The Academy* considered that 'Mr James . . . has read Balzac, if it be possible, just a little too much'.[12] The same views can be gleaned from the American periodicals. The book was described in *The Nation* as 'polished, philosophical . . . absolutely cold-blooded . . . among the best modern studies of society'.[13] *The Galaxy* sensed in James's French and French-Americans 'the air . . . of careful studies from the life',[14] and *Literary World* felt that the solidity of specification was so sustained that 'this bright American book comes perilously near being a French novel, from which may the Lord long deliver us!'[15]

The seminal essay 'The Art of Fiction' (1884) provides the most explicit theoretical exposition of James's views. 'The only reason for the existence of a novel is that it does attempt to represent life' James takes as his most basic formulation of the function of the novel, and it is clear that most of the representation must be in visual terms. The novelist's task is 'the same attempt that we see on the canvas of the painter . . . The analogy between the art of the painter and the art of the novelist is, as far as I am able to see, complete'. The novel seeks 'exactness . . . truth to detail', and his exactness is expressed in description. 'Tiresome analysis of "description" ', James comments ironically, 'are the signs of the "art" that the philistine distrusts'. The novelist must attempt to render 'the look of things, the look that conveys their meaning, to catch the colour, the relief, the expression, the surface, the substance of the human spectacle'.

And he must do so with the objectivity and the conviction of one reporting real events: 'the novel is history . . . it must speak with assurance, with the tone of the historian'.[16]

It is clear then that in considering Hawthorne in 1879 James thought of himself as a writer very different from his subject: he believed himself to be a realist, implicitly and explicitly. But we might bear in mind the fact that fictional practice actually lagged behind his theoretical beliefs, and that he was himself not properly aware of the fact. Significantly, it is a paradox that structurally resembles the exasperation he expressed to Julian Hawthorne.

James's history

James's account of Hawthorne is the application of Taine's formula of 'La race, le milieu et le moment' to Hawthorne's life and works, and he actually quotes it in the pages of his study.[17] The quotation is surely an explicit expression of conviction about the historical approach, in that Taine's tag is quoted, for the purposes of being dismissed, in the pages of the American work that James acknowledges as contributing the facts on which he bases his understanding of the events of Hawthorne's life.[18] To explain Hawthorne, then, he had to explain America in the first half of the nineteenth century.

For James the most salient characteristic of Hawthorne's America was that it had no salient characteristics: it was a place that offered nothing to the observation, there were 'no great things to look out at' (p 383), there was 'a vacancy in the field of vision' (p 352). And in a sense this featurelessness, the lack of things that could be used to make distinctions, characterized it socially too. James refers his primarily English readership to the fact that in one of Hawthorne's novels, *The House of the Seven Gables*, an itinerant odd-job man is on terms of social familiarity with the American equivalents of the Lords of the Manor (p 355). There was simply little to do in Hawthorne's America, even for the educated. James takes Hawthorne's record of a whole evening spent with the Peabodys looking at Flaxman's illustrations to Dante as synecdochically standing for a world where entertainment was extremely scant. It was a world where the artist in particular was at a disadvantage. James remembers that even in his own youth not to be in 'business' was sometimes frowned on (p 342); but even more damaging, that sparseness of social and cultural life simply gave the author nothing to write about. James's list of the negatives of American life (p 351) is too famous to quote; he takes Hawthorne's record of trivia in the American journals to be indicative not of Hawthorne's limitations but of the paucity of things worth recording.

James stresses the moral tone of this world of undifferentiated equals: plain living and high thinking is its note, and he takes as its paradigmatic expression the group of innocents and idealists that made up the population of Brook Farm. It was

> delightfully Arcadian and innocent, and it is certain that there was something peculiar to the clime and race in some of the features of such a life; in the free, frank, and stainless companionship of young men and maidens, in the mixture of manual labour and intellectual flights – dish-washing and aesthetics, wood-chopping and philosophy. (pp 385–6)

For the rest, if there was little by way of history or the dimension of time in America, there was certainly space, and James emphasizes America's natural beauty. He did not take the Transcendentalist line that human culture is properly an expression of nature; rather, history is a building raised over nature, a building that as yet had only 'foundations' (p. 341). James explicitly states the corollary to this notion, that provincial America in Hawthorne's time was closer to nature than a sophisticated culture would have been. He pictures Hawthorne's New England consistently in terms of air and trees, forests and streams. The adjectives James applies throughout to this America are also antithetical to the notion of a place with a past: it is bright, clear, immature, new, and above all 'fresh'.

By realist and historical principles, the whole shapes the part, and James's Hawthorne is accordingly in his personality and his work a reflection of his homeland. He makes much of the fact that Hawthorne was born on the fourth of July, and sees *The Scarlet Letter* as 'absolutely American' (p. 403). James uses exactly the same descriptive words of Hawthorne as of his birthplace: delicate, charming, spontaneous, simple, thin. Hawthorne's life was like that of the nation, thin on events: 'simple . . .

tranquil and uneventful . . . deficient in incident' (p. 319). Even his publishing life is similarly characterized: the second piece of information James offers about his subject is that Hawthorne produced little. His most obvious faculty was that which makes something from nothing: it is Hawthorne's imagination or fancy that James stresses. James emphasizes what he sees to be the uncomplex nature of Hawthorne's mind and thought. What strikes the younger man is his 'serenity' and 'amenity' (p. 339), Hawthorne's 'modest . . . unpretending' genius (p. 320); he had 'no philosophy', was 'an unperplexed intellect' (p. 340). This was most marked in the field of literary theory. 'I am not sure that he had ever heard of Realism', James declares (p. 221). What Hawthorne did have was the high moral tone characteristic of his society, at least in James's version. He was a 'chip off the old block' of his forefathers (p. 325), and showed 'an element of simplicity and rigidity' in his 'plain . . . masculine . . . sensible' moral values (p. 326).

Like America, Hawthorne seems inconsistent with the idea of age. James draws attention to the number of times Hawthorne expressed mistrust of 'old houses, old institutions, long lines of descent' (p. 417). Hawthorne has the perpetual newness characteristic of an unfallen nature: he is natural, spontaneous, unsophisticated, fresh. All of this of course is somewhat in conflict with the idea of a writer who says 'No! in thunder',[19] but James seems unembarrassed by the Puritanic gloom Hawthorne pointed to in himself, and which was identified as his distinctive feature by Emile Montégut, whose essay in *Revue des Deux Mondes* James quotes (p. 339). Hawthorne was a 'Romancier Pessimiste', says James, because this apparent gloominess was not a quirk of personality, a feature of an individual mind: rather, it derived like all Hawthorne's other qualities from his *milieu*. This 'blackness' merely 'stood fixed in the general moral heaven under which he grew up and looked at life' (p. 362).

James's general approach to Hawthorne is realistic, then, and his specific literary approach even more so. 'Hawthorne, to say it again, was not in the least a realist – he was not to my mind enough of one', James says (p. 320), and as he emphasizes here, it is a complaint that runs through his critical biography from beginning to end. Again and again he refers to 'absence of the realistic quality' (p. 320), 'absence . . . of quality of realism' (p 321), 'want of reality' (p. 404). *The Scarlet Letter* shows little of the 'modern realism of research' (p. 404) and in *The Blithedale Romance* we get 'too much out of reality' (p. 422). In tandem with this James condemns the extent of Hawthorne's use of symbolism. In *The Scarlet Letter* there is an 'abuse of the fanciful' (p. 404), and of *The Marble Faun* James says:

> Like all Hawthorne's things, it contains a great many light threads of symbolism, which shimmer in the texture of the tale, but which are apt to break and remain in our fingers if we attempt to handle them . . . The fault of *Transformation* is that the element of the unreal is pushed too far . . . His 'moonshiny romance', he calls it in a letter; and, in truth, the lunar element is a little too pervasive. (p. 447)

Where Hawthorne does make some approach to actuality, he earns James's praise. Despite the complaint about *The Marble Faun* above, 'it may very well be urged in Hawthorne's favour . . . that in *Transformation* he has attempted to deal with actualities more than he did in either of his earlier novels' (pp. 444–5). Zenobia is praised as Hawthorne's 'only very definite attempt at the representation of a character' (p. 379). And despite disclaimers made later in the book about assuming too close a congruence between an artist's model and the finished creation, James suggests that Zenobia's quality derives from her being based on a real person:

> The portrait is full of alteration and embellishment; but it has a greater reality, a greater abundance of detail, than any of his other figures, and the reality was a memory of the lady whom he had encountered in the Roxbury pastoral or among the wood-walks of Concord, with strange books in her hand and eloquent discourse on her lips. (p 379)

James deplores the fact that Hawthorne missed even such opportunities for realistic writing as he had. The *Notebooks* are full of things of no consequence, and 'since a beautiful writer was growing up in Salem, it is a pity that he should not have given himself a chance to commemorate some of the types that flourished in the richest soil of the place' (p 354).

James's *Hawthorne*

It is conventional to praise *Hawthorne* as 'a landmark in the history of American literary criticism', a 'classic'.[20] It is less conventional to notice its many confusions. Alone among modern commentators on the book, Tony Tanner recognizes that *Hawthorne* contains contradictions. He explains that this was because the author's eye was not fixed firmly on his subject:

> What James was really doing in this book was attempting to explore and articulate three matters of urgent interest to him; roughly, the status of America, the peculiar psychology of the American individual, and the problems of the American artist.[21]

These things are certainly true, but Tanner does not note that to look at Hawthorne in this way is inevitable given James's theoretical standpoint: to explain America *is* to explain Hawthorne. The problems that beset *Hawthorne* seem to me to derive from exactly the paradox James expressed to Julian Hawthorne: James's theory told him that Hawthorne should have been no good; but some other faculty in James insisted that he was. It is rather like Huck Finn deciding to go to the devil, but with far less conviction. Testily objecting to James's account of Hawthorne's disadvantages, Maxwell Geismar wonders: 'How did poor Hawthorne manage to write as well as he did? That is the question that haunts the modern reader of James's *Hawthorne*.'[22] Geismar might have added that the question also haunts the book itself.

To begin with, James specifically identifies as Hawthorne's merits the very items he generally claims to be drawbacks. 'The flower of art', James insists, 'blooms only where the soil is deep . . . it takes a great deal of history to produce a little literature' (p. 320). But Hawthorne managed somehow to 'sprout' and 'bloom' in a place with no soil at all, in 'a crevice of that immitigable granite' of New England (p. 320). Not only that, James wanted him to be seen not as a freak or sport, but as distinctively American, as I have tried to show. Provincialness is a curse to the artist, but somehow Hawthorne was a beneficiary of it, for his great distinction was that he expressed his time and place, and he declined when he left it and came to Europe.

Similarly, as we have seen, James throughout complains of Hawthorne's lack of realism, but it is his most obviously non-realistic quality that James finds most distinctive and admirable about him. The tales 'that spring most directly from his fancy . . . constitute his most substantial claim to our attention' (p. 362). 'The real charm' of Hawthorne's writing is 'this purity and spontaneity and naturalness of fancy' (p. 362). James must have been aware of this, for the book is full of feeble disclaimers about the wisdom of not looking too critically at Hawthorne at all. He says of pieces like 'Night Sketches': 'Not to read them would be to do them an injustice . . . , but to bring the machinery of criticism to bear upon them would be to do them a still greater wrong' (pp. 348–9).

The second large confusion was noted by Howells when he reviewed *Hawthorne* for *Atlantic Monthly* in 1880:

> No-one better than Mr James knows the radical difference between a romance and a novel, but he speaks now of Hawthorne's novels, and now of his romances, throughout, as if the terms were convertible; whereas the romance and the novel are as distinct as the poem and the novel . . . Hawthorne's fictions being always and essentially, in conception and performance, romances, not novels, something of all Mr James's special criticism is invalidated by the confusion which, for some reason not made clear, he permits himself.[23]

Hawthorne himself expended a good deal of effort in trying to persuade his readers of exactly this separation, and it is hard to believe that James could have thought that Hawthorne had 'never heard of Realism' in the face of the preface to *The House of the Seven Gables*. However, for one who wants to try all fictions at the bar of realism, the distinction is necessarily invalid. As he explains in 'The Art of Fiction': 'The novel and the romance, the novel of incident and that of character – these clumsy separations seem to me to have been made by critics and readers for their own convenience.' And he goes on to name Hawthorne specifically, claiming that the older writer called 'his story of Blithedale' a romance, 'simply for the pleasantness of the thing'.[24]

A further reason for James's unwillingness to recognize romance as a separate and different mode of fiction must have been that if he recognized Hawthorne as a self-conscious writer, designing his fictions with principles of construction in mind, it would ruin his contention in *Hawthorne* that his subject 'was not a man with a literary theory; he was guiltless of a system' (p. 321). Throughout *Hawthorne* James stresses his subject's simplicity and unintellectual quality: his talent is 'natural' (p. 457), not constructed.

But the final confusion in *Hawthorne* is perhaps the most basic: that is, James subverts his own realist principles by his very techniques in the book. Let us begin with his picture of America. He was confronted with a significant problem: if America was the thinly composed, sparse near-vacancy he pictures, how was it possible to account for his own fictional production? Of course the problem of paucity of subject matter was easily dealt with: he himself had come to Europe, to a 'denser, richer, warmer . . . spectacle' (p. 351). But there remained the problem of how such a place as America could have bred himself, who understood this paucity. The answer was that Hawthorne's America was not James's: it no longer existed.

Hawthorne was 'the last of an earlier race' (p. 162) which had gone out of being with the outbreak of the Civil War. The passage in which James explains this is very interesting. Hawthorne's 'earlier and simpler' (p. 141) generation was unprepared for war, and after it they were in a world foreign to them, in which they had no place:

> The Civil War marks an era in the history of the American mind. It introduced into the national consciousness a certain sense of proportion and relation, of the world being a more complicated place than it had hitherto seemed, the future more treacherous, success more difficult. At the rate at which things are going, it is obvious that good Americans will be more numerous than ever; but the good American, in days to come, will be a more critical person than his complacent and confident grandfather. He has eaten of the tree of knowledge. He will not, I think, be a sceptic, and still less, of course, a cynic; but he will be, without discredit to his well-known capacity for action, an observer. (pp. 427–8)

After the Civil War, then, the distinctive features of Hawthorne's America disappeared. The thin and sparse population is more numerous, despite the usual function of wars to reduce population in the crudest possible way. In place of the simplicity of Hawthorne's world there is complexity, and that complexity is met not with the innocent unphilosophical spontaneity of Hawthorne's generation, but with knowingness. The new American is an 'observer', which Hawthorne never was. 'Observe', 'observer', 'observation' are key words in realist theory. If the new American is an observer, he is a realist. He is in fact Henry James.

What James does not question is that if 'la race, le milieu et le moment' explains the individual, then it must also explain events like the Civil War. But James's references to the war suggest anything but a realist, historicist explanation of it. It was one of the 'rocks ahead' in the future of Hawthorne's America, which his countrymen did not foresee; a 'social revolution', a 'great convulsion', an earthquake, for what had been firm ground became a 'heaving and quaking medium' (p. 427). James's notion of American history is not linear, as a realist's should be, seeing the Civil War as the outcome of a thousand causes small and large; it is right-angled, like Christian or mythic history, in which sudden transformations take place owing to the incursion into human time of the divine will, like the fall of man or the birth of Christ. And indeed James makes this clear by his reference to the tree of knowledge. Hawthorne's America had been a place that was always 'fresh', and such a notion is not only inconsistent with the idea of a place at a point in historical, linear time, but even with the idea of a place at a point in cyclical time, which could be 'fresh' more than once, but not forever new. That is only possible in pre-time, a mythical place.

Paradoxically then, James takes a realist formula to explain Hawthorne, but into the formula inserts mythicized romance terms: Hawthorne is explained as the product of a place and time, but his America is a Garden of Eden.

A similar paradox may be observed by contrasting James's complaints about Hawthorne's lack of realism and over-use of symbolism with the younger authors own practice in representing both Hawthorne and his America. Take his description of Concord:

> Concord . . . would have been a village community operating in excellent conditions. Such a village community was not the least honourable item in the sum of New England civilisation. Its

spreading elms and plain white houses, its generous summers and ponderous winters, its immediate background of promiscuous field and forest, would have been part of the composition. (pp. 389–90)

Though James goes on to give a miscellaneous list of some of the other elements of the 'composition', the kind of list that would not be out of place in one of the descriptive passages from a realist novel, his picture of the place is dominated by the elms, the feature he mentions first. In fact elms overshadow all James's pictures of Hawthorne's New England. Elsewhere they almost seem to make up the population, for he refers to contemporary Concord as having Emerson at one end, Hawthorne at the other, and 'the rows of New England elms between' (p. 393). Although the elms were certainly an actual feature of Concord, they do not function like the kind of metonymic detail a realist novelist would pick out to characterize it. James is surely right in his implication throughout *Hawthorne* that human culture is essentially antithetical to nature. But here is a human fabrication, a town, artificially constructed by definition, represented by James as a natural phenomenon, for he uses trees to 'stand for' it. Placing the actual signs of human fabrication second in a list that is otherwise composed solely of natural phenomena 'naturalizes' the houses. It seems that James is not following the logic of his analysis, but rather that of his repeated characterization of American civilization in Hawthorne's day as 'natural'. The elms are there in the description partly because they were there in the place, but primarily because for James they symbolize the place. They are another feature of the 'Garden'.

This is even more marked in the means James uses to describe Hawthorne himself. If America was a 'natural' civilization, a 'Garden of Eden' congruent with spreading elms and promiscuous field and forest, then Hawthorne would 'naturally' be as he is described, 'the late coming fruit of a tree' (p. 325) or, more insistently, a flower: 'three or four beautiful talents of trans-Atlantic growth are the sum of what the world usually recognises, and in this modest nosegay the genius of Hawthorne is admitted to have the rarest and sweetest fragrance' (p. 320). Hawthorne 'sprouted and bloomed' (p. 320) from the New England granite. He was 'deeply rooted' in New England soil, and 'sprang from the primitive New England stock' (p. 322).

By extension, the works are described in the same way. Of the 'Night-Sketches' James says that 'out of the Salem puddles . . . springs, flower-like, a charming and natural piece of prose' (p. 349). James wonders how it would have felt to have encountered individual 'Twice-Told-Tales' as they appeared in periodicals, these 'dusky flowers in the blossomless garden of American journalism', in 'the first bloom of their freshness' (p. 361). *Mosses from an Old Manse* are 'the duskiest flowers of his invention' (p. 395). And just as James's metaphor organizes his understanding of America's history, so too does it govern his thought here. James comments that 'if we attempt to handle' some of the elements of Hawthorne's stories, they are 'apt to break and remain in our fingers', and this claim that it is a disservice to subject Hawthorne to the test of analytical criticism is often repeated in *Hawthorne*. For James at this time the analytical test would be the test of realism, and as he makes clear in his comments to Julian Hawthorne with which I began, he knew that by this test Hawthorne must fail. But of course we do not put fruits or flowers or natural objects to intellectual tests, only to sensuous ones. What James appreciates then is Hawthorne's 'fragrance' or 'savour' (p. 320) – those things most readily described by the epithet 'fresh'. What I am suggesting is that though James consciously spoke as a realist in writing his critical sketch, he actually wrote as a symbolist, using techniques much like Hawthorne's own. The symbolist could approve what the realist had to fault.

James's metaphors

Another comment from *Hawthorne* will illustrate how James despite his expressed theories followed his literary forebear in his resistance to materiality. Here he praises *The Scarlet Letter*:

> It is beautiful, admirable, extraordinary; it has in highest degree that merit which I have spoken of as the mark of Hawthorne's best things – an indefinable purity and lightness of conception, a quality which in a work of art affects one in the same way as the absence of grossness does in a human being. (p. 403)

Hawthorne is continually called 'light', 'slender', 'thin' or their synonyms in the book, but this lightness is seen as the opposite of two other and on the surface different qualities. Its most obvious antithesis is the one made here: grossness means overweight, with a suggestion of moral failings. But lightness is also seen in opposition to 'denseness', as when he contrasts *The Blithedale Romance* with James Lockhart's *Adam Blair*. *Adam Blair* is praised for superior realism: 'Lockhart was a dense, substantial Briton, with a taste for the concrete, and Hawthorne was a thin New Englander, with a miasmatic conscience' (p. 407).

But elsewhere, where there was not the future of fiction to cloud the issue, he made the alliance that puts 'British', 'realism' and 'corruption' together in a more uncompromising way, and interestingly he chose to do it in connection with the figure that Hawthorne had picked out as symbolizing Britannia at her grossest, the English dowager:

> As for the women I give 'em up: in advance. I am tired of their plainess and stiffness and tastelessness – their dowdy beads, their dirty collars and their linsey woolsey trains. Nay, this is peevish and brutal. Personally (with all their faults) they are well enough. I revolt from their dreary deathly want of – what shall I call it? – Clover Hooper has it – intellectual grace – Minny Temple has it – moral spontaneity.[25]

This letter of 1870 might be seen in the context of another written in the same year on the subject of the untimely death of that very Minny Temple James identifies as the American antithesis to the English women:

> One thought there is that moves me much – that I should be here delving into this alien England in which it was one of her fancies that she had a kind of property. It was not, I think, of the happiest. Every time that I have been out during the last three days, the aspect of things has perpetually seemed to enforce her image by simple contrast and difference. The landscape assents stolidly enough to her death: it would have ministered but scantily to her life. She was a breathing protest against English grossness, English compromises and conventions – a plant of pure American growth.[26]

Another paper could chart the changes in James's critical thinking over the fifteen years or so from the writing of this letter to the writing of *The Bostonians*. Many have already charted the changes in James's fictional practice. But what remains unchanging in James is his habit of thinking metaphorically. It is fascinating to compare this letter about Minny Temple with his reminiscence of her written 44 years later in *Notes of a Son and Brother*:

> ... she was one of the first order, in the sense of the immediacy of the impression she produced, and produced altogether as by the play of her own light spontaneity and curiosity – not, that is, as through a sense of such pressure and such a motive, or through a care for them, in others. 'Natural' to an effect of perfect felicity that we were never to see surpassed is what I have praised the Albany *cousinage* of those years for being; but in none of the company was the note so clear as in this rarest, though at the same time symptomatically palest, flower of the stem; who was natural at more points and about more things, with a greater range of freedom and ease and reach of horizon than any of the others dreamed of.[27]

The vocabulary and symbolic field used to characterize Minny have remained constant, and they are the same vocabulary and symbolic field as those used over a similar period to define Hawthorne. In an 1872 review of Hawthorne's *French and Italian Notebooks* James tells us that Hawthorne 'belonged to the race of magicians, and . . . his genius took nutriment as insensibly – to our vision – as the flowers take the dew . . . his impressions spring from an excessively natural mind'.[28] In an essay introducing Hawthorne in Charles Dudley Warner's *Encyclopaedia of American Literature* (1897) we are told that 'what Hawthorne encountered, he instinctively embroidered, working it over with a fine, slow needle, and with flowers pale, rosy, or dusky, as the case might suggest'.[29] Hawthorne's work is 'a flower of romantic art' in the letter James sent to Robert Rantoul in 1904 to substitute for his appearance at the Hawthorne Centenary celebrations to which he had been invited. Hawthorne's was 'a rare mind' that had been planted in Salem 'as in a parent soil'; 'the serious in him flowered into the grace of art'.[30] Seen in the context of the confusions and contradictions in *Hawthorne*, what the tenacity of this metaphor suggests is that James was not really a materialist, first or last, and he only thought he was one, and did his utmost to look like one, in between. Beneath the surface, he was always in fact more like Hawthorne than like Balzac. If I might refer back to the passage I quote from *The Bostonians* above (see p. 197), having made his extremely concrete evocation of Basil Ransom's New York, the narrator intrudes with a comment that sounds like an apology:

> The establishment was a kind known to New Yorkers as a Dutch grocery; and red-faced, yellow-haired, bare-armed vendors might have been observed to lounge in the doorway. I mention it not on account of any particular influence it may have had on the life or thought of Basil Ransom, but for old acquaintance sake and that of local colour; besides which, a figure is nothing without a setting, and our young man came and went every day, with rather an indifferent, unperceiving step, it is true, among the objects I have briefly designated. (p. 160)

The description is a model of realist analysis. It is strongly visual: the narrator even includes the key-word 'observed'. The point of view resembles what one might extract from a naturalist novel by Zola: he adopts the familiar trope of co-opting a hypothetical looker-on at the scene, who validates the narrator's perceptions as to what anyone might see at the scene, if they had eyes to see. While James does not include Balzacian commentary, he certainly lays claim to Balzac's narrator's authority when he says that he makes his description 'for old acquaintance sake'. The passage even includes a piece of metafiction which enunciates what is perhaps the central tenet of realist theory: 'a figure is nothing without a setting'. The implication of realism is finally that statement taken literally: the setting explains the figure, the figure is an 'x' in an algebraic equation which may be fully deduced from a knowledge of the other terms.

But fascinatingly there is another piece of metafiction, the apology I refer to above: 'I mention it not on account of any particular influence it might have had on the life or thought of Basil Ransom'. The extraordinary thing is that as much as the first piece of metafiction is a formulation of realist principles, this is a flat rejection of them. It hints at a suspicion that all this descriptive effort expended on the material world is a waste of time, that in the end it explains nothing, that for James what Barthes says about description in the novel may be true, that it is a 'luxury of narration' that finally is 'simply enigmatic'.[31]

It is surely the metaphorical 'mind-style' that finally dominates James's thinking about American history, and about his famous literary forebear; and it proved so persistent that it engendered the doubt lurking in even this most 'realistic' passage from *The Bostonians*. Its opposition to historical materialism is what gave rise to the baffled frustration that he expressed to Julian Hawthorne, and to the fact that for eight years or so his fictional practice was actually at odds with his expressed beliefs.

That he should not have been properly conscious of this in 1879 is not unreasonable, however. Tony Tanner is surely right in saying that James was thinking of Hawthorne in the light of his own experience. In America Hawthorne had been confronted by a 'vacancy in the field of vision': he had nothing to write about. James had been confronted by the same absence, and so had come to Europe. Hawthorne had no artistic community in America, and James believed that 'the best things come . . . from the talents that are members of a group' (p. 342). He himself had found just such a group in Paris, and now settled in London had a dense social and artistic context. Hawthorne's opportunity to observe society was constrained by the fact that the society itself was limited and undifferentiated. James in London was in the richest and most varied society in the world, and had opportunities to observe it in all its aspects. More than that, he was welcomed into the very group that created and maintained all those distinctive aspects of culture that he listed as lacking in American social life. The winter that immediately preceded his writing of *Hawthorne* was the one in which he reported to Grace Norton that he had dined out 107 times.[32]

James noted that Hawthorne was 46 before he produced his first novel (p. 345). When he came to Europe at the age of 50 he had only four collections of tales, three novels and some children's stories to his credit.

For James in 1879 alone, *Daisy Miller* had been such a success that the phrase had entered the language and the heroine had inspired a hat.[33] In January 'An International Episode' had appeared in Harper's Half-Hour series; the English edition of *The American* was published in March; the revised edition of *Roderick Hudson* had come out in May; *Confidence* began serialization in August and had come out in book form in both America and Britain in September; *The Madonna of the Future*

and Other Tales was published in October; *Hawthorne* itself
appeared in December. This was 'the conquest of London'
indeed. Tony Tanner puts down some of Hawthorne's attitudes
to a desire on its author's part to ingratiate himself with the
British public: on this evidence he had already won them over
convincingly.

No wonder James was perplexed by Hawthorne. He had
himself done everything contrarily: had been ambitious and not
shown any of Hawthorne's 'want of eagerness' in production
(p. 35); had left America to seek an artistic and social
community, where Hawthorne had stayed and had become
involved with the wider life of his country to the extent of
writing a campaign biography for a President. James had come to
school to the realists where Hawthorne had chosen an old-
fashioned form, the romance. Most of all, James had succeeded
where Hawthorne had failed. But the bafflement expressed to
Julian Hawthorne, the discontinuities of *Hawthorne* itself, and the fact
that the products of his imagination, his novels, should have been out
of alignment with his theories suggests that his success misled him.

Hawthorne was thrust by political preferment and financial
necessity into a European world of materiality and diplomacy,
and was unable to use it imaginatively. With his greater volume
of genius, James was able to take that world, and the theoretical
beliefs about the novel articulated by that world, and make from
them in the mid-1880s a brilliant series of fictions.

But James was heir to the same intellectual influences, the
same 'mind-style' as Hawthorne, and it was a style deeply
sceptical of the visible world of things that is the focus of a mind
like Balzac's. James remained a Hawthorne not a Balzac, an
Isabel Archer not a Madame Merle. While it is a folly to ignore
what the latter lady called 'the envelope of circumstances', it is
not the whole story, and may even be a misleading guide to the
whole story. In the fictions that James wrote in the 1890s and
1900s, the formula from *The Bostonians* is reversed: the setting is
nothing without a figure; a different figure means a different
setting. When F. R. Leavis complains that one of the great
problems of *The Ambassadors* is that Paris is not 'done' for us,[34]
he shows that he has missed the principle on which the novel is
raised: Strether's Paris and Chad's Paris are simply different
places. On that principle, how could a narrator who by

convention can claim final authority set up one single Paris as the 'true' one? And how could the later James have endorsed the earlier historical and material certainties of *Hawthorne*?

Notes

1. Edel L (ed) 1975 *Henry James letters volume II 1875–1883*. Belknap Press, Harvard, Mass, pp 215, 274, 280, 262.
2. Hawthorne J 1938 *The memoirs of Julian Hawthorne* ed Hawthorne E G. Macmillan, New York, p 127.
3. Powers L 1972 *Henry James and the naturalist movement*. Michigan State University Press, Michigan, p 42.
4. Stone E 1964 *The battle and the books: some aspects of Henry James*. Ohio State University Press, Athens, Ohio, p 72.
5. Kelley C P 1965 *The early development of Henry James* 2nd edn. Illinois University Press, Urbana, p 282.
6. James H (1886) 1966 *The Bostonians*. Penguin, Harmondsworth, pp 160–1. Future references will appear in the text in parenthesis.
7. Berthoff W 1965 *The ferment of realism: American literature 1884–1919*. The Free Press, New York, p 104.
8. Powers 1972 pp 58–9.
9. James H 1934 *The art of the novel: critical prefaces by Henry James* ed Blackmur R P. Charles Scribner's Sons, New York, p 25.
10. Edel 1975 p 105.
11. Pollock W 1877 *The American*. The Saturday Review **44** (18 Aug): 214.
12. Saintsbury G 1877 *The American*. The Academy (14 July): 33.
13. Perry T S 1877 James's *American*. The Nation **14** (31 May): 326.
14. Anon 1877 Current literature. The Galaxy **24** (July): 138.
15. Anon 1877 Recent fiction. The Literary World **9** (July): 30.
16. James H 1888 *Partial portraits*. Macmillan, London, pp 378, 390, 382, 380, 379.
17. James H (1879) 1984 *Hawthorne*. Rpt in Edel L (ed) 1984 *Henry James literary criticism: essays on literature, American writers, English writers*. Literary Classics of the United States, New York, p 367. Future references appear in the text in parenthesis.
18. Lathrop G P 1876 *A study of Hawthorne*. James R Osgood, Boston, Mass, p 173.
19. Herman Melville, letter of 16 April 1851. Rpt in Hawthorne J 1885 *Nathaniel Hawthorne and his wife: a biography* (2 vols) 3rd edn. James R Osgood, Boston, Mass, vol 1 p 388.

20. Dupee F W 1956 *Henry James: his life and writings* 2nd edn. Doubleday & Co, New York, p 89; Blair W 1971 Nathaniel Hawthorne. In *Eight American authors: a review of research and criticism* ed Floyd Stovall. W W Norton, New York, p 139.
21. Tanner T 1967 Introduction. *Hawthorne* ed Tony Tanner. Macmillan, London, p 10.
22. Geismar M 1964 *Henry James and his cult.* Chatto & Windus, London, p 34.
23. Howells W D 1880 James's *Hawthorne. Atlantic Monthly* **45** (Feb). Rpt in Cady E H (ed) 1973 *WD Howells as critic.* Routledge & Kegan Paul, London, p 53.
24. James 1888 pp 393, 394.
25. Edel L (ed) 1974 *Henry James letters volume I 1843–1875.* Belknap Press, Harvard, Mass, p 208.
26. Ibid p 228.
27. James H 1914 *Notes of a son and brother.* Macmillan, London, pp 72–3.
28. James H 1872 *The Nation* **14** (14 March): 172–3. Rpt in Crowley J D (ed) 1970 *Hawthorne: the critical heritage.* Routledge & Kegan Paul, London, p 448.
29. James H 1897 Nathaniel Hawthorne. In Warner C D (ed) 1897 *Library of the world's best literature ancient and modern* (30 vols). Peale R S and Hill J A, New York, vol 12. Rpt in Edel L (ed) 1984 *Henry James: literary criticism.* Literary Classics of the United States, New York, p 460.
30. James H 1905 *The proceedings in commemoration of the one hundredth anniversary of the birth of Nathaniel Hawthorne.* Essex Institute, Salem, Mass. Rpt in Edel 1984 p 469.
31. Quoted in Chatman S 1978 *Story and discourse: narrative structure in fiction and film.* Cornell University Press, Ithaca, NY, p 144.
32. Edel 1974 p 240.
33. Edel L (1962) 1978 *Henry James: the conquest of London: 1870–1881.* Avon Books, New York, p 309.
34. Leavis F R (1948) 1962 *The great tradition: George Eliot Henry James Joseph Conrad.* Peregrine Books, Harmondsworth, p 178.

9 Revisioning the American landscape: from Utopia to eco-critique

Renee Slater and Kate Fullbrook

Three Laws
Everything is Connected to Everything
Everything's Got to Go Somewhere
There's No Such Thing as a Free Lunch
                              The Last Whole Earth Catalog

Everything is older than we think.
                  W. G. Hoskins, *The Making of the English Landscape*

Writers concerned with representing the American landscape have inherited a tradition that makes it difficult to *see* the land itself. From the first, literary representation of the North American landscape has been dominated by images of infinitude, vastness, unlimited space. The sublime has been the characteristic mode chosen by American writers when they consider the interplay of nature and culture in their land. The extraordinary variety of the terrain of the continent tends to be read through filters of emotion, inspiration and, at times, terror, in an historically habitual taste for the grandiose interpretation of the land which runs from the divinely appointed readings of the Puritans, through the Burkean and Kantian sublime of the revolutionary and romantic periods, and on to the eco-catastrophists of the present day. This tradition of sublimity operates whether readings of the landscape are cast in positive or negative terms, and whether the land is treated in terms of geological and biological confirmation of political destiny, economic promise, or personal and spiritual enlightenment. And while it has become a truism to note that observations of landscape – anywhere and at any time – are mediated through known patterns of figuration and through already extant ideological frameworks, it is still the case that the American landscape, perhaps more than any, tends to be treated by native and foreign observers alike, as a screen onto which to project Utopian or dystopian imaginings.

The Eurocentric tradition

The key features of the American sublime are, and always have been, emptiness and radical newness. The pertinence of these features is dependent on particular Eurocentric viewpoints, ones which allowed early settlers, especially those from France and England, to read as devoid both of history and of population a landscape which had been inhabited since 12,000 BC, and which, at the time of first contacts with Europeans, had a population of about 2.5 million Native Americans in the area of the continental United States alone.[1] The prehistories which the European colonizers substituted for the actual history of the North American continent were also ancient, but belonged to European traditions rather than to the colonized land. These were mythic prehistories that both drew European settlers to America and erected barriers between them and their experience of the American landscape. The tropes of Eden, the Western Isles, Atlantis, El Dorado, The City on a Hill all carried messages of supernaturally sanctioned Utopian promise which bore little resemblance to the usually hard and confused conditions that the settlers encountered. Further, this generalized European mythos, though it took a variety of forms, tended to promote widespread readings of the American land as actively hostile when it revealed itself as other than edenic.[2]

The most important of these Eurocentric views was that of the Puritans. It is a commonplace that the Puritans regarded the new land as a 'hideous and desolate wilderness, full of wild beasts and wild men', as William Bradford luridly described it in 1650 in his 'History of Plymouth Plantation'. For Cotton Mather the Puritans were a 'people of God settled in those, which were once the devil's territories'. These Puritan fathers did not describe the landscape for its own sake; rather, the New World was seen as the site of the Kingdom of God on earth, a kingdom which it was their destiny to wrest from the wilderness. When the Puritan, Anne Bradstreet, finds herself moved to celebrate the beauties of her new home, she also feels at once the need to moralize them. She closes her 'Contemplations' with a gentle admonition against the dangers of taking pleasure in the natural world: the 'Fond fool . . . takes this earth ev'n for heav'n's bower'.[3] The Puritans' tendency to conceptualize the material world as an analogy for the spiritual world prevented them from *seeing* the material world or examining its phenomena. The Puritan belief that the wilderness was a desert – a waste land emptied of human life by divine providence on their behalf – helped justify the view that the land must be used and peopled by them in order to attain significance and value. Though not all early European arrivals in America were so blinded to the physical and historical actuality of the New World as the Puritans, none were so influential in shaping subsequent American attitudes.

The tendency to read American landscape in transcendent terms – and to be perpetually bewildered and disappointed by experience which fails to deliver transcendence through strictly spatial conquest – is deeply entangled with the strand of the American geopolitical imagination which runs from the 'Frontier Thesis' of Frederick Jackson Turner in the nineteenth century through to the Space Race in the late twentieth. If Utopian promises were unlikely to be fulfilled through Americans' experience of any particular place, their association of such promises with geographical movement remained (and to some extent remains) firm. The American 'elsewhere' is always envisaged as open to possession, as not yet defined, as available for appropriation. The concomitant tendency simply to abandon land that fails to deliver its Utopian promise is the dark side of unrealistic and unrealizable American expectations about the land.

Along with ideas that link emptiness to often unformulated expectations of total fulfilment, there is a network of interlocking cultural assumptions about the land that identify America with the radically new, the modern, the other, the unknown, the future. These ideas, like those regarding the emptiness of America, are European in origin. Robert Lawson-Peebles, for example, cites Amerigo Vespucci, Francis Bacon, John Donne and

John Locke as major contributors to early optimistic notions of the essential novelty of what came to be called the 'New World'.[4] But the idea of novelty carried problems as well as possibilities for writers who tried to formulate a literature to represent America adequately. A distinguished line of American writers running from Washington Irving, through Hawthorne and Fenimore Cooper to Henry James, and on to the expatriate writers of the 1920s stresses the newness of the American land- scape as a sign of the impoverished and irredeemably provincial cultural base which confronts the American writer. In contrast, the European terrain is read as dense with associations. America, from this negative viewpoint, is seen as cursed with novelty, as terrifyingly vacant and unable to give imaginative support to the human consciousnesses which occupy it, which can only struggle senselessly to understand a land lacking the visible marks of history to guide them.

But despite the depth and persistence of this troubled response, the optimistic reading of American newness has always been culturally dominant. From this positive, Jeffersonian stance, the novelty of America is linked to boundless opportunity, to unending possibilities for starting afresh. This is a position which evades history. In terms of the land, it promotes irresponsibility as well as appetite for radical experimentation. The perceived newness of the American landscape also creates other kinds of difficulties. Areas like those west of the Mississippi – the prairies, the Badlands, the Rocky Mountains, the southwestern deserts – cannot be assimilated easily to cognate European experiences of land forms, not even to those features (like the Alps) which are associated with traditions of the sublime. These areas presented deep and sometimes insoluble problems of perception and description for the early westering explorers and settlers. While the characteristic response to American newness was often shallowly optimistic in terms of representations of the land, there were moments when response was near to impossible, where experience seemed to reach out beyond the sublime to silence and incomprehension. The grand landscape without historical associations could generate blankness and anxiety rather than the purging terror characteristic of the European sublime, which always had its dialectical opposite of civilized beauty ready as comfort, should the thrill of the extreme prove overwhelming.[5]

The Emersonian tradition

The American dilemma in relation to the land, then, has always been how to represent what is there, both in immediate and in historical terms, in ways that avoid the distortions of European tropes of the sublime, in ways that resist silence, and which participate in the historical recovery necessary to trace the American experience of the land in patterns that reach both forward and backward in time. The classic answer, given by Emerson and Thoreau, is cultivation of an individual attentiveness to the natural world: an attentiveness so quiet and observant that nature is not disrupted by the solitary human observer who, by virtue of their perceptual humility, is granted experience of a new order of spiritual sublimity and a feeling of unity with the observed landscape. Emerson's famous description of this process in 'Nature' (1836) is a key moment for the development of this alternative attitude toward the American experience of place. 'In the woods', he writes,

> we return to reason and faith. There I feel that nothing can befall me in life, – no disgrace, no calamity (leaving me my eyes,) which nature cannot repair. Standing on the bare ground, – my head bathed by the blithe air, and – uplifted into infinite space, – all mean egotism vanishes. I become a transparent eye-ball; I am nothing; I see all; the currents of the Universal Being circulate through me; I am part or particle of God . . . I am the lover of uncontained and immortal beauty. In the wilderness, I find something more dear and connate than in streets or villages. In the tranquil landscape, and especially in the distant line of the horizon, man beholds somewhat as beautiful as his own nature.[6]

Emerson's viewpoint contains the seeds for a promising kind of apprehension of the American landscape, but it is also fraught with problems. He sidesteps the question of American history by dismissing it altogether. He also evades the endemic American difficulties with directly articulating experience of the land by preferring to describe the effect of his experience of nature on himself. The arrogance of this view, which makes immersion in nature by the solitary individual the source of spiritual sustenance without regard for the other, whether past, present, or future, suited traditional American views. It fitted well with the individualistic tendencies of Emerson's era and provided a fruitful starting point for American writers from Thoreau to Whitman to represent their own experiences of the land in rhapsodic individual modes. (Though, as we shall see later, these writers also operated in perceptual registers unavailable to Emerson.)

But as much as Emerson's transcendental naturism became the keynote for nineteenth-century American writing about the land, the problems it purported to solve remained unaddressed. Emerson's unwillingness actually to engage with either the landscape or his fellow citizens (except as guru and guide) remain the fundamental reasons why his ideas about the land are ultimately inadequate. Emerson's desire is not to see this world but to be lifted out of it and beyond it. He is as much a Utopian as those who wrote about the American land before him. History, for Emerson, is off the map, out of the picture. The Emersonian land remains as empty and as unavailable to history or community as in the problematic Eurocentric versions of the American sublime. Further, the experience Emerson describes as attendant on his radical non-intervention in the landscape (a 'transparent eyeball' is as limited (and as ugly) a synecdoche for the possibilities of human awareness as one can imagine) signals a passion for non-disruption that borders on the desire for annihilation. The hatred of matter here – of body and tree and rock – offers a version of human need as unattuned to general experience as the Puritan reading of the landscape as a religious dystopia of sin emanating from the anger of a righteous God. Emerson's extremist quietism, his version of a personal sublime triggered by thoughts *within* but not *of* that landscape, represented a *cul de sac* in the American search for a way to figure the landscape in ways that would prove both individually and historically satisfying.

It scarcely needs saying that the classic view of the American landscape considered so far, and the knotted problematics of inability to see or represent the land in ways that are simultaneously culturally satisfying and responsible, are overwhelmingly masculinist and imperialist in cast. If the land is seen in terms of a faulty sublimity – as incomprehensible and unspeakable virgin territory available to be used, without understanding, in any way, whether physical or spiritual, an appropriator sees fit – then it is no surprise that women and children (as the signs of culture, continuity and futurity) and all

Native Americans (as signs of the unacknowledged past) are excluded from consideration wherever possible. But they feature in the landscape as absent figures, as the human unconsciousness of writing about the American land whose presence would disrupt the tropes of absolute mastery on one hand, and absolute mystery on the other. If Native Americans are unavoidably brought into the picture, they are treated as part of the wilderness itself, rather than as persons with human ideas and consciousnesses. If women and children appear, they are either sentimentalized or portrayed as interferences with and encumbrances on the project of reading the continent in terms of emptiness, novelty, and lack of limitation.[7] The question for American writers is how to break the myth of limitlessness, how to write their way out of the sublime into a landscape that is finite rather than infinite, how to write their way into time.

The Thoreauvian tradition

The forging of an alternative tradition of seeing American landscape in terms other than those either of the unspeakable sublime or of individualistic satisfaction that is equally grandiose in its demands begins, for modern American literature, with Thoreau, who took Emerson at his word and actually *looked* intently at the landscape he inhabited. Thoreau's lead was followed by writers as diverse as Whitman, who in the very specificity of his epic naming of the places of the continent and its inhabitants gives linguistic substance to the particulars which minutely compose the vastness of America, and Willa Cather, who again by drawing on epic traditions, establishes the pastoral mode of the homesteading ethic as the proper and equal counterbalance to the ethic of unlimited mobility. The general tendency of the modern American writer who has been concerned to represent the land has not been to dismiss the sublime as a pernicious trope through which to read the landscape, but to attempt to infuse the sublime with elements absent in earlier usages. This writing tries to incorporate detailed attention to the land itself and to the creatures who live on it with the history which records the interaction of humanity with the land. The result is a modern American literature of the landscape which, when it is not caught (as much of it still is) in the old tropes of the sublimity of absolute movement characterized by the road and the desert, struggles to read the land in terms of a minute specificity which is spiritually enlightening and historically aware.

Thoreau, the literary naturalist, is the most significant precursor of late twentieth-century writers on landscape whose way of seeing and valuing the natural world is grounded in ethical and spiritual premises different from those of the Puritans and transcendentalists, premises which demand close attention to the natural world for itself.

Thoreau's drive to name the natural world accurately is strongly reinscribed in William Carlos Williams's attempt to 'rename the things seen' in American history in *In the American Grain* (1925). This book of imaginative historical reconstructions is written specifically against the tendency of the Puritan sublime to find 'one thing like another in a world destined for blossom only in "Eternity", all soul, all "emptiness" then here'. The Puritan mind, writes Williams, which shaped the basic principles of American ways of interpreting the land, was fundamentally opposed to looking at the material world. It was, to its especially great loss, 'precluded from SEEING the Indian . . . save as an unformed Puritan'.[8] Williams's point is that within a mental set like that of the Puritans, which reads through experience to a terrain beyond time and precursors, history becomes invisible, and, without history, ethics is impossible. This Puritan heritage of historical blindness leading to ethical incapacity is, in Williams's view, a dangerous element in American culture. As he argues:

> It is an extraordinary phenomenon that Americans have lost the sense, being made up as we are, that what we are has its origin in what *the nation* in the past has been; that there is a source in AMERICA for everything we think or do; that morals affect the food and food the bone, and that, in fine, we have no conception at all of what is meant by moral, since we recognize no ground our own – and that this rudeness rests all upon the unstudied character of our beginnings; and that if we will not pay heed to our own affairs, we are nothing but an unconscious porkyard and oilhole for those, more able, who will fasten themselves upon us.[9]

The answer to this lack of knowledge of and respect for either the past or the present is, for Williams, to abandon the habit of reading the natural world in terms of signs and to learn to touch the land and its creatures while becoming familiar with the records of what has been. Williams points a path many American writers have tried to follow in recent years: to move away from the ideologies of the sublime and the transparent eyeball, spinning out of the landscape into the eternal, and instead to become conscious participants in an environment that reaches responsibly forwards and backwards in history. That responsibility begins to include the greatly extended knowledge of the scientific community about the landscape. Tropes of the sublime do not disappear in American writing about the land but are modified and informed by a new and knowledgeable scientific sublime which does not rely exclusively on prior literary practice.

The contemporary situation

This tendency has gathered pace since the end of the Second World War, so much so that the most distinguished postwar commentators on American landscape can be seen as shaping a new, and temporarily definitive, tradition. Writers like Edward Abbey, Wendell Berry, Annie Dillard, Barry Lopez, Peter Matthiessen, N. Scott Momaday and Gary Snyder are concerned both to describe the land in its physical and historical dimensions and to awaken in their readers a respect for the non-human life of the land. They reassess the conventions which have dominated writing about the landscape and propose different ways of valuing the land.

Unlike the Puritans who saw the New World in terms of unredeemed desolation, these new writers see the empirical world as a source of blessing and revelation (and often of reproach). As wilderness has disappeared, so the value for humanity of its otherness, its silence and loneliness has become ever more apparent. Yet contemporary tropes that attempt to rework the sublime are characterized less by a sense of emptiness than by wonder at the fecundity, diversity, complexity and tenacity of life of all kinds in even the most apparently empty spaces. These recent writers reject the lofty solitary experience of the transcendent Emersonian observer of the landscape and instead adopt the point of view of one representative member of one species who is immersed in it.

Aldo Leopold's *Sand County Almanac* (1949) is the benchmark from which to chart the growth of this new kind of landscape writing. Leopold articulated a 'land ethic' which 'would change the role of *Homo sapiens* from conqueror of the land-community to plain member and citizen of it'.[10] Leopold's profoundly ethically–informed approach to the land implies the need for acute observation of and interest in the particularities of a given landscape. But far from being detached observers of the landscape they survey, human beings are called upon to recognize and to be accountable for the impact of even their most contemplative presence in the natural world.

Wendell Berry moves the formation of this tradition a step further. Berry – poet, essayist and farmer – takes as his subject his native place, an isolated smallholding in Kentucky. In so doing he consciously rejects the American literary tradition which assumes 'that the life of the metropolis is *the* experience, the *modern* experience, and that the life of the rural towns, the farms, the wilderness places is not only irrelevant to our times, but archaic as well because unknown or unconsidered by the people who really matter – that is, the urban intellectuals'.[11]

As a writer who is also a farmer, Berry comes to occupy, in a literal sense, the 'middle ground' defined by Leo Marx as 'somewhere "between", yet in a transcendent relation to, the opposing forces of civilization and nature'.[12] In recognizing and consciously choosing his native landscape as his subject, Berry becomes aware of 'the surprisingly long and difficult nature of *seeing* the country' on which he found himself 'so intricately dependent'.[13] He acknowledges the difficulties a landscape devoid of the associations of European pastoral presents to the writer, but he finds that the intense effort of observation and accumulation of knowledge about a particular place makes the details of the life of that place come clearly into focus. Berry links his desire to bring his native place into being for others with the development of his own linguistic capabilities: 'I began more seriously than ever to learn the names of things . . . and to articulate my observations and memories. My language increased and strengthened.'[14] The American preoccupation with naming becomes, for Berry, a means of responsible relation to his landscape which, in turn, lends concrete specificity to his poetry and the authority of considered experience to his essays.

As a farmer, Berry must contend with the destruction that years of poor husbandry have wrought on the fragile ecology of the Kentucky River watershed. The history of the white man's interaction with the land is inscribed in the eroded valleys and derelict river pastures of the country. The man who farms that land encounters both the signs of and the concrete reality of limitation at every turn of the plough. Berry's personal awareness of what has been lost in the history of casual abuse of the land finds expression in a jeremiad addressed to the nation as a whole and more specifically to a government which subordinates the interests of local communities and economies to those of an increasingly rapacious international absentee economy. Berry has consistently maintained that the land can only be properly cared for by people who know it intimately and who have some stake in it. The depopulation of the countryside and the destruction of rural communities (rural population has declined from 32 per cent of the national population in 1900 to just 3 per cent in 1980)[15] marks for him the end of the Jeffersonian dream of individual economic sufficiency through the prosperity of the land.[16]

Berry's sense of the necessary relation of people to land is, in his own words, religious, and the language he constructs to communicate this sense of reverence, with its biblical rhythms and echoes, proclaims him an inheritor of the religious tradition which moved the early settlers of his country. But Berry is also a political writer who brings the classic clarity of Jeffersonian thought to bear upon the Puritan tendency to read the landscape for divine messages, and the transcendental tendency to feed the individual psyche with rhapsodic intimations of natural affiliations. Berry's relation to the land is rooted in the history of his patient, responsible stewardship of his marginal farm. His smallholding becomes the microcosmic basis for universal speculation on the state of (agri)culture. Like Thoreau, in whose tradition he consciously locates himself, Berry continually interrogates the American ideologies which have so harmed the landscape he contemplates and cultivates. And like Thoreau, who 'travelled a good deal in Concord', Berry declares that in Port Royal, Kentucky, 'as well as any place I can look out my window and see the world'.[17] For Berry, as for Thoreau, the American sublime of long distances and inexhaustible space is replaced by intense and reverent attention to minutiae; the conquering gaze and the habit of heedless movement through the land are rejected in favour of meditative immersion in a distinct and definitive place.

Berry's writing career began in the late 1950s, when his subject matter, like his farm, was regarded as 'marginal'. Now his insistence on the importance of deep knowledge of the particulars of any landscape, and his call for respect and responsibility toward the land, put him at the centre of contemporary 'eco-literature'. In exchanging wonder for reverence he arrives at mystery only at last, through familiarity. In this he is not unlike the Native Americans whose relationship with the land he so much admires. Berry's contemplative project reaches out toward an ethic of inclusion, community and responsible use of the land, rather than to individual self-indulgence or corporate exploit-ation. In this, Berry's work links with that of other commentators on the American landscape who turn to non-Western, non-dualistic ways of apprehending place in the moment, seeking neither revelation nor exaltation nor profit from the land.

The poetry of Gary Snyder provides a clear example of this kind of tendency. Snyder has been an anthropologist, a sinologist, a forest fire lookout, and a student of Zen. His poetry describes simply his immediate experience of the concrete physical world. *Earth House Hold*, a collection of essays published in 1957, gives an indication of the range of Synder's recurring concerns. His governing concept of the household is closely related to the concept of ecology. If a household is a group of persons living under one roof and composing a family extended through time which includes ancestors, descendants and kindred, then the earth household includes all the creatures who live or have lived on the planet. Moving from this position of generosity and inclusion, Snyder is concerned to suggest the sacramental quality of the ordinary, to underline the way in which the daily life of the household can be seen to be meaningful and valuable in its detailed particularity. His sense of the beauty and nobility of common activity derives, at least in part, from his Zen training, which teaches the inestimable value of the present moment, whatever it contains. In Zen the Here-Now is all; as Snyder says, 'there is no other life'.[18] But Snyder's insistence on the connection between the quotidian and the sweep of geologic time reminds modern readers that the human place in the earth household is not privileged over that of other creatures or other times. Snyder thus widens Thoreau's concept of 'Economy' to one that reaches out from the moment and locates present action in the great sweep of time, domesticating the ancient and empty spaces that romantic transcendentalism figured as sublime.

An earlier part of this essay shows how American tropes of the sublime traditionally have depended upon the radical separation of the human from the natural world. To the Native American the landscape the white man has idealized as 'wild' and 'empty' is neither. Its vastness and variety are not occasions for a luxurious *frisson* of terror, nor for self-congratulation at being able to withstand their threat to the cohesion of the identity of the individual, who becomes a titan by resisting the sublime's intimations of insignificance. The Native American ethos is built on a profound sense of being at home in the world, the companion and equal of the other creatures who inhabit it. Where the Puritan sees the natural world as fallen and human beings as depraved, the Native American sees the world as given by the Great Spirit to provide for the needs of all. His ethic is founded on grateful respect for the gift of the material world. The Native American spiritual trajectory is not outward away from this life, but inward toward a fullness of being as a responsible member of the earth household. It is precisely this radically other vision of ethical response to the American land to which Snyder signalled his affinity in his Pulitzer Prize-winning collection of poetry, *Turtle Island* (1974).

As writers attempting to live ecologically responsible lives, both Berry and Snyder look to the example of the Native Americans who, as Berry puts it, 'had the wisdom and the grace to live in this country for perhaps ten thousand years without destroying or damaging any of it'.[19] Barry Lopez, probably the pre-eminent American literary naturalist writing today, opens his highly acclaimed study, *Arctic Dreams* (1986), with a quotation from the Native American writer, N. Scott Momaday:

> Once in his life a man ought to concentrate his mind upon the remembered earth. He ought to give himself up to a particular landscape in his experience; to look at it from as many angles as he can, to wonder upon it, to dwell upon it.[20]

In his encounter with the Arctic, Lopez begins by acknowledging the presence of its indigenous people and accepting that their extensive knowledge of the land can only be gained from living intimately with it. Lopez asks an Inuit what he does when he comes to a new place, and the man replies: 'I listen.'[21] The European mode of the sublime is visual; it constructs man as spectator of the landscape and thereby limits the range of response to it. To 'listen' is to become aware of that which cannot be seen, to perceive and take cognizance of what remains invisible.

Lopez understands that it is only when one enters the land with self-effacing attentiveness and respect that the land opens itself. But, like Berry, he also approaches the land with the intellectual equipment of his own culture. His observations are informed by extensive reading not only in natural history, but in the conventional arts and sciences. Lopez knows the history of European exploration of the Arctic intimately. He has studied the archaeology of prehistoric Arctic cultures. He is a natural scientist. He knows American landscape painting. He understands the optical physics of the Arctic light. All this historical and scientific knowledge enables him to contemplate and apprehend the land from a multiplicity of human ways of knowing which privileges none of them.

Lopez tries always to imagine the wholeness of the land – winter as well as summer; darkness as well as light; pain, violence and death as well as beauty, harmony and order. This attempt 'to get a feeling for the proportions of a full life, one that confronts everything'[22] forestalls any tendency to romanticize the land or to yield to the primitivist illusion that life in remote places is somehow simpler or more innocent than life elsewhere.

Lopez's prodigious knowledge of the natural world renders him alive to the variety and complexity of even so bleak and seemingly empty a place as the Arctic. Nevertheless, he recounts the detail of his immediate sensory experience of the places he observes with the consciousness that 'we all . . . apprehend the land imperfectly, even when we go to the trouble to wander in it. Our perceptions are colored by preconception and desire.'[23] His attempts to understand the land are guided by this humility, and while Lopez has abandoned the sublime as a means of figuring his own relation to the landscape, he remains concerned to investigate the manifold figurations which structure our apprehension of the land. Faced with the ultimate unknowableness of the land, Lopez, like Snyder, Berry, and their Native American precursors, approaches it with a fundamental gesture of respect. He bows before it. Mystery lies at the end of patient, careful, reflective investigation.

It is clear from what has been said so far that the attitude of contemporary American writers to landscape is very different from that of either the Puritans or the early westering settlers. Writers on the landscape today cannot escape the recognition that landscapes are not only real but also 'artifacts of human perception' and figments of human desire.[24] Their work is characterized by attention, respect, studious observation and the attempt to enter imaginatively into the life of a particular landscape in all its detail. It is also characterized by a desire to redeem past moral failures in the treatment of the landscape by a culture whose earlier encounters with the land were marked by a sense of wonder which was quickly displaced with wreckage and waste. Contemporary American writers on the landscape are at times nearly overwhelmed by the scale of destruction wrought on the landscape of their country within a few hundred years, and by the dimensions of what has been lost in the process. All tend to position themselves in their accounts of the landscape as humble exemplars of possible other ways of being. Berry's response is both outraged and robustly didactic. He uses his life as an instance of the possible harmony between human desire and the land in an agricultural context. Snyder is cautiously Utopian. He examines the possibilities for alternative political and economic arrangements which would take account of the planet as well as its current human inhabitants. Exploring the Arctic, Lopez comes face to face with the tremendous pressures to exploit that landscape. He tries to find a way through the contradictions that mark the fissure points between different cultures, desires and dreams that define and lay claim to the land. If he is hopeful, it is a willed hope, and his tone is often melancholy if not tragic.

It comes as no surprise to see that these writers break the bounds of conventional intellectual categories as much as they break through the limitations of the romantic sublime. Their work is as likely to be discussed in theological and scientific journals as in the *Sewanee Review* or in *Western American Literature*. Their writing displaces the traditional discourse of the sublime, with its construction of European man as the detached spectator and heroic master of majestic, limitless and empty American spaces. In its place they forge a discourse of the American landscape which locates human beings in an attentive relation of respect and gratitude for all that the land contains.

Notes

1. Buter K W The Indian legacy in the American landscape. In Conzens M P (ed) 1990 *The making of the American landscape*. Unwin Hyman, London, pp 28, 45.
2. Lawson-Peebles R 1988 *Landscape and written expression in revolutionary America*. Cambridge University Press, Cambridge, p 2.
3. Bradford W Of Plymouth plantation. Rpt in Baym N *et al* (ed) 1985 *The Norton anthology of American literature* (2 vols). Norton, New York, vol 1 p 70; Cotton M The wonders of the invisible world. In Baym 1985 vol 1 p 225; Bradstreet A Contemplations. In Baym 1985 vol 1 p 107.
4. Lawson-Peebles 1988 p 10.
5. Fender S 1989 American landscape and the figure of anticipation. In Gidley M, Lawson-Peebles R (eds) 1989 *Views of American landscapes*. Cambridge University Press, Cambridge, pp 51–63.
6. Emerson R W 1982 *Selected Essays* ed L Ziff. Penguin, Harmondsworth, p 39.
7. See Gidley M 1989 The figure of the Indian in photographic landscapes. In Gidley, Lawson-Peebles (eds) 1989 pp 199–220; Murray D 1988 From speech to text: the making of American Indian autobiographies. In Bell I F A, Adams D K (eds) 1988 *American literary landscapes: the fiction and the fact*. Vision Press, London, pp 29–43. For a study of American women's experience of the land see Kolodny A 1984 *The land before her: fantasy and experience of the American frontier 1630–1860*. University of North Carolina Press, Chapel Hill.
8. Williams W C (1925) 1971 *In the American grain*. Penguin, Harmondsworth, p 125.
9. Ibid p 121.
10. Leopold A 1986 *A Sand County almanac*. Ballantine, New York, pp 240, 261.
11. Berry W A native hill. In Berry W 1981 *Recollected essays, 1965–1980*. North Point Press, Berkeley, Ca, p 78.

12. Marx L 1964 *The machine in the garden: technology and the pastoral ideal in America.* Oxford University Press, Oxford, p 23.
13. Berry W The long-legged house. In Berry 1981 pp 42–3.
14. A native hill. In Berry 1981 p 79.
15. Jackson K T 1985 *Crabgrass frontier: the suburbanization of the United States.* Oxford University Press, Oxford, p 173.
16. Wendell W Sept 1992 Conservation and local economy. Lecture given at Dartington Conference.
17. The long-legged house. In Berry 1981 p 66.
18. Snyder G 1974 *Turtle Island.* New Directions, New York, p 63.
19. A native hill. In Berry 1981 p 85.
20. Lopez B 1987 *Arctic Dreams.* Picador, London, p ix.
21. Ibid p 257.
22. Ibid p 244.
23. Ibid p 257.
24. Ibid p 256.

10 William Carlos Williams and the reconstruction of America

Les Arnold

All that will be new in America will be anti-Puritan.
It will be of another root.

In the American Grain

In *Yes, Mrs Williams*, William Carlos Williams assembled a 'personal record' of his mother out of conversations he had written down between 1924 and her death in 1949, aged 101. The book, originally published in 1959, has a foreword to its 1982 edition by Williams's son, Eric. In justifying the need for his father's book about 'this obscure little woman', Eric Williams reads her as

> this product of a tropical hotbed on a West Indian island, this multinational mongrel gentlewoman transplanted to a north temperate zone suburb of a major metropolis that was infested with WASP entrepreneurs who cared not a *centimo* for her religious, social, or cultural background.[1]

Curtly dismissing his grandfather as 'an Anglophile travelling-man citizen of Great Britain', Eric celebrates his grandmother's life – '(H.R.H. equals Her Royal Highness equals Helene Raquel Hoheb)' – and sees his own family not as Europeans but as 'spawn of the Caribbean'.[2] In both foreword and book, son and father direct their anger and resentment against the dominance of white Anglo-Saxon Protestantism – or WASPness – recognizing in part its embodiment in the distant figure of English father and grandfather, as a dominant orthodoxy which refuses to acknowledge any other source, historical, cultural, linguistic, for America.

Williams chose to transcribe his mother talking, certain that in the speech of this 'multinational francophile *senora*', moving between English, French and Spanish, he could indicate the multiplicity of the New World's ethnic 'mix', and implicitly indict any singular and simplistic reading of American culture and nationhood.[3] The tension between his English father, whom Williams coldly observed 'never became a citizen of the United States', and his mother, half French and half a 'mixed breed, the Hohebs, Monsantos',[4] serves as a useful analogue for those wider aesthetic tensions which underpin his writing. By consistently interrogating purposive, white, protestant maleness, identified as an essential part of a prevalent Puritanism, Williams deliberately kept alive another source for himself and for America. That source was especially registered in the talk of women, in the confidences of his female friends and patients, but most especially in his conversations with Flossie, his wife, and with his mother and grandmother. As his writing evolves, the voices of women join those of other unacknowledged citizens of the New World – Hispanics, Indians, blacks, the poor – in Williams's attempt to reconstruct America out of the unauthorized histories of its marginalized peoples.

Williams's reconstruction of America was angry and violent and began in the writer's consistent determination to defeat himself. Rejecting Baudelairean excesses, which he identified with an exalted vision of the 'artist' and the artist's necessary separateness from the material world, Williams's 'furious wish was to be normal, undrunk, balanced in everything'. He continues in his *Autobiography*:

> I would marry . . . have children and still write, in fact, therefore to write. I would not court disease, live in the slums for the sake of art, give lice a holiday. I would not 'die for art,' but live for it, grimly! and work, work, work (like Pop), beat the game and be free (like Mom, poor soul) to write, write as I should write, for the sheer drunkenness of it . . .[5]

Self-defeat confirmed Williams as a writer *within* a community, and his long residence in Rutherford as physician-poet suggests an awareness that the writer's first responsibility in his rewriting of America was to give voice to his town's inhabitants, among whom were many of his own patients.

In *Paterson* Williams constructs a city to house his voiceless poor, confirming his desire to remain a part of society, rather than an artist in isolation. In all his writings Williams explored ways of *opening* compositions so that 'roughness' or lack of literary finish would suggest the state of being human. The condition of 'openness' was for Williams an expression of contempt for WASPness and its closed forms where 'vain curlicues' displaced the urgent *news* about local and national environments which Williams believed good writing must communicate.[6] WASPness was synonymous with the falsification of America and the betrayal of the New World consciousness. Against it Williams built *Paterson* as a kind of newspaper, using, in Glauco Cambon's words, 'a montage technique' of loosely juxtaposed facts that would destroy what was generally accepted as 'news'.[7] In 'Asphodel, That Greeny Flower', Williams argued:

> it is difficult
> to get the news from poems
> yet men die miserably every day
> for lack
> of what is found there.[8]

Closed art – the art of New York's 'literary boilermakers' – offered by contrast only artifice or 'clever drawing' which resulted in 'legend' and the mystification and enshrinement of both Literature and other written forms such as the seamless prose of Madison Avenue.[9]

Self-defeat led inevitably to other, more violent attempts to defeat Puritanism in all its written forms. His early poems, influenced by his close friendship with painters such as Charles Sheeler and Charles Demuth, record Williams in the act of purging himself of literary 'excesses'. Williams deliberately burned off unwanted flesh – adjective, adverb, whatever delayed the reader in his/her reading of the poem. Such poetry is charged with an urgency – 'so much depends' – which sees in the act of reading a liberation from cultural restraints, a freeing of the reader to read his/her world for the first time.[10] Interestingly, in *Kora in Hell*, Williams associates this need for re-vision with the figure of his mother:

Thus, seeing the thing itself without forethought or afterthought but with great intensity of perception, my mother loses her bearings or associates with some disreputable person or translates a dark mood . . . She is a despoiled, molted castaway but by this power she still breaks life between her fingers.[11]

Williams began to clear the ground for the building of his city-text, *Paterson*, with his deconstruction of literary 'models' in the 1920s. *Kora in Hell* (1920), *Spring and All* (1923), *The Great American Novel* (1923) and *In the American Grain* (1925) are attempts – angry, violent, mischievous – to represent the American writer's task as initially one of destruction. What has to be de-created, Williams argues, is no less than the concept of 'literature' itself. His aim was to destroy past concepts of poetry, including what, in *Spring and All*, he calls those 'Traditionalists of Plagiarism' whose Puritan mind-set dominates thinking about it.[12]

Decolonizing 'literature' begins in the improvisational freedom of *Kora in Hell* where the release of repressed energies suggests an analogue to the larger freedoms Williams seeks from a dominant WASP ideology. *Kora* is informed by a principle of regeneration, figured in Kora-Persephone herself, which indicates a potential for renewal within the repressive 'hell' Williams identifies as both New York and his own consciousness.[13] Although, in the arrangement of its materials, *Kora* adopts a public posture, the text is constantly interrupted by irrepressible outbursts of exuberant energy. The 'Whee!' and 'Ah!' of the writer point to an enthusiasm and urgency which seek always to disturb, disrupt and finally subvert.

Both *The Great American Novel* and *Spring and All* continue the task of subversion. *Novel*, for example, rejects narrative continuities and the 'impertinence' of literary time. It contrives a 'hero' out of a 'little dusty car' and grounds its aesthetic not in other literary models but in the anecdotes of a doctor's life and reading.[14] *Novel* accommodates details of childbirth and hysterectomy, stories of the Mayor Indians, fragments of Mormon history and of Williams's domestic life. It rejects, most significantly, the concept of literary 'finish' and offers instead a principle of inclusiveness which informs all Williams's later work, particularly *Paterson*.

Spring challenges not only the concept of a volume of poems but also of poetry itself, reading it as part of a writing process from which prose cannot be excluded. The American writer, Williams judged, must confront and clear away this colonial debris before the building of a new American literature could begin. His parodies of the 1920s work to counter Literature's spurious 'mechanics' which subordinated materials to casual functions and overt transitions. The deliberate discontinuities of his parodies in both *Novel* and *Spring* are the result of Williams's belief in a radical newness.

What Williams wanted was nothing less than a new beginning. His New World, linked inexorably to a new mind, embodied in a new national literature and informed by a new historical vision, is the single consistent subject of his writing. Spring, the image of Kora-Persephone, 'Nuevo Mundo!',[15] all registered that newness which for Williams indicated the world cleared of its ideological detritus and *seen* for the first time as, for example, by the Dutch sailors in Nick Carraway's sentimentalizing vision at the close of *The Great Gatsby*. Seeing clearly signifies a freedom from a distorting puritan morality, a judgemental view which provides, Williams believed, 'a constant barrier between the reader and his consciousness of immediate contact with the world'.[16]

In the American Grain

'Of course History', Williams argued in *Kora*, 'is an attempt to make the past seem stable and of course it's all a lie'.[17] The documentary sources of American history named individuals and events in the American past but did not 'reveal' history. History, like Place, remained for Williams 'that secret and sacred presence', which it was the writer's responsibility to uncover.[18] His function, he argued in his prefatory note to *In the American Grain*, was to 'separate out from the original records some flavour of an actual peculiarity', drawing from his assembled sources 'the strange phosphorous of the life, nameless under an old mis-appellation'. Conventional histories were little more than 'legend' sugared by a 'sentimental overlay'. History had entered the service of the state, its meanings and usefulness enshrined in time past and perpetuating a myth of progress which had culminated in the 'glories' of a twentieth-century New York puritanism which Williams describes as 'an atrocious thing, a kind of mermaid with a corpse for tail'.[19] *In the American Grain* seeks to uncover the New World wilderness buried beneath accretions of 'civilized' documentary judgements. What Williams sought in all his searches through materials was nothing less than the 'spirit of place' itself and that spirit was equated with a prevailing female principle which consistently resisted the efforts of male explorers and writers like himself.

Their very inertness was an essential part of the documents' function for those later 'puritans' who retained a vested interest in encoding a singular reading of the American past, particularly as that view privileged them as first citizens. Popular History offered only 'heroes of antiquity' conceived by 'emotional grandeur'.[20] Asserting a national narrative in which white Christian Adams took possession of a receptive New World Garden, settling a recalcitrant wilderness, taming wildness both within and without, its historians, Williams believed, established a textual Mount Rushmore of, for example, Washingtons and Franklins which had become formalized as a monument to white, protestant maleness. Such narratives ignored the contribution to national life of later waves of immigrants and indeed the rights and the very existence of America's native peoples. *In the American Grain* corrects this reading by reassessing documentary sources and by asserting that the very touchstone of American national identity is not the puritan 'spirit' but the Indian and those, like the Catholic missionary, Père Sebastian Rasles, who retained sympathetic understanding of the Indian. 'I do believe the average American to be an Indian', Williams argued, 'but an Indian robbed of his world'.[21]

The Puritans never understood the newness of their New World, foisting upon it a pale imitation of the Old and building a stockade-mentality – 'horrid walls' – to defend its orthodoxies against the wilderness.[22] Their refusal to acknowledge newness is captured in their fear of 'touch' which extends from relations with their women to their inability to make contact with the new world about them. Instead of registering its newness and accommodating it within structures which celebrated its difference from Europe, the Puritans worked by principles of exclusion, shutting out what they did not understand and revealing for Williams both a failure of nerve and a repression of instinct. For understanding of the New World they substituted purposive action; for love they substituted violence. In coming to terms with the earliest 'gathers' Williams identifies the source for America in the twentieth century which he reads as 'the most lawless country in the civilized world, a panorama of murders, perversions, a terrific ungoverned strength, excusable only because of the horrid beauty of its great machines'.[23]

In the American Grain scratches beneath the imposed culture of puritanism to resurrect the Indian whom Williams equates with the spirit of the land itself. The Indian *is* the New World incarnate and his relationship to that World is the essential metaphor for Williams's own relationship to his world and the poetics which result from it.

Williams's deconstruction of authorized history is uncompromising. He angrily violates the apparent objectivity of WASP historians by tinkering with documents; he rejects the narrative continuities of historical texts by asserting the immediacy of History and establishes an alternative reading of America which owes much to non-white, non-protestant, non-male perspectives. To find literal room for those voices Williams dialogizes the language of written documents and begins, particularly in 'The Advent of the Slaves', to counter the proprieties of American New England, writing with the broken energies of marginalized people talking:

> dancing, singing with the wild abandon of being close, closer, closest together; waggin', wavin', weavin', shakin'; or alone, in a cabin, at night, in the stillness, in the moonlight – bein' nothin' – with gravity, with tenderness – they arrive and 'walk all over God's heaven –'[24]

In this way *In the American Grain* reflects the beginnings of the writer's obsessive need to accommodate voices other than his own, to represent American history not from a single vision but through a multiplicity of responses to it. Such voices work to subvert not only that history's monolithic nature but more especially his own authorial voice as that voice threatens to assert its own tyranny.

In the American Grain is informed by Williams's revision of American history, although it is difficult to say whether the work is itself a 'history' or a long poem. In it Williams re-examines familiar documents such as the Norse sagas or Cotton Mather's 'record' of the Salem witchcraft trials and the work of earlier historians such as Filson, Daniel Boone's biographer, to resurrect individual energies withering within a strongly judgemental viewpoint. He also attempts to reconstruct the voices of historical presences by stylistically recreating those who, like the 'Indians' under Montezuma, would otherwise have no voice, and rewrites those like Erik the Red who would otherwise remain victims of a dominant orthodoxy, excluded from a WASP vision which equates the beginning of American history with Protestantism and the landing of the Pilgrim Fathers. *In the American Grain* thus offers a history written and ghost-written from multiple perspectives, where Indian and Puritan engage in a dialogue rooted in a documented past the relevance of which dominates twentieth-century American thought. Williams therefore provides not historical continuity but temporal simultaneity.

In *In the American Grain* history is always present, immediate and part of the writer's consciousness as s/he engages with the 'moment'.[25] Either writers are condemned by their own words and their writings stand as testimony to various failures of instinct or vision, or they are rewritten by Williams and kept alive. The historically 'exiled' Aaron Burr, for example, is brought back from public shame and exclusion to speak in his own words in 'The Virtue of History'; Erik the Red is translated into a muscular idiom which speaks of his singleness of vision and freedom from self-pity. Such chapters argue that history is made by individuals – 'great' men who in the main do not receive the recognition they deserve from Puritan historians reading them from a singular viewpoint. *In the American Grain* places these men against leaderless Puritans each of whom, small and several, 'shrank from an imagination that would sever him from the rest'. One individual singled out by Williams, for example, is Samuel de Champlain whom he reads through Parkman's biography. His chapter, 'The Founding of Quebec', not only interrogates Parkman's writing of Champlain but re-sees what Parkman records, interrupting the record to make Parkman's history 'present' and immediate, and bringing Champlain back to life from his written shroud:

Parkman says 'Champlain was a man all for the theme and purpose, nothing for himself.' Good Lord, these historians! By that I understand the exact opposite of what is written: a man all for himself – but gently, with love, with patience, unwilling to endure the smallest fracture of his way of doing. He knew Champlain and followed Champlain in everything. See if I am not right.[26]

History is thus the record of the historian's active engagement with his materials – how he presents, interprets, foists his own visions upon, his apparent subject. Williams's emphasis in his chapter on Champlain is to show the writer thinking through and with his materials – Champlain *and* Parkman – generating questions which lead to an imaginative recreation based upon an authenticated source. What Williams achieves is a doubleness of vision as both Williams *and* Parkman write Daniel Boone. The acquisition by Williams of individuals, redeemed from a static past by either a new language or a new look at familiar documents, generates historical justification for Williams's real subject – his own writing.

Paterson

In Williams's work the search to uncover the New World, the search for a new language to articulate it and the search for new forms of organization to accommodate it are inextricable. Writing is the means by which the old Puritan mind-set can finally be laid to rest. As a process or journey itself – though one without purposive 'direction'[27] – it can represent the individual mind moving about the world, crossing that space or wilderness which *is* America seen for the first time, and refusing all shelter within alien and imposed literary forms. Writing, too, rejects the idea of settlement. Like the movement of the Passaic River which structures *Paterson*, it has its phases, its moods, its quiet backwaters, its rapid torrents, but it is always moving, and in that movement lies the essential counterbalance to poorly founded and ill-considered social and literary structures. It is indeed only during the act of writing that American space can be quickened to life. The spirit of place, Williams argues, cannot be confined with the crab to a box which seeks only to contain and mutilate it.[28] It is, rather, uncovered by the imagination as the writer moves among his materials, refusing to subsume their voices within his own, acknowledging his partiality, generating energies which may not substantiate any spuriously coherent view of that spirit but which attempt to release them in the writer's sudden shock of recognition. The 'spirit of place', the New World's stench, the wilderness and American space, exist only in the writer's writing. Like Williams himself, struggling to place writing in the activities of his life as doctor, it ceases to exist when the writing stops.

The need to write, and fear of the responsibilities it placed upon him, occupied Williams throughout his life. Writing was an act of decolonization, an act of liberation, a declaration of independence from domestic constraints and expectations. Much of Williams's writing is characterized by intense surges of energy, a fearful joy at the abundance of the materials through which he tries to find his way and an accompanying frustration that there seems no way of accommodating it. Such surges suspend normal rules of grammar, delay syntax or reverse it, thwart a reader's expectations. Books begin with their endings and once ended can begin again. In this un- and non-grammatical headlong rush an ill-defined reality is touched and acknowledged. Writing's freedom, however, is illusory. In *The Desert Music*, for example, Williams begins with that break in consciousness, figured by a dash, which suggests a poem is triggered. What follows is a restatement of the aesthetic baggage he carries within and an awareness of the painful self-realization in which he is already involved. Anxious to rediscover on another writing journey that elusive spirit of place, and yet fearing his own inability to make himself yet again complete the process and confirm himself poet, Williams prevaricates, dodging where possible into local bars to avoid the touch of the world outside. Understanding the writing process, alert to responsibility, Williams's development as writer is related to sharpening his skills as he moves among his materials, making connections. It is a journey whose purpose is defined by the poet in what Wallace Stevens called 'the act of finding what will suffice'.[29]

This journey, however, is not attempted alone. The written materials through which the writer makes his way are documents culled from a variety of historical, personal and social sources.

Each document releases into the writer's path a voice or series of voices which the writer acknowledges, responds to, but does not finally assimilate. The writer's need is to stay open to new experiences, to recognize the inappropriateness of such assimilation and to cope with the failure inevitable in such a recognition. 'The poet', Williams wrote in 'The Poem Paterson', the last chapter of his *Autobiography*, 'thinks with his poem, in that lies his thought and that in itself is the profundity'.[30] The result of Williams's rejection of the poem as net is an open composition alive to accidents and imperfections which might suddenly reveal the hidden 'spirit of place'. The innumerable difficulties such a rejection of a safety net imposes upon the writer are implicit in the difficulties of building *Paterson*.

In selecting Paterson, New Jersey, as site for his city-text, Williams was mindful of the need to ground his reconstruction of American history in a *local* community. Williams *knew* Paterson, had walked its river, observed its impressive falls, read its city-guides and researched its history. Paterson was, after all, only a few miles from the town of Rutherford where Williams had been born and where he had lived as physician-poet for more than 50 years. Williams had local knowledge. He had heard Billy Sunday preach; he had talked with John Reed who had written the collaged *Seven Days That Shook The World* and organized the Paterson workers' pageant. In particular he knew its inhabitants, had heard their voices and as a compulsive collector of such data had recorded those voices, probably on prescription blanks. He was immersed in its 'spirit of place', and fired by an awareness that local history, written or at least redistributed by an enthusiastic 'amateur', would reveal an America previously undiscovered by professional historians writing at a level of generalization.

Williams's reconstruction of American history and his implicit rewriting of America take shape in this local emphasis and his belief, citing John Dewey, that 'the local is the only universal, upon that all art builds'.[31] *Paterson* embodies Williams's belief that good writing begins in particulars, not in 'vague categories', and that a poet writes 'as a physician works, upon a patient, upon the thing before him, in the particular to discover the universal'.[32] The commitment to realize the city's own history, and the corollary awareness that a place had to be found for those inhabitants of the city who had no other way of making a contribution to that history, dominates Williams's building of his city-text.

But it was the Passaic River, flowing through the city and through its various and discrete phases, which finally convinced Williams he had chosen wisely. Despite pollutants and industrial waste, the Passaic flowed on. In its very movement Williams recognized an image of the writing energies he needed to make use of if he were to activate those written materials he had assembled for his poem. As they came more and more to hand the materials remained inert. The past of Paterson remained locked inside a colonial language which recorded but did not re-enact the past. Paterson present, Williams argued, needed knowledge of its past before it could understand its fallen condition, and the reader, as in *In the American Grain*, needed to understand the reasons for that fall if s/he were to come to an understanding of America. The writer's task was to find a way of making that past significantly present and in the image of the Passaic he understood both the energy required and the poem's methodology.

Williams had in mind the four phases of the river to structure his work, beginning with the relatively unpolluted river upstream above Paterson, and continuing with the falls, the river below the falls and closing – in his original conception of the poem – with the river meeting the sea in the area of the Chesapeake Bay. In this way Williams had both a visible principle whereby a local knowledge could be dispersed and made 'universal', and a strong image of the phases of writing itself – from moods of pastoral quietude to angry cascades of 'thinking' for which the writer struggles to find a language.

The river, however, served a far more specific purpose, embodying in its own history both a political and a literary principle. In the nineteenth century the falls had been used to generate power for SUM, the Society of Useful Manufactures, a company owned in part by Alexander Hamilton, with his vision of a federal city to meet the country's needs. *Paterson*, the city-text, is a reply to this federal exploitation of Paterson's local resources, and a fierce celebration of the local which registers contempt for literary and political 'federalism'.

The interrelatedness of his interest in the reconstruction of

America and his local emphasis as writer can be better understood by looking in further detail at Williams's interest in Paterson's weaving industry. SUM's 'prominant purpose', Williams argued, was 'the manufacture of cotton goods' by harnessing the power of the falls. In addition, it would produce 'cassimeres, wall papers, books, felt and straw hats, shoes, carriages, pottery, bricks, pots, pans and buttons needed in the United States', but its main product remained cotton goods.[33] SUM, under the direction of Alexander Hamilton, came thus to embody for Williams a negation of Paterson's 'spirit of place'. Its local industries included fine-quality woollen weaving and George Washington, for instance, had worn a Paterson coat at his first inaugural. SUM was for Williams another example of colonialism by federal intervention in local economics and of the imposition of a generalized national vision, fiscal, industrial, political, upon a particular locale. It exploited natural and human resources to produce cheap goods of poor quality. The power of the falls, central to Williams's belief in that 'abundance' within and without the individual, was thus harnessed to make what Williams called in *Paterson* Book Five an 'age of shoddy'.[34]

His reply to the age of shoddy, and the culmination of his interest in weaving, was *Paterson* Book Five, founded upon the Unicorn tapestries in the Cloisters 'annexe' to the Metropolitan Museum of Modern Art. Williams's interest in the tapestries begins in their means of production and continues in the integration of production methods, community vision and central motifs. The tapestries, dating from the fifteenth century and of French origin, offered Williams evidence of the continuities of both the natural and human world, and suggested a direct response to Hamilton and the machinery of SUM. Beginning as a 'cartoon', worked upon by an entire community, the tapestries articulated a quality of endeavour based not on profit motive but on a detailed attention to the registering of their world. Against what Williams saw as the 'indifference' coursing his own society he juxtaposed a society's love glimpsed in the tapestry-makers' art. Implicit in the Cloisters tapestries is a political statement, an active example of a democratic community which is given voice by its participation in art. The mind which organizes the vision of the tapestries owes their realization to that community. The tapestries confirmed for Williams that the artist was a functioning member of his community, and that his doubts about the authority – and 'colonising impulse' – of a singular vision could be allayed by the methodologies implicit in them. The community who weaved the Cloisters tapestries have their contemporary counterparts in the inhabitants of Paterson and their voices which Williams weaves together in *Paterson*.

Williams's attention, however, remains on the weaving process itself. It underpins an important local industry while embodying the principles whereby Williams 'unravels' and 'combs' through his materials using the warp and weft of prose and poetry in an attempt to 'weave' the poem into whole cloth.[35] Williams thus uncovers in his thinking through his materials an analogue to the writing process. Weaving similarly describes the movement of Indians through the locale. As Williams walks through Garrett Mountain Park he sees 'across the old swale – a dry wave in the ground / tho' marked still by the line of Indian alders', and remembers 'they [the Indians] would weave / in and out, unseen, among them along the stream'.[36]

In identifying weaving as a principle of movement associated with the Indians, Williams finds local confirmation of his poetics. Rejecting purposive movement – the subsuming 'direction' of colonial 'literature' – and substituting instead an indirection allows both the writer freedom to move among his materials and the reader freedom to evaluate that process and the materials through which the writer imaginatively journeys.

Williams's conception of *Paterson* as weaving or tapestry is the simple culmination of his desire to connect things up. Having much admired Juan Gris's collage compositions from the 1920s, Williams had made early use of Gris's analogy of the painterly 'fabric' in his attempts to define the appearance of a similar fabric in the poetry of Marianne Moore. Weaving signified the means whereby the maker, in accepting responsibility for materials, integrated them within a composition while retaining the integrity of individual elements. In *Paterson* the prose extracts confirm a public presence in a poem in which the poet, by thinking aloud, always runs the danger of too intense an introspection. They function deliberately to defeat the poet in his inevitable impulse to 'colonise' America for himself. Their voices clamour incessantly throughout *Paterson* for a place in its rewriting.

Williams knew his attempts to acknowledge his world's 'abundance' would end in failure. Conceptually, the poem – 'an image large enough to embody the whole knowable world about me' – was always too ambitious.[37] But such a failure, far from diminishing the poem and the poet's sense of his responsibilities, serves rather to strengthen the poet's resolve to continue. 'Failure', particularly failure to replicate the glutinous stability of Puritanism, is the condition necessary to defeat its ideological need for a spurious coherence. And failure also ensures the self-defeat which commits the writer to the continuing pursuit of his 'quest'. Although *Paterson* was originally conceived in four books, published between 1946 and 1951, Book Five appeared in 1958 and fragments of a sixth book were discovered in Williams's papers on his death in 1963.

Notes

1. Williams W C (1959) 1982 *Yes Mrs Williams: a personal record of my mother*. Macgibbon & Kee, London, p ix.
2. Ibid pp xv, xvi.
3. Ibid p ix.
4. Ibid p 3.
5. Williams W C (1951) 1967 *The autobiography of William Carlos Williams*. Random House, New York, p 51.
6. Williams W C 1969 *Selected essays of William Carlos Williams*. New Directions, New York, p 129.
7. Cambon G 1963 *The inclusive flame: studies in American poetry*. Indiana University Press, Bloomington, p 15.
8. Asphodel, That Greeny Flower. In Williams W C (1962) 1968 *Pictures from Breughel and other poems*. MacGibbon & Kee, London, pp 161–2.
9. William W C (1925) 1966 *In the American grain*. MacGibbon & Kee, London, p 105; Williams 1969 pp 232, 140.
10. *Spring and all*. In Williams W C 1970 *Imaginations: five experimental prose pieces* ed Webster Schott. MacGibbon & Kee, London, p 138.
11. *Kora in Hell*. In Williams 1970 p 8.
12. *Spring and all*. In ibid p 94.
13. *Spring and all*. In ibid p 116.
14. *The great American novel*. In Ibid pp 213, 171.
15. *The great American novel*. In ibid p 181.

16. *Spring and all*. In ibid p 88.
17. *Kora in Hell*. In ibid p 41.
18. Williams 1967 p 390.
19. Williams 1966 p 115.
20. Ibid p 174.
21. Ibid p 128.
22. Ibid p 129.
23. Ibid p 86.
24. Ibid p 209.
25. *Spring and all*. In Williams 1970 p 89.
26. Williams 1966 p 69.
27. Williams W C 1963 *Paterson*. New Directions, New York, p 28.
28. Williams 1969 p 188.
29. Stevens W 1955 Of modern poetry. *The collected poems of Wallace Stevens*. Faber & Faber, London, p 239.
30. Williams 1967 p 391.
31. Ibid p 391.
32. Ibid p 391.
33. Williams 1963 p 91.
34. Ibid p 266.
35. Ibid pp 15, 25, 100.
36. Ibid pp 67–8.
37. Ibid p 391.

PART II
Selected Documents

The Constitution of the United States, 1787

Reprinted from Heffner R D (ed) 1965 *A Documentary History of the United States* 2nd edn. New American Library, New York, pp 24–34.

We the People of the United States, in order to form a more perfect union, establish justice, insure domestic tranquility, provide for the common defence, promote the general welfare, and secure the blessings of liberty to ourselves and our posterity, do ordain and establish this Constitution for the United States of America.

ARTICLE I

Sec 1 All legislative powers herein granted shall be vested in a Congress of the United States, which shall consist of a Senate and House of Representatives.

Sec 2 The House of Representatives shall be composed of members chosen every second year by the people of the several States, and the electors in each State shall have the qualifications requisite for electors of the most numerous branch of the State legislature.

No person shall be a Representative who shall not have attained to the age of twenty-five years, and been seven years a citizen of the United States, and who shall not, when elected, be an inhabitant of that State in which he shall be chosen.

Representatives and direct taxes shall be apportioned among the several States which may be included within this Union, according to their respective numbers, which shall be determined by adding to the whole number of free persons, including those bound to service for a term of years, and excluding Indians not taxed, three-fifths of all other persons. The actual enumeration shall be made within three years after the first meeting of the Congress of the United States, and within every subsequent term of ten years, in such manner as they shall by law direct. The number of Representatives shall not exceed one for every thirty thousand, but each State shall have at least one Representative; and until such enumeration shall be made, the State of New Hampshire shall be entitled to choose three, Massachusetts eight, Rhode Island and Providence Plantations one, Connecticut five, New York six, New Jersey four, Pennsylvania eight, Delaware one, Maryland six, Virginia ten, North Carolina five, South Carolina five, and Georgia three.

When vacancies happen in the representation from any State, the executive authority thereof shall issue writs of election to fill such vacancies.

The House of Representatives shall choose their Speaker and other officers; and shall have the sole power of impeachment.

Sec 3 The Senate of the United States shall be composed of two Senators from each State, chosen by the legislature thereof, for six years, and each Senator shall have one vote.

Immediately after they shall be assembled in consequence of the first election, they shall be divided as equally as may be into three classes. The seats of the Senators of the first class shall be vacated at the expiration of the second year, of the second class at the expiration of the fourth year, and of the third class at the expiration of the sixth year, so that one-third may be chosen every second year; and if vacancies happen by resignation, or otherwise, during the recess of the legislature of any State, the executive thereof may make temporary appointments until the next meeting of the legislature, which shall then fill such vacancies.

No person shall be a Senator who shall not have attained to the age of thirty years, and been nine years a citizen of the United States, and who shall not, when elected, be an inhabitant of that State for which he shall be chosen.

The Vice-President of the United States shall be President of the Senate, but shall have no vote, unless they be equally divided.

The Senate shall choose their other officers, and also a President pro tempore, in the absence of the Vice-President, or when he shall exercise the office of President of the United States.

The Senate shall have the sole power to try all impeachments. When sitting for that purpose, they shall be on oath or affirmation. When the President of the United States is tried, the Chief Justice shall preside: and no person shall be convicted without the concurrence of two-thirds of the members present.

Judgment in cases of impeachment shall not extend further than to removal from office, and disqualification to hold and enjoy any office of honor, trust or profit under the United States: but the party convicted shall nevertheless be liable and subject to indictment, trial, judgment, and punishment, according to law.

Sec 4 The times, places and manner of holding elections for Senators and Representatives, shall be prescribed in each State by the legislature thereof; but the Congress may at any time by law make or alter such regulations, except as to the places of choosing Senators.

The Congress shall assemble at least once in every year, and such meeting shall be on the first Monday in December, unless they shall by law appoint a different day.

Sec 5 Each house shall be the judge of the elections, returns and qualifications of its own members, and a majority of each shall constitute a quorum to do business; but a smaller number may adjourn from day to day, and may be authorized to compel the attendance of absent members, in such manner, and under such penalties as each House may provide.

Each house may determine the rules of its proceedings, punish its members for disorderly behaviour, and, with the concurrence of two-thirds, expel a member.

Each house shall keep a journal of its proceedings, and from time to time publish the same, excepting such parts as may in their judgment require secrecy; and the yeas and nays of the members of either house on any question shall, at the desire of one-fifth of those present, be entered on the journal.

Neither house, during the session of Congress shall, without the consent of the other, adjourn for more than three days, nor to any other place than that in which the two Houses shall be sitting.

Sec 6 The Senators and Representatives shall receive a compensation for their services, to be ascertained by law, and paid out of the Treasury of the United States. They shall in all cases, except treason, felony and breach of the peace, be privileged from arrest during their attendance at the session of their respective Houses, and in going to and returning from the same; and for any speech or debate in either House, they shall not be questioned in any other place.

No Senator or Representative shall, during the time for which he was elected, be appointed to any civil office under the authority of the United States which shall have been created, if the emoluments whereof shall have been increased during such time; and no person holding any office under the United States, shall be a member of either House during his continuance in office.

Sec 7 All bills for raising revenue shall originate in the House of Representatives; but the Senate may propose or concur with amendments as on other bills.

Every bill which shall have passed the House of Representatives and the Senate, shall, before it becomes a law, be presented to the President of the United States; if he approve he shall sign it, but if not he shall return it, with his objections to that house in which it shall have originated, who shall enter the objections at large on their journal, and proceed to reconsider it. If after such reconsideration two-thirds of that house shall agree to pass the bill, it shall be sent, together with the objections, to the other house, by which it shall likewise be reconsidered, and if approved by two-thirds of that house, it shall become a law. But in all such cases the votes of both houses shall be determined by yeas and nays, and the names of the persons voting for and against the bill shall be entered on the journal of each house respectively. If any bill shall not be returned by the President within ten days (Sundays excepted) after it shall have been presented to him, the same shall be a law, in like manner as if he had signed it, unless the Congress by their adjournment prevent its return, in which case it shall not be a law.

Every order, resolution, or vote to which the concurrence of the Senate and House of Representatives may be necessary (except on a question of adjournment) shall be presented to the President of the United States; and before the same shall take effect, shall be approved by him, or being disapproved by him, shall be repassed by two-thirds of the Senate and House of Representatives, according to the rules and limitations prescribed in the case of a bill.

Sec 8 The Congress shall have power to lay and collect taxes, duties, imposts, and excises, to pay the debts and provide for the common defence and general welfare of the United States; but all duties, imposts, and excises shall be uniform throughout the United States;

To borrow money on the credit of the United States;

To regulate commerce with foreign nations, and among the several States, and with the Indian tribes;

To establish a uniform rule of naturalization, and uniform laws on the subject of bankruptcies throughout the United States;

To coin money, regulate the value thereof, and of foreign coin, and fix the standard of weights and measures;

To provide for the punishment of counterfeiting the securities and current coin of the United States;

To establish post-offices and post-roads;

To promote the progress of science and useful arts, by securing for limited times to authors and inventors the exclusive right to their respective writings and discoveries;

To constitute tribunals inferior to the Supreme Court;

To define and punish piracies and felonies committed on the high seas, and offences against the law of nations;

To declare war, grant letters of marque and reprisal, and make rules concerning captures on land and water;

To raise and support armies, but no appropriation of money to that use shall be for longer term than two years;

To provide and maintain a navy;

To make rules for the government and regulation of the land and naval forces;

To provide for calling forth the militia to execute the laws of the Union, suppress insurrections and repel invasions;

To provide for organizing, arming, and disciplining the militia, and for governing such part of them as may be employed in the service of the United States, reserving to the States respectively the appointment of the officers, and the authority of training the militia according to the discipline prescribed by Congress;

To exercise exclusive legislation in all cases whatsoever over such district (not exceeding ten miles square) as may, by cession of particular

States, and the acceptance of Congress, become the seat of the Government of the United States, and to exercise like authority over all places purchased by the consent of the Legislature of the State in the same shall be, for the election of forts, magazines, arsenals, dockyards, and other needful buildings; and

To make all laws which shall be necessary and proper for carrying into execution the foregoing powers, and all other powers vested by this Constitution in the Government of the United States, or in any department or officer thereof.

Sec 9 The migration or importation of such persons as any of the States now existing shall think proper to admit, shall not be prohibited by the Congress prior to the year one thousand eight hundred and eight, but a tax or duty may be imposed on such importation, not exceeding ten dollars for each person.

The privilege of the writ of habeas corpus shall not be suspended, unless when in cases of rebellion or invasion the public safety may require it.

No bill of attainder or ex post facto law shall be passed.

No capitation, or other direct, tax shall be laid, unless in proportion to the census or enumeration herein before directed to be taken.

No tax or duty shall be laid on articles exported from any State.

No preference shall be given by any regulation of commerce or revenue to the ports of one State over those of another: nor shall vessels bound to, or from, one State, be obliged to enter, clear, or pay duties in another.

No money shall be drawn from the Treasury but in consequence of appropriations made by law; and a regular statement and account of receipts and expenditures of all public money shall be published from time to time.

No title of nobility shall be granted by the United States: and no person holding any office of profit or trust under them, shall, without the consent of the Congress, accept of any present, emolument, office, or title, of any kind whatever, from any king, prince or foreign State.

Sec 10 No State shall enter into any treaty, alliance, or confederation; grant letters of marque and reprisal; coin money, emit bills of credit; make any thing but gold and silver coin a tender in payment of debts; pass any bill of attainder, ex post facto law, or law impairing the obligation of contracts, or grant any title of nobility.

No State shall, without the consent of the Congress, lay any imposts or duties on imports or exports, except what may be absolutely necessary for executing its inspection laws; and the net produce of all duties and imposts, laid by any State on imports or exports, shall be for the use of the Treasury of the United States; and all such laws shall be subject to the revision and control of the Congress.

No State shall, without the consent of Congress, lay any duty of tonnage, keep troops, or ships of war in time of peace, enter into any agreement or compact with another State, or with a foreign power, or engage in war, unless actually invaded, or in such imminent danger as will not admit of delay.

ARTICLE II

Sec 1 The executive power shall be vested in a President of the United States of America. He shall hold his office during the term of four years, and, together with the Vice-President, chosen for the same term, be elected, as follows:

Each State shall appoint, in such manner as the legislature thereof may direct, a number of electors, equal to the whole number of Senators and Representatives to which the State may be entitled in the Congress: but no Senator or Representative, or person holding an office of trust or profit under the United States, shall be appointed an elector.

The electors shall meet in their respective States, and vote by ballot for two persons, of whom one at least shall not be an inhabitant of the same State with themselves. And they shall make a list of all the persons voted for, and of the number of votes for each; which list they shall sign and certify, and transmit sealed to the seat of the Government of the United States, directed to the President of the Senate. The President of the Senate shall, in the presence of the Senate and House of Representatives, open all the certificates, and the votes shall then be counted. The person having the greatest number of votes shall be the President, if such number be a majority of the whole number of electors appointed; and if there be more than one who have such majority, and have an equal number of votes, then the House of Representatives shall immediately choose by ballot one of them for President; and if no person have a majority, then from the five highest on the list the said house shall in like manner choose the President. But in choosing the President, the votes shall be taken by States, the representation from each State having one vote; a quorum for this purpose shall consist of a member or members from two-thirds of the States, and a majority of all the States shall be necessary to a choice. In every case, after the choice of the President, the person having the greatest number of votes of the electors shall be the Vice-President. But if there should remain two or more who have equal votes, the Senate shall choose from them by ballot the Vice-President.

The Congress may determine the time of choosing the electors, and the day on which they shall give their votes, which day shall be the same throughout the United States.

No person except a natural-born citizen, or a citizen of the United

States, at the time of the adoption of this Constitution, shall be eligible to the office of President; neither shall any person be eligible to that office who shall not have attained to the age of thirty-five years, and been fourteen years a resident within the United States.

In case of the removal of the President from office, or of his death, resignation, or inability to discharge the powers and duties of the said office, the same shall devolve on the Vice-President, and the Congress may by law provide for the case of removal, death, resignation, or inability, both of the President and Vice-President, declaring what officer shall then act as President, and such officer shall act accordingly, until the disability be removed, or a President shall be elected.

The President shall, at stated times, receive for his services, a compensation, which shall neither be increased nor diminished during the period for which he shall have been elected, and he shall not receive within that period any other emolument from the United States, or any of them.

Before he enter on the execution of his office, he shall take the following oath or affirmation: 'I do solemnly swear (or affirm) that I will faithfully execute the office of President of the United States, and will to the best of my ability, preserve, protect, and defend the Constitution of the United States.'

Sec 2 The President shall be Commander-in-Chief of the Army and Navy of the United States, and of the militia of the several States, when called into the actual service of the United States; he may require the opinion, in writing, of the principal officer in each of the executive departments, upon any subject relating to the duties of their respective offices, and he shall have power to grant reprieves and pardons for offences against the United States, except in cases of impeachment.

He shall have power, by and with the advice and consent of the Senate, to make treaties, provided two-thirds of the Senators present concur; and he shall nominate, and by and with the advice and consent of the Senate, shall appoint ambassadors, other public ministers and consuls, judges of the Supreme Court, and all other officers of the United States, whose appointments are not herein otherwise provided for, and which shall be established by law: but the Congress may by law vest the appointment of such inferior officers, as they think proper, in the President alone, in the courts of law, or in the heads of departments.

The President shall have power to fill up all vacancies that may happen during the recess of the Senate, by granting commissions which shall expire at the end of their next session.

Sec 3 He shall from time to time give to the Congress information of the states of the Union, and recommend to their consideration such measures as he shall judge necessary and expedient; he may, on extraordinary occasions, convene both houses, or either of them, and in case of disagreement between them, with respect to the time of adjournment, he may adjourn them to such time as he shall think proper; he shall receive ambassadors and other public ministers; he shall take care that the laws be faithfully executed, and shall commission all the officers of the United States.

Sec 4 The President, Vice-President and all civil officers of the United States, shall be removed from office on impeachment for, and conviction of, treason, bribery, or other high crimes and misdemeanors.

ARTICLE III

Sec 1 The judicial power of the United States, shall be vested in one Supreme Court, and in such inferior courts as the Congress may from time to time ordain and establish. The judges, both of the supreme and inferior courts, shall hold their offices during good behaviour, and shall, at stated times, receive for their services, a compensation, which shall not be diminished during their continuance in office.

Sec 2 The judicial power shall extend to all cases, in law and equity, arising under this Constitution, the laws of the United States, and treaties made, or which shall be made, under their authority; to all cases affecting ambassadors, other public ministers and consuls; to all cases of admiralty and maritime jurisdiction; to controversies to which the United States shall be a party; to controversies between two or more States; between a State and citizens of another State; between citizens of different States, between citizens of the same State claiming lands under grants of different States, and between a State, or the citizen thereof, and foreign States, citizens or subjects.

In all cases affecting ambassadors, other public ministers and consuls, and those in which a State shall be party, the Supreme Court shall have original jurisdiction. In all the other cases before mentioned, the Supreme Court shall have appellate jurisdiction, both as to law and fact, with such exceptions, and under such regulations as the Congress shall make.

The trial of all crimes, except in cases of impeachment, shall be by jury; and such trial shall be held in the State where the said crimes shall have been committed; but when not committed within any State, the trial shall be at such place or places as the Congress may by law have directed.

Sec 3 Treason against the United States, shall consist only in levying war against them, or in adhering to their enemies, giving them aid and comfort. No person shall be convicted of treason unless on the testimony of two witnesses to the same overt act, or on confession in open court.

The Congress shall have power to declare the punishment of treason, but no attainder of treason shall work corruption of blood, or forfeiture except during the life of the person attainted.

ARTICLE IV

Sec 1 Full faith and credit shall be given in each State to the public acts, records, and judicial proceedings of every other State. And the Congress may by general laws prescribe the manner in which such acts, records, and proceedings shall be provided, and the effect thereof.

Sec 2 The citizens of each State shall be entitled to privileges and immunities of citizens in several States.

A person charged in any State with treason, felony, or other crime, who shall flee from justice, and be found in another State, shall on demand of the executive authority of the State from which he fled, be delivered up, to be removed to the State having jurisdiction of the crime.

No person held to service for labor in one State, under the laws thereof, escaping into another, shall, in consequence of any law or regulation therein, be discharged from such service or labor, but shall be delivered up on claim of the party to whom such service or labor may be due.

Sec 3 New States may be admitted by the Congress into this Union; but no new States shall be formed or erected within the jurisdiction of any other State; nor any State be formed by the junction of two or more states; or parts of States, without the consent of the legislatures of the States concerned as well as of the Congress.

The Congress shall have power to dispose of and make all needful rules and regulations respecting the territory or other property belonging to the United States; and nothing in this Constitution shall be so construed as to prejudice any claims of the United States, or of any particular State.

Sec 4 The United States shall guarantee to every State in this Union a republican form of government, and shall protect each of them against invasion; and on application of the legislature, or of the executive (when the legislature cannot be convened) against domestic violence.

ARTICLE V

The Congress, whenever two-thirds of both houses shall deem it necessary, shall propose amendments to this Constitution, or, on the application of the legislature of two-thirds of the several States, shall call a convention for proposing amendments, which, in either case, shall be valid to all intents and purposes, as part of this Constitution, when ratified by the legislatures of three-fourths of the several States, or by conventions in three-fourths thereof, as the one or the other mode of ratification may be proposed by the Congress; provided that no amendment which may be made prior to the year one thousand eight hundred and eight shall in any manner affect the first and fourth clauses in the ninth section of the first article; and that no State, without its consent, shall be deprived of its equal suffrage in the Senate.

ARTICLE VI

All debts contracted and engagements entered into, before the adoption of this Constitution, shall be valid against the United States under this Constitution, as under the Confederation.

This Constitution, and the laws of the United States which shall be made in pursuance thereof; and all treaties made, or which shall be made, under the authority of the United States, shall be the supreme law of the land; and the judges in every State shall be bound thereby, anything in the Constitution or laws of any State to the contrary notwithstanding.

The Senators and Representatives before mentioned, and the members of the several State legislatures, and all executive and judicial officers, both of the United States and of the several States, shall be bound by oath or affirmation, to support this Constitution; but no religious test shall ever be required as a qualification to any office or public trust under the United States.

ARTICLE VII

The ratification of the conventions of nine States, shall be sufficient for the establishment of this Constitution between the States so ratifying the same.

Done in convention by the unanimous consent of the States present, the seventeenth day of September in the year of our Lord one thousand seven hundred and eighty-seven and of the independence of the United States of America the twelfth. In witness whereof, we have hereunto subscribed our names...

Preface to *The Leather-Stocking Tales* by James Fenimore Cooper (1850)

Reprinted from Perkins G, Bradley S, Beatty R C, Long E H (eds) 1985 *The American tradition in literature* 6th edn. Random House, New York, pp 535–8.

This series of stories, which has obtained the name of 'The Leather-Stocking Tales', has been written in a very desultory and inartificial manner. The order in which the several books appeared was essentially different from that in which they would have been presented to the world, had the regular course of their incidents been consulted. In 'The Pioneers', the first of the series written, the Leather-Stocking is represented as already old, and driven from his early haunts in the forest, by the sound of the axe, and the smoke of the settler. 'The Last of the Mohicans', the next book in order of publication, carried the readers back to a much earlier period in the history of our hero, representing him as middle-aged, and in the fullest vigor of manhood. In 'The Prairie', his career terminates, and he is laid in his grave. There, it was originally the intention to leave him, in the expectation that, as in the case of the human mass, he would soon be forgotten. But a latent regard for this character induced the author to resuscitate him in 'The Pathfinder', a book that was not long after succeeded by 'The Deerslayer', thus completing the series as it now exists.

While the five books that have been written were originally published in the order just mentioned, that of the incidents, insomuch as they are connected with the career of their principal character, is, as has been stated, very different. Taking the life of the Leather-Stocking as a guide, 'The Deerslayer' should have been the opening book, for in that work he is seen just emerging into manhood, to be succeeded by 'The Last of the Mohicans', 'The Pathfinder', 'The Pioneers', and 'The Prairie'. The arrangement embraces the order of events, though far from being that in which the books first appeared. 'The Pioneers' was published in 1822; 'The Deerslayer' in 1841; making the interval between them nineteen years. Whether these progressive years have had a tendency to lessen the value of the last-named book by lessening the native fire of its author, or of adding somewhat in the way of improved taste and a more matured judgement, is for others to decide.

If anything from the pen of the writer of these romances is at all to outlive himself, it is, unquestionably, the series of 'The Leather-Stocking Tales'. To say this, is not to predict a very lasting reputation for the series itself, but simply to express the belief it will outlast any, or all, of the works from the same hand.

It is undeniable that the desultory manner in which 'The Leather-Stocking Tales' were written, has, in a measure, impaired their harmony, and otherwise lessened their interest. This is proved by the fate of the two books last published, though probably the two most worthy an enlightened reader's notice. If the facts could be ascertained, it is probable the result would show that of all of those (in America, in particular) who have read the three first books of the series, not one in ten has a knowledge of the existence even of the two last. Several causes have tended to produce this result. The long interval of time between the appearance of 'The Prairie' and that of 'The Pathfinder', was itself a reason why the later books of the series should be overlooked. There was no longer novelty to attract attention, and the interest was materially impaired by the manner in which events were necessarily anticipated, in laying the last of the series first before the world. With the generation that is now coming on the stage this fault will be partially removed by the edition contained in the present work, in which the several tales will be arranged solely in reference to their connexion with each other.

The author has often been asked if he had any original in his mind, for the character of Leather-Stocking. In a physical sense, different individuals known to the writer in early life, certainly presented themselves as models, through his recollections; but in a moral sense this man of the forest is purely a creation. The idea of delineating a character that possessed little of civilization but its highest principles as they are exhibited in the uneducated, and all of savage life that is not incompatible with these great rules of conduct, is perhaps natural to the situation in which Natty was placed. He is too proud of his origin to sink into the condition of the wild Indian, and too much of a man of the woods not to imbibe as much as was at all desirable, from his friends and companions. In a moral point of view it was the intention to illustrate the effect of seed scattered by the way side. To use his own language, his 'gifts' were 'white gifts', and he was not disposed to bring on them discredit. On the other hand, removed from nearly all the temptations of civilized life, placed in the best associations of that which is deemed savage, and favourably disposed by nature to improve such advantages, it appeared to the writer that his hero was a fit subject to represent the better qualities of both conditions, without pushing either to extremes.

There was no violent stretch of the imagination, perhaps, in supposing one of civilized associations in childhood, retaining many of his earliest lessons amid the scenes of the forest. Had these early impressions, however, not been sustained by continued, though casual connexion with men of his own color, if not of his own caste, all our information goes to show he would soon have lost every trace of his origin. It is believed that sufficient attention was paid to the particular circumstances in which this individual was placed to justify the picture of his qualities that has been drawn. The Delawares early attracted the attention of missionaries, and were a tribe unusually influenced by their precepts and example. In many instances they became Christians, and cases occurred in which their subsequent lives gave proof of the efficacy of the great moral changes that had taken place within them.

A leading character in a work of fiction has a fair right to the aid which can be obtained by a poetical view of the subject. It is in this view, rather than in one more strictly circumstantial, that Leather-Stocking has been drawn. The imagination has no great task in portraying to itself a being removed from everyday inducements to err, which abound in civilized life, while he retains the best and simplest of his early impressions; who sees God in the forest; hears him in the winds; bows to him in the firmament that o'ercanopies all; submits to his sway in a humble belief of his justice and mercy; in a word, a being who finds the impress of the Deity in all the works of nature, without any of the blots produced by the expedients, and passion, and mistakes of man. This is the most that has been attempted in the character of Leather-Stocking. Had this been done without any of the drawbacks of humanity, the picture would have been, in all probability, more pleasing than just. In order to preserve the *vrai-semblable*, therefore, traits derived from the prejudices, tastes, and even the weaknesses of his youth, have been mixed up with these higher qualities and longings, in a way, it is hoped, to represent a reasonable picture of human nature, without offering to the spectator a 'monster of goodness'.

It has been objected to these books that they give a more favorable picture of the red man than he deserves. The writer apprehends that much of this objection arises from the habits of those who have made it. One of his critics, on the appearance of the first work in which Indian character was portrayed, objected that its 'characters were of the school of Heckewelder, rather than of the school of nature'. These words quite probably contain the substance of the true answer to the objection. Heckewelder was an ardent, benevolent missionary, bent on the good of the red man, and seeing in him one who had the soul, reason, and characteristics of a fellow-being. The critic is understood to have been a very distinguished agent of the government, one very familiar with Indians, as they are seen at the councils to treat for the sale of their lands, where little or none of their domestic qualities come in play, and where, indeed, their evil passions are known to have the fullest scope. As just would it be to draw conclusions of the general state of American society from the scenes of the capital, as to suppose that the negotiating of one of these treaties is a fair picture of Indian life.

It is the privilege of all writers of fiction, more particularly when their works aspire to the elevation of romances, to present the *beau-idéal* of their characters to the reader. That it is which constitutes poetry, and to suppose that the red man is to be represented only in the squalid misery or in the degraded moral state that certainly more or less belongs to his condition, is, we apprehend, taking a very narrow view of an author's privileges. Such criticism would have deprived the world of even Homer.

'Where I lived, and what I lived for', from *Walden, or life in the woods* by H D Thoreau (1854)
Reprinted from Perkins G, Bradley S, Beatty R C, Long E H (eds) 1985 *The American tradition in literature* 6th edn. Random House, New York, pp 1009–11.

At a certain season of our life we are accustomed to consider every spot as the possible site of a house. I have thus surveyed the country on every side within a dozen miles of where I live. In imagination I have bought all the farms in succession, for all were to be bought, and I knew their price. I walked over each farmer's premises, tasted his wild apples, discoursed on husbandry with him, took his farm at his price, at any price, mortgaging it to him in my mind; even put a higher price on it, – took everything but a deed of it, – took his word for his deed, for I dearly love to talk – cultivated it, and him too to some extent, I trust, and withdrew when I had enjoyed it long enough, leaving him to carry it on. This experience entitled me to be regarded as a sort of real-estate broker by my friends. Wherever I sat, there I might live, and the landscape radiated from me accordingly. What is a house but a *sedes*, a seat? – better if a country seat. I discovered many a site for a house not likely to be soon improved, which some might have thought too far from the village, but to my eyes the village was too far from it. Well, there I might live, I said; and there I did live, for an hour, a summer and a winter life; saw how I could let the years run off, buffet the winter through, and see the spring come in. The future inhabitants of this region, wherever they may place their houses, may be sure that they have been anticipated. An afternoon sufficed to lay out the land into orchard, woodlot, and pasture, and to decide what fine oaks or pines should be left to stand before the door, and whence each blasted tree could be seen to the best advantage; and then I let it lie, fallow perchance, for a man is rich in proportion to the number of things which he can afford to let alone.

My imagination carried me so far that I even had the refusal of several farms, – the refusal was all I wanted, – but I never got my fingers burned by actual possession. The nearest that I came to actual possession was when I bought the Hollowell place, and had begun to sort my seeds, and collected materials with which to make a wheelbarrow to carry it on or off with; but before the owner gave me a deed of it, his wife – every man has such a wife – changed her mind and wished to keep it, and he offered me ten dollars to release him. Now, to speak the truth, I had but ten cents in the world, and it surpassed my arithmetic to tell, if I was that man who had ten cents, or who had a farm, or ten dollars, or all together. However, I let him keep the ten dollars and the farm too, for I had carried it far enough; or rather, to be generous, I sold him the farm for just what I gave for it, and, as he was not a rich man, made him a present of ten dollars, and still had my ten cents, and seeds, and materials for a wheelbarrow left. I found thus that I had been a rich man without any damage to my poverty. But I retained the landscape, and I have since annually carried off what it yielded without a wheelbarrow. With respect to landscapes,–

I am monarch of all I survey,
My right there is none to dispute.

I have frequently seen a poet withdraw, having enjoyed the most valuable part of a farm, while the crusty farmer supposed that he had got a few wild apples only. Why, the owner does not know it for many years when a poet has put his farm in rhyme, the most admirable kind of invisible fence, has fairly impounded it, milked it, skimmed it, and got all the cream, and left the farmer only the skimmed milk.

The real attractions of the Hollowell farm, to me, were; its complete retirement, being about two miles from the village, half a mile from the nearest neighbor, and separated from the highway by a broad field; its bounding on the river, which the owner said protected it by its fogs from frosts in the spring, though that was nothing to me; the gray color and ruinous state of the house and barn, and the dilapidate fences, which put such an interval between me and the last occupant; the hollow and lichen-covered apple trees, gnawed by rabbits, showing what kind of neighbors I should have; but above all, the recollection I had of it from my earliest voyages up the river, when the house was concealed behind a dense grove of red maples, through which I heard the house-dog bark. I was in haste to buy it, before the proprietor finished getting out some rocks, cutting down the hollow apple trees, and grubbing up some young birches which had sprung up in the pasture, or, in short, had made any more of his improvements. To enjoy these advantages I was ready to carry it on; like Atlas, to take the world on my shoulders, – I never heard what compensation he received for that, – and do all those things which had no other motive or excuse but that I might pay for it and be unmolested in my possession of it; for I knew all the while that it would yield the most abundant crop of the kind I wanted if I could only afford to let it alone. But it turned out as I have said.

All that I could say, then, with respect to farming on a large scale, (I have always cultivated a garden,) was, that I had had my seeds ready. Many think that seeds improve with age. I have no doubt that time discriminates between the good and the bad; and when at last I shall plant, I shall be less likely to be disappointed. But I would say to my fellows, once for all, As long as possible live free and uncommitted. It makes but little difference whether you are committed to a farm or the county jail.

Old Cato, whose 'De Re Rustica' is my 'Cultivator' says, and the only translation I have seen makes sheer nonsense of the passage, 'When you think of getting a farm, turn it thus in your mind, not to buy greedily; nor spare your pains to look at it, and do not think it enough to go round it once. The oftener you go there the more it will please you, if it is good.' I think I shall not buy greedily, but go round and round it as long as I live, and be buried in it first, that it may please me the more at last.

'Hawthorne', from *Hawthorne* by Henry James (1879)

Reprinted from Edel L (ed) 1984 *Henry James literary criticism: essays on literature, American writers, English writers.* Literary Classics of the United States, New York, pp 319–21, 427–8.

It will be necessary, for several reasons, to give this short sketch the form rather of a critical essay than of a biography. The data for a life of Nathaniel Hawthorne are the reverse of copious, and even if they were abundant they would serve but in a limited measure the purpose of the biographer. Hawthorne's career was probably as tranquil and uneventful a one as ever fell to the lot of a man of letters; it was almost strikingly deficient in incident, in what may be called the dramatic quality. Few men of equal genius and of equal eminence can have led on the whole a simpler life. His six volumes of Note-Books illustrate this simplicity; they are a sort of monument to an unagitated fortune. Hawthorne's career had few vicissitudes or variations; it was passed for the most part in a small and homogeneous society, in a provincial, rural community; it had few perceptible points of contact with what is called the world, with public events, with the manners of his time, even with the life of his neighbours. Its literary incidents are not numerous. He produced, in quantity, but little. His works consist of four novels and the fragment of another, five volumes of short tales, a collection of sketches, and a couple of story-books for children. And yet some account of the man and the writer is well worth giving. Whatever may have been Hawthorne's private lot, he has the importance of being the most beautiful and most eminent representative of a literature. The importance of the literature may be questioned, but at any rate, in a field of letters, Hawthorne is the most valuable example of the American genius. That genius has not, as a whole, been literary; but Hawthorne was on his limited scale a master of expression. He is the writer to whom his countrymen most confidently point when they wish to make a claim to have enriched the mother-tongue, and, judging from present appearances, he will long occupy this honourable position. If there is something very fortunate for him in the way that he borrows an added relief from the absence of competitors in his own line and from the general flatness of their literary field that surrounds him, there is also, to a spectator, something almost touching in his situation. He was so modest and delicate a genius that we may fancy him appealing from the lonely honour of a representative attitude – perceiving a painful incongruity between his imponderable literary baggage and the large conditions of American life. Hawthorne on the one side is so subtle and slender and unpretending, and the American world on the other is so vast and various and substantial, that it might seem to the author of The Scarlet Letter and the Mosses from an Old Manse, that we render him a poor service in contrasting his proportions with those of a great civilization. But our author must accept the awkward as well as the graceful side of his fame; for he has the advantage of pointing a valuable moral. This moral is that the flower of art blooms only where the soil is deep, that it takes a great deal of history to produce a little literature, that it needs a complex social machinery to set a writer in motion. American civilisation has hitherto had other things to do than to produce flowers, and before giving birth to writers it has wisely occupied itself with providing something for them to write about. Three or four beautiful talents of trans-Atlantic growth are the sum of what the world usually recognises, and in this modest nosegay the genius of Hawthorne is admitted to have the rarest and sweetest fragrance.

His very simplicity has been in his favour; it has helped him to appear complete and homogeneous. To talk of his being national would be to force the note and make a mistake of proportion; but he is, in spite of the absence of the realistic quality, intensely and vividly local. Out of the soil of New England he sprang – in a crevice of that immitigable granite he sprouted and bloomed. Half of the interest that he possesses for an American reader with any turn for analysis must reside in his latent New England savour; and I think it no more than just to say that whatever entertainment he may yield to those who know him at a distance, it is an almost indispensable condition of properly appreciating him to have received a personal impression of the manners, the morals, indeed of the very climate, of the great region of which the remarkable city of Boston is the metropolis. The cold, bright air of New England seems to blow through his pages, and these, in the opinion of many people, are the medium in which it is most agreeable to make the acquaintance of that tonic atmosphere. As to whether it is worth while to seek to know something of New England in order to extract a more intimate quality from The House of Seven Gables and The Blithedale Romance, I need not pronounce; but it is certain that a considerable observation of the society to which these productions were more directly addressed is a capital preparation for enjoying them. I have alluded to the absence in Hawthorne of that quality of realism which is now so much in fashion, an absence in regard to which there will of course be more to say; and yet I think I am not fanciful in saying that he testifies to the sentiments of the society in which he flourished almost as pertinently (proportions observed) as Balzac and some of his descendants – M M Flaubert and Zola – testify to the manners and morals of the French people. He was not a man with a literary theory; he was guiltless of a system, and I am not sure that he had ever heard of Realism, this remarkable compound having (although it was invented some time earlier) come into general use only since his death. He had certainly not proposed to himself to give an account of the social idiosyncrasies of his fellow-citizens, for his touch on such points is always light and vague, he has none of the apparatus of an historian, and his shadowy style of portraiture never suggests a rigid standard of accuracy. Nevertheless he virtually offers the most vivid reflection of New England life that has found its way into literature. His value in this respect is not diminished by the fact that he has not attempted to portray the usual Yankee of comedy, and that he has been almost culpably indifferent to his opportunities for commemorating the variations of colloquial English that may be observed in the New World. His characters do not express themselves in the dialect of the Biglow Papers – their language indeed is apt to be too elegant, too delicate. They are not portraits of actual types, and in their phraseology there is nothing imitative. But none the less, Hawthorne's work savours thoroughly of the local soil – it is redolent of the social system in which he had his being . . .

The three American novels

This last invidious allusion is to the disposition, not infrequent at the North, but by no means general, to set a decisive limit to further legislation in favour of the cherished idiosyncrasy of the other half of the country. Hawthorne takes the license of a sympathetic biographer in speaking of his hero's having incurred obloquy by his conservative attitude on the question of Slavery. The only class in the American world that suffered in the smallest degree, at this time, from social persecution, was the little band of Northern Abolitionists, who were as unfashionable as they were indiscreet – which is saying much. Like most of his fellow-countrymen, Hawthorne had no idea that the respectable institution which he contemplated in impressive contrast to humanitarian 'mistiness', was presently to cost the nation four long years of bloodshed and misery, and a social revolution as complete as any the world has seen. When this event occurred, he was therefore proportionately horrified and depressed by it; it cut from beneath his feet the familiar ground which had long felt so firm, substituting a heaving and quaking medium in which his spirit found no rest. Such was the bewildered sensation of that earlier and simpler generation of which I have spoken; their illusions were rudely dispelled, and they saw the best of all possible republics given over to fratricidal carnage. This affair had no place in their scheme, and nothing was left for them but to hang their heads and close their eyes. The subsidence of that great convulsion has left a different tone from the tone it found, and one may say that the Civil War marks an era in the history of the American mind. It introduced into the national consciousness a certain sense of proportion and relation, of the world being a more complicated place than it had hitherto seemed, the future more treacherous, success more difficult. At the rate at which things are going, it is obvious that good Americans will be more numerous than ever; but the good American, in days to come, will be a more critical person than his complacent and confident grandfather. He has eaten of the tree of knowledge. He will not, I think, be a sceptic, and still less, of course, a cynic; but he will be, without discredit to his well-known capacity for action, an observer. He will remember that the ways of the Lord are inscrutable, and that this is a world in which everything happens; and eventualities, as the late Emperor of the French used to say, will not find him intellectually unprepared. The good American of which Hawthorne was so admirable a specimen was not critical, and it was perhaps for this reason that Franklin Pierce seemed to him a very proper President.

'Basil Ransom's New York', from *The Bostonians* by Henry James (1886)

Reprinted from Henry James (1966) *The Bostonians*. Penguin, Harmondsworth, pp 160–1.

Basil Ransom lived in New York, rather far to the eastward, and in the upper reaches of the town; he occupied two small shabby rooms in a somewhat decayed mansion which stood next to the corner of the Second Avenue. The corner itself was formed by a considerable grocer's shop, the near neighbourhood of which was fatal to any pretensions Ransom and his fellow-lodgers might have had in regard to gentility of situation. The house had a red, rusty face, and faded green shutters, of which the slats were limp and at variance with each other. In one of the lower windows was suspended a fly-blown card, with the words 'Table Board' affixed in letters cut (not very neatly) out of coloured paper, of graduated tints, and surrounded with a small band of stamped gilt. The two sides of the shop were protected by an immense pent-house shed, which projected over a greasy pavement and was supported by wooden posts fixed in the curbstone. Beneath it, on the dislocated flags, barrels and baskets were freely and picturesquely grouped; an open cellarway yawned beneath the feet of those who might pause to gaze too fondly on the savoury wares displayed in the window; a strong odour of smoked fish, combined with a fragrance of molasses, hung about the spot; the pavement, towards the gutters, was fringed with dirty panniers, heaped with potatoes, carrots, and onions; and a smart, bright waggon, with the horse detached from the shafts, drawn up on the edge of the abominable road (it contained holes and ruts a foot deep, and immemorial accumulations of stagnant mud), imparted an idle, rural, pastoral air to a scene otherwise perhaps expressive of a rank civilization. The establishment was of the kind known to New Yorkers as a Dutch grocery; and red-faced, yellow-haired, bare-armed vendors might have been observed to lounge in the door-way. I mention it not on account of any particular influence it may have had on the life or the thoughts of Basil Ransom, but for old acquaintance sake and that of local colour; besides which, a figure is nothing without a setting, and our young man came and went every day, with rather an indifferent, unperceiving step, it is true, among the objects I have briefly designated. One of his rooms was directly above the street-door of the house; such a dormitory, when it is so exiguous, is called in the nomenclature of New York a 'hall bedroom'. The sitting-room, beside it, was slightly larger, and they both commanded a row of tenements no less degenerate than Ransom's own habitation – houses built forty years before, and already sere and superannuated. These were also painted red, and the bricks were accentuated by a white line; they were garnished, on the first floor, with balconies covered with small tin roofs, striped in different colours, and with an elaborate iron lattice-work, which gave them a repressive, cage-like appearance, and caused them slightly to resemble the little boxes for peeping unseen into the street, which are a feature of oriental towns. Such posts of observation commanded a view of the grocery on the corner, of the relaxed and disjointed roadway, enlivened at the curbstone with an occasional ash-barrel or with gas-lamps drooping from the perpendicular, and westward, at the end of the truncated vista, of the fantastic skeleton of the Elevated Railway, overhanging the transverse longitudinal street, which it darkened and smothered with the immeasurably spinal column and myriad clutching paws of an ante-diluvian monster. If the opportunity were not denied me here, I should like to give some account of Basil Ransom's interior, of certain curious persons of both sexes, for the most part not favourites of fortune, who had found an obscure asylum there; some picture of the crumpled little table d'hote, at two dollars and a half a week, where everything felt sticky, which went forward in the low-ceiled basement, under the conduct of a couple of shuffling negresses, who mingled in the conversation and indulged in low, mysterious chuckles when it took a facetious turn. But we need, in strictness, concern ourselves with it no further than to gather the implication that the young Mississippian, even a year and a half after that momentous visit of his to Boston, had not made his profession very lucrative.

'The Significance of the Frontier in American History' by Frederick Jackson Turner (1893)

Reprinted from Heffner R D (ed) 1965 *A Documentary History of the United States* 2nd edn. New American Library, New York, pp 183–91.

In a recent bulletin of the Superintendent of the Census for 1890 appear these significant words: 'Up to and including 1880 the country had a frontier of settlement, but at present the unsettled area has been so broken into by isolated bodies of settlement that there can hardly be said to be a frontier line. In the discussion of its extent, its westward movement, etc, it can not, therefore, any longer have a place in the census reports.' This brief official statement marks the closing of a great historic movement. Up to our own day American history has been in a large degree the history of the colonization of the Great West. The existence of an area of free land, its continuous recession, and the advance of American settlement westward, explain American development.

Behind institutions, behind constitutional forms and modifications, lie the vital forces that call these organs into life and shape them to meet changing conditions. The peculiarity of American institutions is the fact that they have been compelled to adapt themselves to the changes of an expanding people – to the changes involved in crossing a continent, in winning a wilderness, and in developing at each area of this progress out of the primitive economic and political conditions of the frontier into the complexity of city life. Said Calhoun in 1817, 'We are great, and rapidly – I was about to say fearfully – growing!' So saying, he touched the distinguishing feature of American life. All peoples show development; the germ theory of politics has been sufficiently emphasized. In the case of most nations, however, the development has occurred in a limited area; and if the nation has expanded, it has met other growing peoples whom it has conquered. But in the case of the United States we have a different phenomenon. Limiting our attention to the Atlantic coast, we have the familiar phenomenon of the evolution of institutions in a limited area, such as the rise of representative government; the differentiation of simple colonial governments into complex organs; the progress from primitive industrial society, without division of labor, up to manufacturing civilization. But we have in addition to this a recurrence of the process of evolution in each western area reached in the process of expansion. Thus American development has exhibited not merely advance along a single line, but a return to primitive conditions on a continually advancing frontier line, and a new development for that area. American social development has been continually beginning over again on the frontier. This perennial rebirth, this fluidity of American life, this expansion westward with its new opportunities, its continuous touch with the simplicity of primitive society, furnish the forces dominating American character. The true point of view in the history of this nation is not the Atlantic coast, it is the Great West. Even the slavery struggle . . . occupies its important place in American history because of its relation to westward expansion.

In this advance, the frontier is the outer edge of the wave, the meeting point between savagery and civilization. Much has been written about the frontier from the point of view of border warfare and the chase, but as a field for the serious study of the economist and the historian it has been neglected.

The American frontier is sharply distinguished from the European frontier, a fortified boundary line running through dense populations. The most significant thing about the American frontier is, that it lies at the hither edge of free land. In the census reports it is treated as the margin of that settlement which has a density of two or more to the square mile. The term is an elastic one, and for our purposes does not need sharp definition. We shall consider the whole frontier belt, including the Indian country and the outer margin of the 'settled area' of the census reports. This paper will make no attempt to treat the subject exhaustively; its aim is simply to call attention to the frontier as a fertile field for investigation, and to suggest some of the problems which arise in connection with it.

In the settlement of America we have to observe how European life entered the continent, and how America modified and developed that life and reacted in Europe. Our early history is the study of European germs developing in an American environment. Too exclusive attention has been paid by institutional students to the Germanic origins, too little to the American factors. The frontier is the line of most rapid and effective Americanization. The wilderness masters the colonist . . . at the frontier the environment is at first too strong for the man. He must accept the conditions which it furnishes, or perish, and so he fits himself into the Indian clearings and follows the Indian trails. Little by little he transforms the wilderness, but the outcome is not the old Europe, not simply the development of Germanic germs . . . The fact is, that here is a new product that is American. At first, the frontier was the Atlantic coast. It was the frontier of Europe in a very real sense. Moving westward, the frontier became more and more American. As successive terminal moraines result from successive glaciations, so each frontier leaves its traces behind it, and when it becomes a settled area the region still partakes of the frontier characteristics. Thus the advance of the frontier has meant a steady movement away from the influence of Europe, a steady growth of independence on American lines. And to study this advance, the men who grow up under these conditions, and the political, economic, and social results of it, is to study the really American part of our history . . .

In these successive frontiers we find natural boundary lines which have served to mark and to affect the characteristics of the frontiers, namely: the 'fall line'; the Allegheny Mountains; the Mississippi; the Missouri where its direction approximates north and south; the lines of the arid lands, approximately the ninety-ninth meridian; and the Rocky Mountains. The fall line marked the frontier of the seventeenth century; the Alleghenies that of the eighteenth; the Mississippi that of the first quarter of the nineteenth; the Missouri that of the middle of this century (omitting the California movement); and the belt of the Rocky Mountains and the arid tract, the present frontier. Each was won by a series of Indian wars.

At the Atlantic frontier one can study the germs of processes repeated at each successive frontier. We have the complex European life sharply precipitated by the wilderness into the simplicity of primitive conditions. The first frontier had to meet its Indian question, its question of the disposition of the public domain, of the means of intercourse with older settlements, of the extension of political organization, of religious and educational activity. And the settlement of these and similar questions for one frontier served as a guide for the next. The American student needs not to go to the 'prim little townships of Sleswick' for illustration of the law of continuity and development. For example, he may study the origin of our land policies in the colonial land policy; he may see how the system grew by adapting the statutes to the customs of the successive frontiers. He may see how the mining experience in the lead regions of Wisconsin, Illinois, and Iowa was applied to the mining laws of the Sierras, and how our Indian policy has been a series of experimentations on successive frontiers. Each tier of new States has found in the older ones material for its constitutions. Each frontier has made similar contributions to American characters . . .

But with all these similarities there are essential differences, due to the place element and the time element . . .

It would be a work worth the historian's labors to mark these various frontiers and in detail compare one with another. Not only would there result a more adequate conception of American development and characteristics, but invaluable additions would be made to the history of society.

Loria, the Italian economist, has urged the study of colonial life as an aid in understanding the stages of European development, affirming that colonial settlement is for economic science what the mountain is for geology, beginning to light primitive stratifications. 'America', he says, 'has the key to the historical enigma which Europe has sought for centuries in vain, and the land which has no history reveals luminously the course of universal history.' There is much truth in this. The United States lies like a huge page in the history of society. Line by line as we read this continental page from West to East we find the record of social evolution. It begins with the Indian and the hunter; it goes on to tell of the disintegration of civilization; we read the annals of the pastoral stage in ranch life; the exploitation of the soil by the raising of unrotated crops of corn and wheat in sparsely settled farming communities; the intensive culture of the denser farm settlement; and finally the manufacturing organization with city and factory system. This page is familiar to the student of census statistics, but how little of it has been used by our historians. Particularly in eastern States this page is a palimpsest. What is now a manufacturing State was in an earlier decade an area of intensive farming. Earlier yet it had been a wheat area, and still earlier the 'range' had attracted the cattle-herder. Thus Wisconsin, now developing manufacture, is a State with varied agricultural interests. But earlier it was given over to almost exclusive grain-raising, like North Dakota at the present time.

. . . Having now roughly outlined the various kinds of frontiers . . . we may next inquire what were the influences on the East and on the Old World . . .

First, we note that the frontier promoted the formation of a composite nationality for the American people. The coast was preponderantly English, but the later tides of continental immigration flowed across to the free lands. This was the case from the early colonial days. The Scotch-Irish and the Palatine Germans, or 'Pennsylvania Dutch', furnished the dominant element in the stock of the colonial frontier. With these peoples were also the freed indented servants, or redemptioners, who at the expiration of their time of service passed to the frontier . . . Very generally these redemptioners were of non-English stock. In the crucible of the frontier the immigrants were Americanized, liberated, and fused into a mixed race, English in neither nationality nor characteristics. The process has gone on from the early days to our own. Burke and other writers in the middle of the eighteenth century believed that Pennsylvania was 'threatened with the danger of being wholly foreign in language, manners and perhaps even inclinations'. The German and Scotch-Irish elements in the frontier of the South were only less great. In the middle of the present century the German element in Wisconsin was already so considerable that leading publicists looked to the creation of a German state out of the commonwealth by concentrating their colonization. Such examples teach us to beware of misinterpreting the fact that there is a common English speech in America into a belief that the stock is also English.

In another way the advance of the frontier decreased our dependence on England. The coast, particularly of the South, lacked diversified industries, and was dependent on England for the bulk of its supplies. In the South there was even a dependence on the Northern colonies for articles of food . . . Before long the frontier created a demand for merchants. As it retreated from the coast it became less and less possible for England to bring her supplies directly to the consumer's wharfs, and carry away staple crops, and staple crops began to give way to diversified agriculture for a time. The effect of this phase of the frontier upon the northern section is perceived when we realize how the advance of the frontier aroused seaboard cities like Boston, New York, and Baltimore to engage in rivalry for what Washington called 'the extensive and valuable trade of a rising empire'.

The legislation which most developed the powers of the national government, and played the largest part in its activity, was conditioned on the frontier. Writers have discussed the subjects of tariff, land, and internal improvement as subsidiary to the slavery question . . . This is a wrong perspective. The pioneer needed the goods of the coast, and so the grand series of internal improvement and railroad legislation began, with potent nationalizing effects. Over internal improvements occurred great debates, in which grave constitutional questions were discussed. Sectional groupings appear in the votes, profoundly significant for the historian. Loose construction increased as the nation marched westward. But the West was not content with bringing the farm to the factory. Under the lead of Clay – 'Harry of the West' – protective tariffs were passed, with the cry of bringing the factory to the farm. The disposition of the public lands was a third important subject of national legislation influenced by the frontier . . .

It is safe to say that the legislation with regard to land, tariff, and internal improvements – the American system of the nationalizing Whig party – was conditioned on frontier ideas and needs. But it was not merely in legislative action that the frontier worked against the sectionalism of the coast. The economic and social characteristics of the frontier worked against sectionalism. The men of the frontier had closer resemblances to the Middle region than to either of the other sections. Pennsylvania had been the seed-plot of frontier emigration, and, although she passed on her settlers along the Great Valley into the west of Virginia and the Carolinas, yet the industrial society of these Southern frontiersmen was always more like that of the Middle region than like that of the tide water portion of the South, which later came to spread its industrial type throughout the South.

The Middle region, entered by New York harbor, was an open door to all Europe. The tide water part of the South represented typical Englishmen, modified by a warm climate and servile labor, and living in baronial fashion on great plantations; New England stood for a special English movement, Puritanism. The Middle region was less English than the other sections. It had a wide mixture of nationalities, a varied society, the mixed town and county system of local government, a varied economic life, many religious sects. In short, it was a region mediating between New England and the South, and the East and the West. It represented that composite nationality which the contemporary United States exhibits, that juxtaposition of non-English groups, occupying a valley or a little settlement, and presenting reflections of the map of Europe in their variety. It was democratic and non-sectional, if not national; 'easy, tolerant and contented'; rooted strongly in material prosperity. It was typical of the modern United States. It was least sectional, not only because it lay between North and South, but also because with no barriers to shut out its frontiers from its settled region, and with a system of connecting waterways, the Middle region mediated between East and West as well as between North and South. Thus it became the typically American region. Even the New Englander, who was shut out from the frontier by the Middle region, tarrying in New York or Pennsylvania on his westward march, lost the acuteness of his sectionalism on the way.

. . . This nationalizing tendency . . . transformed the democracy of Jefferson into the national republicanism of Monroe and the democracy of Andrew Jackson. The West of the War of 1812, the West of Clay, and Benton and Harrison, and Andrew Jackson, shut off by the Middle States and the mountains from the coast sections, had a solidarity of its own with national tendencies. On the tide of the Father of Waters, North and South met and mingled into a nation. Interstate migration went steadily on – a process of cross-fertilization of ideas and institutions. The fierce struggle of the sections over slavery on the western frontier does not diminish the truth of this statement; it proves the truth of it. Slavery was a sectional trait that would not down, but in the West it could not remain sectional. It was the greatest of frontiersmen who declared: 'I believe this Government cannot endure permanently half slave and half free. It will become all of one thing or all of the other.' Nothing works for nationalism like intercourse within the nation. Mobility of population is death to localism, and the western frontier worked irresistibly in unsettling population. The effect reached back from the frontier and affected profoundly the Atlantic coast and even the Old World.

But the most important effect of the frontier has been in the promotion of democracy here and in Europe. As has been indicated, the frontier is productive of individualism. Complex society is precipitated by the wilderness into a kind of primitive organization based on the family. The tendency is anti-social. It produces antipathy to control and particularly to any direct control. The tax-gatherer is viewed as a representative of oppression . . . Frontier conditions prevalent in the colonies are important factors in the explanation of the American Revolution, where individual liberty was sometimes confused with absence of all effective government. The same conditions aid in explaining the difficulty of instituting a strong government in the period of the confederacy. The frontier individualism has from the beginning promoted democracy.

The frontier States that came into the Union in the first quarter of a century of its existence came in with democratic suffrage provisions, and had reactive effects of the highest importance upon the older States whose peoples were being attracted there. An extension of the franchise became essential. It was *western* New York that forced an extension of suffrage in the constitutional convention of that State in 1821; and it was *western* Virginia that compelled the tide water region to put a more liberal suffrage provision in the constitution framed in 1830, and to give to the frontier region a more nearly proportionate representation with the tide water aristocracy. The rise of democracy as an effective force in the nation came in with western preponderance under Jackson and William Henry Harrison, and it meant the triumph of the frontier – with all of its good and with all of its evil elements . . .

So long as free land exists, the opportunity for a competency exists, and economic power secures political power. But the democracy born of free land, strong in selfishness and individualism, intolerant of administrative experience and education, and pressing individual liberty beyond its proper bounds, has its dangers as well as its benefits. Individualism in America has allowed a laxity in regard to government affairs which has rendered possible the spoils system and all the manifest evils that follow the lack of a highly developed civic spirit. In this connection may be noted also the influence of frontier conditions in permitting lax business honor, inflated paper currency and wild-cat banking. The colonial and revolutionary frontier was the region whence emanated many of the worst forms of an evil currency. The West in the War of 1812 repeated the phenomenon on the frontier of that day, while the speculation and wild-cat banking of the period of the crisis of 1837 occurred on the new frontier belt of the next tier of States. Thus each one of the periods of lax financial integrity coincides with periods when a new set of frontier communities had arisen, and coincides in area with these successive frontiers, for the most part. The recent Populist agitation is a case in point. Many a State that now declines any connection with the tenets of the Populists, itself adhered to such ideas in an earlier stage of the development of the State. A primitive society can hardly be expected to show the intelligent appreciation of the complexity of business interests in a developed society. The continual recurrence of these areas of paper money agitation is another evidence that the frontier can be isolated and studied as a factor in American history of the highest importance . . .

From the conditions of frontier life came intellectual traits of profound importance. The works of travelers along each frontier from colonial days onward describe certain common traits, and these traits have, while softening down, still persisted as survivals in the place of their origin, even when a higher social organization succeeded. The result is that to the frontier the American intellect owes its striking characteristics. That coarseness and strength combined with acuteness and inquisitiveness; that practical, inventive turn of mind, quick to find expedients; that masterful grasp of material things, lacking in the artistic but powerful to effect great ends; that restless, nervous energy; that dominant individualism, working for good and for evil, and withal that buoyancy and exuberance which comes with freedom – these are traits of the frontier, or traits called out elsewhere because of the existence of the frontier. Since the days when the fleet of Columbus sailed into the waters of the New World, America has been another name for opportunity, and the people of the United States have taken their tone from the incessant expansion which has not only been open but has even been forced upon them. He would be a rash prophet who would assert that the expansive character of American life has now entirely ceased. Movement has been its dominant fact, and, unless this training has no effect upon a people, the American energy will continually demand a wider field for its exercise. But never again will such gifts of free land offer themselves. For a moment, at the frontier, the bonds of custom are broken and unrestraint is triumphant. There is no *tabula rasa*. The stubborn American environment is there with its imperious summons to accept its conditions; the inherited ways of doing things are also there; and yet, in spite of environment, and in spite of custom, each gate of escape from the bondage of the past; and freshness, and confidence, and scorn of older society, impatience of its restraints and its ideas, and indifference to its lessons, have accompanied the frontier. What the Mediterranean Sea was to the Greeks, breaking the bond of custom, offering new experiences, calling out new institutions and activities, that, and more, the ever retreating frontier has been to the United States directly, and to the nations of Europe more remotely. And now, four centuries from the discovery of America, at the end of a hundred years of life under the Constitution, the frontier has gone, and with its going has closed the first period of American history.

'Paterson'

From William Carlos Williams (1963) *Paterson* Book I. New Directions, New York, pp 83–4.

> Great riches shall be yours!
> I wasn't born here. I was born in what we call
> over here the Old Country. But it's the same
> people, the same kind of people there as here
> and they're up to the same kind of tricks as over
> here – only there isn't as much money
> over there – and that makes the difference.
>
> My family were poor people. So I started to work
> when I was pretty young.
> – Oh, it took me a long time! but
> one day I said to myself, Klaus, that's my name,
> Klaus, I said to myself, you're a success.
> You have worked hard but you have been
> lucky.
> You're
> rich – and now we're going to enjoy ourselves.

Hamilton saw more clearly than anyone else with what urgency the new government must assume authority over the States if it was to survive. He never trusted the people, 'a great beast,' as he saw them and held Jefferson to be little better if not worse than any.

So I came to America!

Especially in the matter of finances a critical stage presented itself. The States were inclined to shrug off the debt incurred during the recent war – each state preferring to undertake its own private obligations separately. Hamilton saw that if this were allowed to ensue the effect would be fatal, to future credit. He came out with vigor and cunning for 'Assumption,' assumption by the Federal Government of the national debt, and the granting to it of powers of taxation without which it could not raise the funds necessary for this purpose. A storm followed in which he found himself opposed by Madison and Jefferson.

But when I got here I soon found out that I
was a pretty small frog in a mighty big pool. So
I went to work all over again. I suppose
I was born with a gift for that sort of thing.
I throve and I gloried in it. And I thought then
that I was happy. And I was – as happy
as money could make me.

But did it make me GOOD?

He stopped to laugh, healthily, and
his wan assistants followed him
forcing him out – grinning against
the rocks with wry smiles.

NO! he shouted, bending
at the knees and straightening himself up
violently with the force of his emphasis – like
Beethoven getting a crescendo out of an orchestra – NO!

It did *not* make me good. (His clenched fists
were raised above his brows.) I kept on making
money, more and more of it, but it didn't make
me good.

America the golden!
with tricks and money
damned
like Altgeld sick
and molden
we love thee bitter
land

Like Altgeld on the
corner
seeing mourners
pass
we bow our heads
before thee
and take our hats
in hand

'Witness: the story of a middle-class family'
From Whittaker Chambers 1979 *Witness: the story of a middle class family* 2nd edn. Regnery, South Bend, Indiana, pp 146–53.

XXV

Sometimes, as I sat translating Minna von Barnhelm, I would hear in the distance the shuffling feet of the Home Guard and fifes playing 'Little Shaver'. For the World War that my grandfather had predicted had come, and added a new element of turmoil to my mind. The First World War was in my thoughts day and night; I felt it with an intensity with which I never felt World War II. My family was traditionally Francophile. I was brought up to believe that Paris was less the capital of a country than the capital of Light. The German advance through Belgium filled us almost with as much consternation as if we had been invaded ourselves. I can still remember the Sunday morning when I picked up the newspaper and saw the headlines about the Battle of the Marne. I felt that I was experiencing an authentic miracle. After that, I lived day by day through the deadlock of the trench war on the Western Front. My grandfather had sent me a big military map of Europe, showing forts and naval bases. It covered almost one wall of my room. I had marked out the fronts with rubber bands. Every night before I went to bed, I moved the bands to correspond with the day's communiques.

The war was the direct cause of my Russian studies. After the Russian Revolution (which interested me only as it affected Allied strategy), my mother decided that we might be fighting the Russians soon. She urged me to prepare for a career in the military intelligence by studying Russian. I had only Thimm's *Russian Self-Taught*, which consisted chiefly of vocabularies. These my mother patiently heard me repeat day after day until I had learned two or three thousand Russian words. I never learned Russian grammar, though I learned to read Russian type and to write Russian script.

I planned to get into the war as soon as I finished high school – a plan that I did not share with my mother. The false armistice was a tremendous blow. But as soon as it was denied, I saw that there was no time to lose. In New York City, one day, I had passed the British recruiting office and made a careful note of its address. The day after the false armistice, I left a note for my family, saying that I had gone to enlist. I walked into the British recruiting office and offered my services to the Empire. A stiff English officer looked me up and down. 'Hell, boy', he said, 'the war's over'. I slunk home. My family was amused. It should have been handwriting on the wall.

As nobody seemed able to help me, I strove to help myself. I sought refuge in those places where I had always found it. I became a haunter of the woods and fields. I would set out by myself before the family was stirring in the morning and spend whole days in the woods, which required of me only that I be silent, patient and harmless. In return, nature gave me the peace that it gives to anyone who comes to see and hear and not to change.

Those woods, and their lakes and streams, were then a part of the Brooklyn waterworks system. They have become a part of the New York State park system, and thousands pass through them in a day. In those days, I had them almost entirely to myself. I seldom met another person. I could soon find my way about them even at night, as I sometimes used to do. For I never found the loneliness of the woods at night as disturbing as people by daylight. I soon knew their birds, plants and insects as well as I knew my way along their trails. Only those who really live close to nature can understand the elation I felt when I first discovered where the seagulls roosted seven miles from the sea, or the shallow stream in the dense woods where all the robins in the area bathed just at sunrise, or the one brook where a cardinal flower grew, or my first pinxter bush in bloom.

I presently discovered that the life below the surface of shallow ponds was as absorbing as the life on their shores. It reached a climax in the fore-spring when the alder catkins were bursting with pollen and the ice was still rotting on the pools. Through the ice I used to watch the watery world below coming back to life after winter, while the toads came down to the lowlands to deposit their masses of jellied eggs or the frogs unwound their slimy ribbons in the shallows. In these pursuits, I could not always take off my shoes in time to follow an exciting specimen. I learned simply to wade in with my shoes on. This habit so impressed one of my schoolmates that he remembered it through the years, and was able to testify to it, as an example of my bizarre behavior, during the first Hiss trial.

In time, my ear became so sensitive that, sitting silently, I could sometimes hear the tiny tearing sound that a caterpillar makes in gnawing a leaf, and by following it, locate him. My eye, too, became sensitized, so that the slightest movement, the waving of grass stems, the way a leaf hung when the others were blowing, or the way a twig vibrated, always meant something and often something terrible, since nature, under the leaves, is a vast concealment and pursuit. I still retain this power to pick out minute movements in nature. But I have lost the power to sit silent for an hour, mentally alert, but physically lulled by the sun and the smell of plants each of which has a distinct odor. It was not necessary to sit motionless, but only to make those slow and explicit motions which said that I was not in hiding and did not mean attack. I never had to move much to observe the life of fields and woods, for its inquisitiveness is equal to its fear, and the woods and fields sooner or later drew near to observe me. I was a part of nature myself. In that habit of identification with nature is a healing peace more medicinal than herbs. Undoubtedly it carried me through the worse of my adolescence.

During those quiet sessions, I was not only observing the life of the woods. I was making inner and outer observations of another kind, trying to sort out my thoughts about myself, my family and our dislocations both of which made me a fugitive in the woods. I sensed that one dislocation was connected with the other. I felt that the failure of my family was in part a failure of the life in which it found itself. But since I had no grasp of why these things were so, I was chiefly engaged in adding up the ways in which they were so. By degrees I told myself:

I am an outcast. My family is outcast. We have no friends, no social ties, no church, no organization that we claim and that claims us, no community. We could scarcely be more foreign in China than in our alienation from the life around us. If we tried to share with it our thoughts, it would draw away, uncomprehending. If it tried to share its hopes with us, we would draw away, uncomprehending. It does not want what we want. We do not want what it wants. It puts the things of the world first. We put the things of the mind first. It knows what it wants better than we know what we want. They are simple things. It measures happiness and success in terms of money, comfort, appearances and what it calls pleasure. I, for one, would not want to live a life in which money, comfort, appearances and pleasure mean success. There is something wrong with a people that measures its happiness and success in those terms. It has lost its mind. It has no mind; it has only activity. 'What shall be said', I had written, for I was writing more and more, 'of those who have destroyed the mind of a nation?'

But if there was something wrong with the life around us, there was also something wrong with us. Compared to us, the life around us was orderly and happy. We were not happy. Beneath our quiet, we were wretchedly unhappy. We were not a family. Our home was not a home. My father was not a father. My mother was not a mother. He was nothing. She was trying to be both father and mother. She dominated through her love, which was genuine, tender and sacrificing, but was dangerous. I felt it around me like coils, interposing between me and reality, coddling my natural weakness, to keep the world away from me, but also to keep me away from the world. 'My mother does not want me to grow up', I thought, 'because she does not want me to go away from her'. As the life around me had no mind, only activity, my mother had no plans, and few hopes – not many of them.

That left me absolutely alone. My family could give me no support against the alien world, from which the whole influence of our life divided me. And I felt about our family, a foreboding, an indefinable sense of doom, which I would also share unless I found the strength to free myself from it. I doubted that I had that strength. I decided to find out.

I did not understand that the malady of the life around me from which I retreated into the woods, and the malady of the life of my family, from which I was about to retreat into the world, were different manifestations of the same malady – the disorder that overtakes society and families when a world has lost its soul. For it was not its mind that the life around me had lost, though I thought so as a boy and was to continue to think so for almost twenty years, but its way, because it had lost its soul. I was about to set out from those quiet woods (to which I would return only at the decisive moment of the Hiss Case) on a lifelong quest for that lost way, first in personal, then in revolutionary, then in religious terms.

XXVI

It was the summer I graduated from high school. My mother wanted me to go on to college. My father was opposed. So was I, but for different reasons. I had had enough of school. I needed a job, but I was peculiarly helpless in finding one in the white-collar world where it was taken for granted that I should look, but where we had no roots. My father refused to interest himself in the problem.

I decided to solve it for myself, to leave home, to make my own way, to turn my back on that middle-class world of white collars in which our claim to belong seemed to me a pretense unjustified by any reality. I knew that this announcement would cause wild emotional scenes, tearful charges of ingratitude and lack of love. Because I was a boy, I slipped away secretly, and, because I was a boy, and because even a wanderer likes to have a destination, I headed for Mexico.

XXVII

Few boys run away from happy homes. The world is too wide; it is easier to stay put. I left my unhappy home with a wrench that I could barely master. Once or twice, I was on the point of turning back. I kept on chiefly because I knew more about the unhappiness behind me than about the loneliness of the world ahead. I had a little money of my own – ten dollars possibly. I bought a ticket to Baltimore. It seems prophetic, but I was simply heading south, and Baltimore was about as far as I could go on the money I had.

I reached Baltimore for the first time on a singeing Saturday afternoon. I was wearing my graduation suit – the first suit of my own I had had. I wandered in the stunning heat until I found an old flea-bag opposite the Calvert Station. There I took a room. There I met my first bedbugs and learned that there are worse things than a shabby house: there are filthy rooms.

On Monday morning, after I had paid my bill, I had just enough money left for a newspaper, rolls and a cup of coffee. The coffee was a declaration of independence. I had never been allowed to drink coffee. In the newspaper, among the help wanted ads, I found that Engel & Hevenor, contractors, were hiring on laborers for a street railway job in Washington. Their address was on Eutaw Street. Seventeen years later, in underground days, I would live on its upper extension. Eutaw Place, where Alger Hiss, who was a young boy in that same city on that morning of my first job hunt, would sometimes visit me.

Engel & Hevenor's headquarters was an empty store. Outside, on the sidewalk, a hard-faced young man in shirtsleeves was doing the hiring. A long line of men of all nationalities and all styles of rough faces and rough clothes, stretched away for a block. These had passed the hiring test; they already had jobs.

The test was simple. When a man asked for a job, the hiring boss said: 'Stick out your hands'. If the hands were callused, the man was sent to fall in at the end of the line. I was wearing a hat, my trim graduation suit with jacket (although it was hot), and my tie was neatly tied. The hiring boss took one startled look at me (one way or another, my appearance always seems to work against me). 'Stick out your hands', he said. They were soft, of course. 'Can't use you'.

I turned away, with crushing defeat in my eyes, and walked down the line of life's successes, trying to look invisible. Every man in the line knew what had happened. As I neared the end, hands reached out and pulled me through the line to the far side, where I was largely out of sight of the hiring boss, who was busy with others. Somebody said: 'Give me your hat'. Somebody else grabbed the hat from my hand, folded it and stuffed it in his pocket. 'Mess up your hair'. 'Take off that tie'. 'Take off your coat'. Somebody snatched my jacket and passed it down the line. Somebody else scooped muck out of the gutter and made me rub it on my hands. Then they made room for me in the line.

It was moving. A boss, standing at the head, was handing out transportation to Washington. The man behind me said: 'Keep moving. Take a ticket. He won't know you'. I shuffled along with the rest. I stood before the transportation boss. I reached out my grimy hand for a ticket. He slapped one into the palm. I walked past him. The line followed. The faces remained expressionless.

In a rough group, an insurgence from the netherworld that made respectable Baltimoreans turn to stare, we marched to the Washington, Baltimore and Annapolis railroad station. We crowded together in a special coach – special in the sense that it was old and shabby. On the train, somebody handed me back my hat and jacket.

The proletariat and I had met. The wretched of the earth that stretched out their hands and claimed me for their own because they understood my need. In four minutes, they had done for me what others failed to do in a lifetime. They taught me that there is a level of humanity where compassion is a reflex of distress, and, in that sense, they humanized my soul for the rest of my life.

XXVIII

We piled off the W B & A train on New York Avenue in Washington. The job lay just beyond. For a mile or so, the Engel & Hevenor company was tearing up street railway tracks or laying new ones. It was a little like a daylight scene from Hell. In places, big fires were burning and asphalt pots were belching blackly. For several blocks, the asphalt of the street and the concrete around the tracks had been cut out by pneumatic drills and picks and shoveled away. Elsewhere, picks and drills were clattering, air compressors were throbbing, the noise was deafening. In places, the earth had been scooped out around the tracks and the excavation shored up with timbers. Men, shoveling, picking, hammering, drilling, swarmed over the construction and destruction.

I gave an assumed name, Charles Adams, to a straw boss, who handed me a badge with a number. Then I was attached to a gang whose boss wore a sweat-drenched silk shirt with peppermint candy stripes (post-war prosperity had not faded yet). He was a big, reserved, pleasant-looking man with a walrus moustache, who moved slowly among the men, giving a quiet order here, a quiet suggestion there, sometimes gently taking a tool from a laborer's hand and showing him how to do the same job with less effort and more effect. He never raised his voice. The men respected him deeply – in part, because he had been a construction boss on a New York subway job and knew every detail of the work, in part, because he was fearless about what they most feared – the third rail.

Sometimes, in cutting up concrete between the tracks, the stuttering, unwieldy pneumatic drills would go through the surface. The blade of the drill would touch the third rail below and the drill would stick there, burning with a brilliant blue electric light. The drillers wore heavy gloves and the shock of contact seemed to hurl them off the drills, so that I never saw anyone hurt in this way. Calmly, the boss would walk over to the blazing drill. Deliberately, he would take off his battered felt hat, punched with holes. He would fold it, wrap it around the drill handle and lug out the heavy tool.

When I was turned over to him, he had stared at me a moment a little curiously. Then he went and got a short cold chisel and a short-handled sledge and set me to cracking the nuts on the bolts that tied the rail plates together. I worked doggedly in the killing sun. Once in a while I caught the boss watching me. Once he came over and told me not to grip the sledge and the chisel so tight. He did not mention my hands though he glanced at them. Ten minutes after I started working there was scarcely any skin left on palms or fingers. In that condition, I worked with them through the afternoon.

At quitting time, we piled into a street car on our way to a boarding house, not far from the Capitol, where we all ate around trestle tables in a long bleak room. There was nothing in it but those tables, the fold chairs and a mantelpiece on which stood two small plaster busts. Across the flattened base of each was printed a name: Mozart.

The food was prison fare; meat that was unidentifiable, and lapped in a greasy suspect stew. Potatoes were the filler. Dessert was nearly always the same – bread, the refuse from the last meal, glued into a pudding and concealed in a glutinous sauce that reminded me of masses of toad eggs in my boyhood (not far in the past – though one day made it seem like a decade). We were always ravenously hungry, and while we sometimes grumbled at the food, we always wolfed it, washing out the more questionable tastes with unlimited coffee.

By a selective seniority system, some of the men slept upstairs in the boarding house. Most of them, perhaps a hundred or more, drifted after supper to a barracks a few blocks away. There in a big hall, dingy and bare, and reeking of disinfectant, were a hundred or so beds, most of them double-deckers. Each man had his bed under which he kept his few belongings.

I slumped down on my bed with my clothes on. My skinless hands were burning. A tall, lean, middle-aged man with an elusive face in which dissipation lurked, walked over to my bed. 'Let me see your hands', he said. He examined them as if he had been a doctor. 'I'm an old soldier', he said, 'and I know what to do for these'.

He rummaged among his things and brought up two bottles of iodine. 'I am going to hold your wrist tight', he said, 'because when I pour this on your hand, it's going to burn like hell, and you're going to jump'. A crowd of men had slipped over and stood quietly watching.

My doctor uncorked the first iodine bottle, and, like a doctor, he talked to distract me. 'My name's York', he said, and unruffled by the listening gallery, added, 'I had a good upbringing. You know what's the matter with me? Women. Keep away from them'. (How often I was to hear that one.) While he talked, he emptied the whole bottle of iodine over the palm and fingers of my hand. I managed not to wince and even to smile. Then York grasped my other hand and emptied the other bottle over that.

The men drifted away as quietly as they had drifted up. I knew that I had passed a test. In a short time, my hands healed with calluses that should have got me a job anywhere.

XXIX

Learning to do my different jobs kept me busy; the heavy physical work kept me exhausted. At first, in the evening, I would collapse on my bed at once and fall into a deep sleep. Gradually, I hardened. Then I began to look at the men around me.

They were my first International. Practically every European nationality was represented. Yet they had no nationality, just as they had no homes. That was the difference between them and other men: they were the men who had no homes at all. They had reached that bleak barracks in the unheroic course of a working-man's everlasting search for work which, as Tolstoy has noted, beggars the wanderings of Odysseus. The job was the nearest thing to home they felt. Few of them spoke English and I found that my scrappy knowledge of half a dozen languages was one way I could get to know them.

I worked day after day beside a silent, sour, potato-faced Russian. One day I got tired of this mute companionship. I pointed to the rails and said 'Zheleznaya daroga' (railroad). The Russian froze, leaning on his pick and repeated after me in a rapt voice, as if the words were a phrase of music: 'Zheleznaya daroga'. Thereafter, when we got bored with the work and our silence, we would hold that kind of one-word conversation. He would point to something and I would give the Russian word for it, if I knew it. If I didn't, he would tell me the word. We never progressed beyond that. But he seemed perfectly satisfied.

There was a burly, surly Pole who ran the cement mixer near me on the job. In the barracks, he had the bed next to mine. Sometimes, as I fell asleep, I would hear him coughing his lungs out. Sometimes, his coughing woke me at night. After speaking to him once or twice and getting no response, I decided that he was ill-tempered, and gave it up. One day I asked somebody about him. I was told: 'Paul's got TB. The cement dust is killing him'. So I took to greeting him again. Usually, he merely grunted and kept on shovelling cement and sand. One day I found him sitting on a pile of blocks beside the cement mixer. 'How are you, Paul?' I asked. 'I die soon', he said, 'some day I die soon'.

There was a Belgian, a Fleming, a wiry, sallow, hawk-faced young man, who sometimes spoke French to me. I think he doubted how much I understood, for one day he dove into his suitcase and brought up a copy of *Madame Bovary*. He opened it at random and said: 'Translate'. I translated a page, haltingly. 'If you can read Flaubert', he said, 'you can read anything'. Thereafter, he spent much time with me. Our conversations, on the sweating job or in the disinfected barracks, were persistently literary, though on a somewhat narrow range. For, outside of *Madame Bovary*, he seemed to have read nothing but the novels of Emile Zola, whose massive social tracts he admired tremendously and talked about continually. ' 'E 'ave written many books', he said to me one day as if that were the first time we had touched the subject, 'many books, beautiful books, and so filthy. But 'e 'ave written one book – listen, *La Reve* – so piure that it can be read by the piurest virgin'. I have never read this immaculate book, but in his anonymous memory (for I cannot recollect his name), I hope to do so before I die.

The Belgian said that he had been the boss of several gangs of native rubber gatherers in Malaya. He had fabulous stories of slave driving with whips, of monumental heat in which the workers sometimes dropped dead and were simply left to rot to be gnawed by beasts or insects. He was sincerely puzzled that I should find that a little horrible, for he was completely without pity or mercy, as if his reactions were on a different range from the human, more like a bird of prey's.

He brought the jungle creepily alive, with slow muddy rivers, a nocturnal pulsation of men, beasts and bugs and tales of king cobras stalking rubber gatherers in lonely huts. He insisted that men could make a fortune in a short time, gathering rubber (he had made a fortune himself, but lost it, according to the usual tale, on women). He begged me to go back to the East with him, and he began to teach me Flemish, for he planned that we should go to the Dutch East Indies. For a while I was strongly tempted, thinking that I heard my future coming up like thunder out of Chine cross the bay. But I did not like or trust him. I thought that he would not hesitate to kill me, and would scarcely know that he had done it, if I were in the way. And there was something about his yellowish complexion, his taut gestures and the way the pupil of his eye would contract to a fine point that made me guess at madness, drugs or less mentionable things. I gradually detached myself from him.

'Arctic dreams'

From Barry Lopez 1987 *The Country of the Mind*. Picador, London, pp 254–6.

This is an old business, walking slowly over the land with an appreciation of its immediacy to the senses and in anticipation of what lies hidden in it. The eye alights suddenly on something bright in the grass – the chitinous shell of an insect. The nose tugs at a minute blossom for some trace of arctic perfume. The hands turn over an odd bone, extrapolating, until the animal is discovered in the mind and seen to be moving in the land. One finds anomalous stones to puzzle over, and in footprints and broken spiderwebs the traces of irretrievable events.

During those summers I found, too, the molted feathers of ducks washed up in great wrack lines, in heaps, on the beach. Undisturbed in shallow waters on the lagoon side, I found hoofprints of caribou, as sharp as if the animals had stepped there in fresh clay only a moment before. They must have crossed over in late spring, on the last of the ice. I squatted down wherever the evidence of animals was particularly strong amid the tundra's polygon fractures. Where Canada geese had cropped grass at the edge of a freshwater pond; at the skull of a ringed seal carried hundreds of yards inland by ice, or scavengers; where grass had been flattened by a resting fox.

I saw in the sea face of a low bench of earth along the beach the glistening edge of an ice lens that underlay the tundra. The surface layers of plants and dirt overhung it like a brow-thatch of hair. I tried persistently but without success to sneak up on the flocks of feeding geese. I lost and regained images of ptarmigan against the ground, because of their near-perfect camouflage. I brought back to the cabin to set on a shelf by my bed castings of the landscape, to keep for a while and wonder over. The fractured intervertebral disk of a belukha whale. The prehistoric-looking exoskeleton of a marine isopod. And handfuls of feathers. Tangible things from my gentle interrogations, objects to which some part of a pervasive and original mystery still clung.

In the sometimes disconcerting summary which is a photograph, Pingok Island would seem bleak and forsaken. In winter it disappears beneath whiteness, a flat white plain extending seaward into the Beaufort Sea ice and landward without a border into the tundra of the coastal plain. The island emerges in June, resplendent with flowers and insects and birds, only to disappear again in a few months beneath the first snowstorms. To a Western imagination that finds a stand of full-crowned trees heartening, that finds the flight and voice of larks exhilarating, and the sight of wind rolling over fields of tall grass more agreeable, Pingok seems impoverished. When I arrived on the island, I, too, understood its bleak aspect as a category, the expression of something I had read about or been told. In the weeks during which I made some passing acquaintance with it, its bleakness was altered, however, the prejudice we exercise against such landscapes, imagining them to be primitive, stark, and pagan, became sharply apparent. It is in a place like this that we would unthinkingly store poisons or test weapons, land like the deserts to which we once banished our heretics and where we once loosed scapegoats with the burden of our transgressions.

The differing landscapes of the earth are hard to know individually. They are as difficult to engage in conversation as wild animals. The complex feelings of affinity and self-assurance one feels with one's native place rarely develop again in another landscape. It is a convention of Western thought to believe all cultures are compelled to explore, that human beings seek new land because their economies drive them onward. Lost in this valid but nevertheless impersonal observation is the notion of a simpler longing, of a human desire for a less complicated life, for fresh intimacy and renewal. These, too, draw us into new landscapes. And desire causes imagination to misconstrue what it finds. The desire for wealth, for revivification, for triumph, as much or more than scientific measurement and description, or the imperatives of economic expansion, resolves the geography of a newfound landscape.

Notes on contributors

Les Arnold was Head of English at Bath College of Higher Education until his death in 1992. His collected poems appear in *Joy riding*.

Regina Barreca teaches feminist theory and modern British literature at the University of Connecticut and is co-editor of the journal *LIT: literature interpretation theory*. She is the editor of two books, *Last laughs: perspectives on women and comedy* and *Sex and Death in Victorian Literature*. She is also the author of *They used to call me Snow White . . . but I drifted*, a book on women's strategic use of humour.

Robert Burchell is professor of American history at the University of Manchester and Director of the David and Mary Eccles Centre at the British Library. He has written books on westward expansion, and on the San Francisco Irish, and is editor of *The end of Anglo-America: historical essays in the study of cultural divergence*. He is a former chairman of the British Association for American Studies.

Gavin Cologne-Brookes is lecturer in English at Bath College of Higher Education. He is the author of *The novels of William Styron: from harmony to history*. He is currently working on a study of the novels of Joyce Carol Oates.

Mary Ellison teaches American Studies at the University of Keele. She has written extensively on black music, and on recent black history. She is author of *Extensions of the blues* and *Lyrical protest: Black music's struggle against discrimination*.

Antony Easthope is professor of English at Manchester Metropolitan University. He is author of a number of books on critical theory, and of a book on masculinity, *What a man's gotta do: the masculine myth in popular culture.*

Christopher Mulvey is professor of English and American Studies at King Alfred's College, Winchester. He is author of *Anglo-American landscapes* and *Transatlantic Manners*, and editor of a collection of essays, *New York: city as text.*

Alun Munslow is Head of Historical Studies at Staffordshire University and Treasurer of the British Association for American Studies. He writes on American cultural history and has published in the *Journal of American Culture, Journal of American Studies* and *Proceedings of the Massachusetts Historical Society.* He is author of *Discourse and Culture: The Creation of America: 1870–1920* and co-author (with Owen R. Ashton) of *Our American cousins* and *Henry D Lloyd's Critiques of American Capitalism, 1881–1903.*

Neil Sammells is Dean of Humanities at Bath College of Higher Education. He is the author of a book on Tom Stoppard, and one of the editors of *Irish Studies Review.* He is also one of the general editors of the *Crosscurrents* series.

David Seed is senior lecturer in English and American literature at Liverpool University. He has written books on Joseph Heller and Thomas Pyncheon, and on the novelist and screenwriter Rudolph Wurlitzer. He has also written fiction for children. His most recent work is an edited volume, *Anticipations: essays on early science fiction and its precursors.*

Renee Slater (Senior Lecturer in Literary Studies) and **Kate Fullbrook** (Principal Lecturer in Literary Studies) have taught American literature together for the past five years at the University of the West of England, Bristol. Their interests include the adversarial tradition in American literature and American women's writing. Kate Fullbrook has published book-length studies on Katherine Mansfield and on ethics in twentieth-century women's fiction. Renee Slater's research interests include autobiography and representation of landscape.

David Timms is Head of Quality Support at Bath College of Higher Education. He has taught English and American literature at the universities of Leicester and Manchester, and at Bath College of Higher Education. He is author of a book on Philip Larkin, a pamphlet on Nathaniel Hawthorne, and of articles on nineteenth-century American literature and contemporary English poetry.

Select Bibliography

Altieri C 1984 *Self and sensibility in contemporary American poetry.* Cambridge University Press, Cambridge.

Ambrose S E 1983 *Rise to globalism: American foreign policy since 1938.* Penguin, Harmondsworth.

Bailyn B 1967 *The ideological origins of the American revolution.* Harvard University Press, Cambridge, Mass.

Baker H A Jr 1980 *The journey back: issues in black literature and criticism.* University of Chicago Press, Chicago.

Banta M 1978 *Failure and success in America: a literary debate.* Princeton University Press, Princeton, NJ.

Barreca R 1991 *They used to call me Snow White . . . but I drifted: women's strategic use of humor.* Viking, New York.

Barrett L K 1975 *American literary racism 1790–1890.* Greenwood Press, Westport, Conn.

Baym N 1978 *Women's fiction: a guide to novels by and about women in America 1820–1870.* Cornell University Press, Ithaca, NY.

Bercovitch S, Jehlen M (ed) 1987 *Ideology and classic American literature.* Cambridge University Press, Cambridge.

Berthoff W 1965 *The ferment of realism: American literature 1884–1919.* Free Press, New York.

Berthoff W 1979 *A literature without qualities: American writing since 1945.* University of California Press, Berkeley and Los Angeles.

Bigsby C W E 1982 *A critical introduction to twentieth-century American drama* (3 vols). Cambridge University Press, Cambridge.

Boles J B 1984 *Black Southerners 1619–1869.* University Press of Kentucky, Lexington.

Bolt C 1974 *A history of the USA.* Macmillan, London.

Brown D 1970 *Bury my heart at Wounded Knee.* Barnie and Jenkins.

Chase R V 1957 *The American novel and its traditions.* Doubleday, Garden City, NY.

Clarke G (ed) 1990 *The new American writing since 1970.* Vision Press, London.

Conn P 1983 *The divided mind: ideology and imagination in America 1898–1917.* Cambridge University Press, Cambridge.

Conn P 1989 *Literature in America: an illustrated history*. Cambridge University Press, Cambridge.

Conzen M P 1990 *The making of the American landscape*. Unwin Hyman, London.

Couser G T 1979 *American autobiography: the prophetic mode*. University of Massachussetts Press, Amherst, Mass.

Cowley M 1934 *Exile's return: a literary odyssey of the 1920's*. W W Norton, New York.

Cronon W, Miles G, Gitlin J (eds) 1992 *Under an open sky: rethinking America's Western past*. W W Norton, New York.

Dickstein M 1977 *Gates of Eden: American culture in the sixties*. Basic Books, New York.

Donaghue D 1987 *Reading America: essays on American literature*. Knopf, New York.

Drinnon R 1980 *Facing West: the metaphysics of Indian-hating and empire-building*. Minnesota University Press, Minneapolis.

Epstein D 1977 *Sinful tunes and spirituals: Black folk music to the Civil War*. University of Illinois Press, Urbana.

Fetterley J 1978 *The resisting reader: a feminist approach to American fiction*. Indiana University Press, Bloomington.

Fiedler L 1967 *Love and death in the American novel* 2nd edn. Jonathan Cape, New York.

Fiedler L 1982 *What was literature? Class culture and mass society*. Simon & Schuster, New York.

Fisher M M 1983 *Negro slave songs in the United States*. Cornell University Press, Ithaca, NY.

Gidley M and Lawson-Peebles R (eds) 1990 *Views of American landscapes*. Cambridge University Press, Cambridge.

Gray R 1986 *Writing the South: ideas of an American region*. Cambridge University Press, Cambridge.

Grossman J R (ed) 1994 *The frontier in American culture*. University of California Press, Berkeley.

Hallberg R 1985 *American poetry and culture 1945–1980*. Harvard University Press, Cambridge, Mass.

Harding V 1981 *There is a river: the Black struggle for freedom in America*. Harcourt Brace Jovanovitch, New York.

Hirshey G 1984 *Nowhere to run: the history of soul music*. Macmillan, London.

Homberger E 1986 *American writers and radical politics 1900–39: equivocal commitments*. Macmillan, Basingstoke.

Jackson Lears T, Fox R W (eds) 1983 *The culture of consumption: critical essays in American history 1880–1980*. Pantheon, New York.

Karl F 1983 *American fictions 1940–1980: a comprehensive history and critical evaluation*. Harper & Row, New York.

Kenner H 1975 *A homemade world: the American modernist writers.* Knopf, New York.

King R H 1980 *A Southern renaissance: the cultural awakening of the American South 1930–1955.* Oxford University Press, Oxford.

Kolodny A 1984 *The land before her: fantasy and experience of the American frontier 1630–1860.* University of North Carolina Press, Chapel Hill.

Kroes R (ed) 1988 *High brow meets low brow: American culture as an intellectual concern.* Free University Press, Amsterdam.

Kroes R, Van de Bilt E (eds) 1988 *The US constitution after 200 years.* Free University Press, Amsterdam.

Lawrence D H 1923 *Studies in classic American literature.* Seltzer, New York.

Lawson-Peebles R 1988 *Landscape and written expression in revolutionary America: the world turned upside down.* Cambridge University Press, Cambridge.

Lewis R 1959 *The American Adam: innocence, tragedy and tradition in America.* Chicago University Press, Chicago.

Maddox L 1991 *Removals: nineteenth-century American literature and the politics of Indian affairs.* Oxford University Press, New York.

Marx L 1967 *The machine in the garden: technology and the pastoral ideal in America.* Oxford University Press, Oxford.

Mazzaro J 1980 *Postmodern American poetry.* University of Illinois Press, Urbana.

Medhurst M J et al 1990 *Cold war rhetoric: strategy, metaphor and ideology.* Greenwood Press, Westport, Conn.

Messent P 1990 *New readings in the American novel: narrative theory and its application.* Macmillan, Basingstoke.

Miller P 1953 *The New England mind: the seventeenth century.* Harvard University Press, Cambridge, Mass.

Milner C M et al 1994 *The Oxford history of the American West.* Oxford University Press, New York.

Morison S E 1960 *The intellectual life of colonial New England.* Cornell University Press, Ithaca, NY.

Morrison T 1990 *Playing in the dark: whiteness and the literary imagination.* Harvard University Press, Cambridge, Mass.

Munslow A 1992 *Discourse and culture: the creation of America.* Routledge, London.

Norton M B 1980 *Liberty's daughters: the revolutionary experience of American women 1750–1800.* Little, Brown, Boston, Mass.

Novick P 1988 *That noble dream: the 'objectivity question' and the American historical profession.* Cambridge University Press, Cambridge.

O'Brien M 1979 *The idea of the American South 1920–1941.* John Hopkins University Press, Baltimore.

Ostriker A S 1986 *Stealing the language: the emergence of women's poetry in America*. Beacon Press, Boston, Mass.

Perkins D 1987 *A history of modern poetry from the 1890s to the high modernist mode*. Harvard University Press, Cambridge, Mass.

Pizer D 1984 *Realism and naturalism in nineteenth-century American literature* 2nd edn. University of Southern Carolina Press, Carbondale, Ill.

Poirier R 1966 *A world elsewhere: the place of style in American literature*. Oxford University Press, New York.

Rappaport A 1975 *A history of American diplomacy*. Macmillan, New York.

Ray R B 1985 *A certain tendency of the American cinema 1930–1980*. Princeton University Press, Princeton, NJ.

Reising R 1986 *The unusable past: theory and the study of American literature*. Methuen, London.

Riley G 1988 *The female frontier: a comparative view of women on the prairie and the plains*. University Press of Kansas, Lawrence, Kan.

Schmitz N 1983 *Of Huck and Alice: humorous writing in American literature*. Minnesota University Press, Minneapolis.

Shaw P 1981 *American patriots and the rituals of revolution*. Harvard University Press, Cambridge, Mass.

Silber I (ed) 1964 *Soldier songs and home-front ballads of the Civil War*. Oak Publications, New York.

Silverman K 1976 *A cultural history of the American revolution: painting, music, literature and the theatre in the colonies and the United States from the Treaty of Paris to the inauguration of George Washington, 1763–1789*. Crowell, New York.

Slotkin R 1950 *Regeneration through violence: the mythology of the American frontier 1600–1860*. Wesleyan University Press, Middletown, Conn.

Southern E 1971 *The music of Black Americans: a history*. W W Norton, New York.

Spindler M 1983 *American literature and social change: William Dean Howells to Arthur Miller*. University of Indiana Press, Bloomington.

Stepto R 1979 *From behind the veil: a study of Afro-American narrative*. University of Illinois Press, Urbana, Ill.

Stone A E 1992 *The return of Nat Turner: history, literature and cultural politics in sixties America*. University of Georgia Press, Athens, Ga.

Strout C 1981 *The veracious imagination: essays on American history, literature and biography*. Wesleyan University Press, Middletown, Conn.

Susman W 1984 *Culture as history: the transformation of American society in the twentieth century*. Pantheon Books, New York.

Tanner T 1971 *City of words: American fiction 1950–70.* Jonathan Cape, London.

Tichi C 1979 *New World, new earth: environmental reform in American literature from the puritans through Whitman.* Yale University Press, New Haven, Conn.

Tirro F 1977 *Jazz: a history.* W W Norton, New York.

Trilling L 1950 *The liberal imagination: essays on literature and society.* Viking Press, New York.

Waggoner H H 1984 *American poets from the puritans to the present* 2nd edn. Louisiana State University Press, Baton Rouge.

Walker N 1988 *A very serious thing: women's humor and American culture.* Minnesota University Press, Minneapolis.

Walsh M 1981 *The American frontier revisited.* Humanities Press, Atlantic Highlands, NJ.

Washington M 1987 *Invented lives: narratives of Black women 1860–1960.* Doubleday, New York.

Wilson E 1962 *Patriotic gore: studies in literature of the American Civil War.* Deutsch, London.

Index